LEARNING JA____

Hiragana and Katakana

+Plus Kanji

Workbook For Beginners

*SELF-STUDY FOR LEARNING TO READ, WRITE AND
SPEAK JAPANESE*

EXPANDED EDITION (1)

JUST REALITY

**Learning Japanese Workbook for
Beginners Hiragana-Katakana and Kanji**

First Edition: July 17, 2021 Mie – Japan
ISBN-13: 979-8538977383 (Paperback)

Limit of Liability / Disclaimer of Warranty

The author and publisher make no representations or warranties with respect to the accuracy or completeness of the contents of this work and expressly disclaim all warranties, including, without limitation, warranties of fitness for a particular purpose. No warranty may be created or extended by sales or promotional materials.

The advice and strategies contained herein are not suitable for every individual. By providing information or links to other companies or websites, the publisher and the author do not guarantee, approve or endorse the information or products available at any linked websites or mentioned companies or persons, nor does a link indicate any association with or endorsement by the publisher or author.

This publication is designed to provide information with regard to the subject matter covered. It is offered or sold with the understanding that neither the publisher nor the author is engaged in rendering legal, accounting, or other professional service. If legal advice or other expert assistance is required, the services of a competent professional should be sought. Neither the publisher nor the author shall be liable for any loss or loss of profit or any other commercial damages, including but not limited to special, incidental, consequential, or other damages.

TABLE OF CONTENTS

ありがとうございます *arigatou gozaimasu*

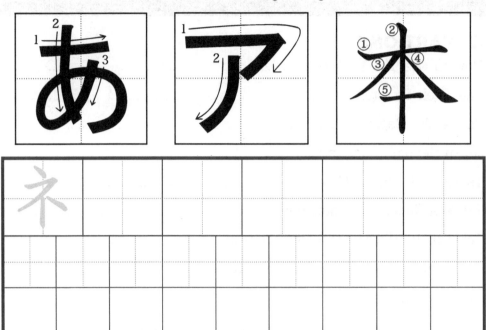

Congratulations on buying this book and setting out on the road to learning Japanese! Language learning can help you begin to think differently, make more friends, and increase your understanding of the world around you.

First of All

I'd like to give you a little background information. The Japanese language has three characters: Hiragana, Katakana, and Kanji. You must learn all three character sets to read Japanese and study beyond a beginner's level.

How to Use This Book (1-2)

- Write the character in the boxes and pay attention to stroke order.
- Use the book exercises to assess your understanding and measure your progress.
- Get free **Online audio** files are available on **justreality1.com** recorded by a native Japanese speaker, covering Hiragana, Katakana, Kanji characters, vocabulary, and lessons.
- To download the audio files for free, simply enter your email address, and a **zipped** file will be sent to your email.
- When you're having trouble understanding a particular section, re-read it and review the exercises that correspond to it until you feel comfortable moving on.

Notes:

1. Hiragana and katakana syllables have the same pronunciation.
2. The answer key for exercises is also included with the audio files.
3. Do not try to study all of the characters at once, take your time and keep practicing.

Here are two basic ways that kanji characters can be read:

Kunyomi: is normally used for a standalone Kanji without Hiragana attached to it.
For example, the words for the four directions—north, south, east, and west are pronounced as 北 (kita), 南 (minami), 東 (higashi), and 西 (nishi), respectively, all in Kunyomi.

Onyomi: is mostly used with two or more Kanji in a Japanese word, for example, two Kanji compound words like 法律 (houritsu), 家族 (kazoku), 衣服 (ifuku).

Ⓐ 月 ①③④		Ⓑ	
	MEANING	Month, Moon	
	ONYOMI	ガツ、ゲツ Gatsu, Getsu	Ⓕ
	KUNYOMI	つき Tsuki	
	Ⓒ **EXAMPLE**	**EXAMPLE SENTENCE**	
Ⓖ	いちがつ 一月　　Ichigatsu　– January こんげつ 今月　　Kongetsu　– This Month げつようび 月曜日　Getsuyoubi – Monday	きょう　　げつようび 今日は、月曜日です。 Kyou wa Getsuyoubi desu. Today is Monday.	Ⓓ

✓ **Review** ☐**Awesome!** ☐**Excellent!** ☐**Good!** ☐**Average!** ☐**Poor!** Ⓔ

A. Kanji stroke order
B. English meaning
C. Example words
D. Example sentence
E. Review your writing
F. The official Kanji reading
G. Stroke order diagrams and writing instructions

■ Trace the number and write the characters horizontally from left to right and from top to bottom.

How This Book is Structured

This book is comprised of four parts, and each part is followed by a vocabulary list. It includes Hiragana and Katakana as well as Kanji and **Rōmaji** with English meanings and Furigana.

Font Size and Formatting

- Some text is highlighted in the book.
- Font size used are: 10, 11, 12, 14, 16 and 18.
- Font size is 12 and 14 points or higher for footnotes, table captions, and hints.
- All essential tables have a header rows, captions, alternative text, and cell padding.

Dedicated and Made For

This book is designed for those who want to learn how to read, write and speak basic Japanese for living and working in Japan, including Hiragana, Katakana, and Kanji characters. It is also useful for students and travellers, Japanese culture lovers, and watchers of Japanese anime and dramas.

Upon Completing This Book

Learners will have gained the ability to:

- Learners will be able to recognize and read/write all 46 basic Hiragana and Katakana characters, as well as the additional 33 Youon Hiragana-Katakana, sounds, and the 20 Dakuten and 5 Handakuten modifications. They will also have learned about 103 of the most commonly used Kanji.

- You will also be able to understand basic spoken vocabulary and use it in everyday communicative situations.

- Acquired proficiency in Japanese greetings, number counting, expressing ages, and discussing dates, weeks, months, and years.

- Learners will have a solid understanding of Japanese pronunciation and the writing system, encompassing Kanji, Furigana, Romaji, and the concept of small "tsu".

- Read and write basic Japanese texts and simple stories, and understand the main points of short news articles and essays.

The book contents are tailored to cover essential vocabulary, and patterns necessary for passing the Japanese Language Proficiency Test at Level N5. The vocabulary and scenarios presented in this book have been designed for beginner levels associated with the JLPT Level 5. It also incorporates advanced-level examples that are highly beneficial.

To provide the correct reading of kanji, hiragana will be placed above them. This practice, known as furigana, is commonly used in comic books and other publications, ensuring accurate kanji pronunciation for readers.

Examples:

Furigana

にほんご　まな
日本語を学びたいです。(Nihongo wo manabitai desu.) I want to learn Japanese.

The vocabulary, Hiragana, Katakana, Kanji, and lessons are arranged by numbers, and the audio files indicate the numbers in Japanese instead of English. To follow along with the audio and understand the words, you will need to learn the Japanese numbers from one to ten first.

Numbers	Hiragana	Reading
1	いち	(ichi)
2	に	(ni)
3	さん	(san)
4	よん	(yon)
5	ご	(go)

Numbers	Hiragana	Reading
6	ろく	(roku)
7	しち	(shichi)
8	はち	(hachi)
9	きゅう	(kyuu)
10	じゅう	(juu)

Good luck as you embark on this new undertaking to increase your understanding of the Japanese people and their wonderful culture. Let's get started.
Turn the page and begin your journey.

Currency: Yen (¥)
Emperor and Empress: Naruhito and Masako
Prime Minister: Fumio Kishida
Government: Constitutional Democracy Official
Language: Japanese
Religion: Shintou, Buddhism, Christianity, Other
Population: 125.8 million (as of 2020)
Writing Systems: Hiragana, Katakana, Kanji
National Sport: Sumou
Popular Sport: Baseball and Soccer

HOKKAIDOU
北海道
SAPPORO
PACIFIC OCEAN
SEA OF JAPAN
AOMORI
AKITA
IWATE
YAMAGATA
SENDAI
KYOTO
京都
FUKUSHIMA
HYOGO
兵庫
OSAKA
大阪
IBARAKI
CHIBA
HIROSHIMA
広島県
TOKYO
東京都
KANAGAWA
NAGOYA
FUKUOKA
MIE
ISE SHIMA
NAGASAKI
NARA
奈良
OKINAWA

Japan is an island nation, consisting of an entire archipelago of 6,852 islands. Despite this huge number, it consists of five major islands Hokkaidou, Honshuu, Shikoku, Kyuushuu, and Okinawa that account for about 97% of its total area.

The island of Honshuu, the mainland of Japan, is a very large residential area. Japan has been divided into 47 administrative prefectures, spread over eight traditional regions.

Famous Things

Japan is famous for natural sights like cherry blossoms, bamboo forests and Mount Fuji; technology like Japanese cars and bullet trains; karaoke and vending machines; cultural values; popular anime and manga; and food like ramen and sushi. It's also known for its shrines, temples and onsen (hot springs).

Major Cities

Tokyo-Yokohama-Sapporo-Nagoya-Osaka-Kobe-Kyoto-Nara-Hiroshima-Fukuoka-Okinawa.

Famous Foods

Sushi & Sashimi ,Tempura, Curry Rice, Miso Soup, Udon, Ramen, Okonomiyaki, Yakitori, etc.

Basic Hiragana

あ **a**	い **i**	う **u**	え **e**	お **o**
か **ka**	き **ki**	く **ku**	け **ke**	こ **ko**
さ **sa**	し **shi**	す **su**	せ **se**	そ **so**
た **ta**	ち **chi**	つ **tsu**	て **te**	と **to**
な **na**	に **ni**	ぬ **nu**	ね **ne**	の **no**
は **ha**	ひ **hi**	ふ **hu**	へ **he**	ほ **ho**
ま **ma**	み **mi**	む **mu**	め **me**	も **mo**
や **ya**		ゆ **yu**		よ **yo**
ら **ra**	り **ri**	る **ru**	れ **re**	ろ **ro**
わ **wa**				を **wo**
ん **n**				

Dakuten

が **ga**	ぎ **gi**	ぐ **gu**	げ **ge**	ご **go**
ざ **za**	じ **zi(ji)**	ず **zu**	ぜ **ze**	ぞ **zo**
だ **da**	ぢ **di(ji)**	づ **du**	で **de**	ど **do**
ば **ba**	び **bi**	ぶ **bu**	べ **be**	ぼ **bo**

Handakuten

ぱ **pa**	ぴ **pi**	ぷ **pu**	ぺ **pe**	ぽ **po**

Youon

きゃ **kya**	きゅ **kyu**	きょ **kyo**
しゃ **sha(sya)**	しゅ **shu(syu)**	しょ **sho(syo)**
ちゃ **cha(tya)**	ちゅ **chu(tyu)**	ちょ **cho(tyo)**
にゃ **nya**	にゅ **nyu**	にょ **nyo**
ひゃ **hya**	ひゅ **hyu**	ひょ **hyo**

みゃ **mya**	みゅ **myu**	みょ **myo**
りゃ **rya**	りゅ **ryu**	りょ **ryo**

ぎゃ **gya**	ぎゅ **gyu**	ぎょ **gyo**
じゃ **zya(ja)**	じゅ **zyu(ju)**	じょ **zyo(jo)**

びゃ **bya**	びゅ **byu**	びょ **byo**
ぴゃ **pya**	ぴゅ **pyu**	ぴょ **pyo**

Sokuon

つ **tsu**
pause (no sound, small "tsu")

THE BASIC 46 HIRAGANA CHARACTERS

SPECIAL GROUPS OF CHARACTERS

HIRAGANA - ADDITIONAL SOUNDS YOUON

Table of Katakana Characters

Basic Katakana

ア **a**	イ **i**	ウ **u**	エ **e**	オ **o**
カ **ka**	キ **ki**	ク **ku**	ケ **ke**	コ **ko**
サ **sa**	シ **shi**	ス **su**	セ **se**	ソ **so**
タ **ta**	チ **chi**	ツ **tsu**	テ **te**	ト **to**
ナ **na**	ニ **ni**	ヌ **nu**	ネ **ne**	ノ **no**
ハ **ha**	ヒ **hi**	フ **hu**	ヘ **he**	ホ **ho**
マ **ma**	ミ **mi**	ム **mu**	メ **me**	モ **mo**
ヤ **ya**		ユ **yu**		ヨ **yo**
ラ **ra**	リ **ri**	ル **ru**	レ **re**	ロ **ro**
ワ **wa**				ヲ **wo**
ン **n**				

Dakuten

ガ **ga**	ギ **gi**	グ **gu**	ゲ **ge**	ゴ **go**
ザ **za**	ジ **zi(ji)**	ズ **zu**	ゼ **ze**	ゾ **zo**
ダ **da**	ヂ **di(ji)**	ヅ **du**	デ **de**	ド **do**
バ **ba**	ビ **bi**	ブ **bu**	ベ **be**	ボ **bo**

Handakuten

パ **pa**	ピ **pi**	プ **pu**	ペ **pe**	ポ **po**

Youon

キャ **kya**	キュ **kyu**	キョ **kyo**
シャ **sha(sya)**	シュ **shu(syu)**	ショ **sho(syo)**
チャ **cha(tya)**	チュ **chu(tyu)**	チョ **cho(tyo)**
ニャ **nya**	ニュ **nyu**	ニョ **nyo**
ヒャ **hya**	ヒュ **hyu**	ヒョ **hyo**

ミャ **mya**	ミュ **myu**	ミョ **myo**
リャ **rya**	リュ **ryu**	リョ **ryo**

ギャ **gya**	ギュ **gyu**	ギョ **gyo**
ジャ **zya(ja)**	ジュ **zyu(ju)**	ジョ **zyo(jo)**

ビャ **bya**	ビュ **byu**	ビョ **byo**
ピャ **pya**	ピュ **pyu**	ピョ **pyo**

Sokuon

ツ **tsu**
pause (no sound, small "tsu")

The Basic 103 Kanji Characters

一	二	三	四	五
六	七	八	九	十
百	千	万	水	火
木	天	土	北	東
西	南	左	右	日
月	花	魚	空	山
川	雨	本	目	口
耳	手	足	人	母
父	女	男	子	小
中	大	上	下	何
行	見	言	語	食
飲	会	学	休	買
聞	来	立	生	話
出	読	入	書	後
古	高	安	多	新
少	長	白	分	時
間	週	年	今	先
前	午	半	店	外
電	道	毎	友	名
金	円	車	駅	気
国	社	校		

This book contains 103 Kanji for Japan Language Proficiency Test N5.

There Are Three Types of Letters in Japanese

1. **Hiragana:** These characters represent phonetic sounds and are employed for particles, words, and components of words.

2. **Katakana:** These characters also represent phonetic sounds, but they are specifically used for foreign or loan words.

3. **Kanji:** These characters, derived from Chinese, are used to depict the root or stem of words, conveying both meaning and sound.

We suggest you start learning Hiragana, then Katakana, and then Kanji. If you learn Hiragana first, it will be easier to learn katakana next.

Hiragana will help you learn Japanese pronunciation properly, read Japanese beginner textbooks, and write sentences in Japanese.

Japanese will become a lot easier to study after having learned Hiragana. Also, as you will be able to write sentences in Japanese, you will be able to write emails in Hiragana. Katakana will help you read Japanese menus at restaurants. Hiragana and Katakana will be a good help to your Japanese study.

Furigana

Furigana is Hiragana and Katakana characters written in small forms above Kanji to show the pronunciation, Furigana is used in kids 'books and Japanese language textbooks for learners to teach the reading of unknown Kanji.

Rōmaji

In addition to the three Japanese character systems, you will see the Roman alphabet used to spell out sounds in Japan. **Rōmaji** (ローマ字) or the Romanized letters may be used where Japanese text is targeted at non-Japanese speakers, such as on street signs, dictionaries, textbooks, and passports.

Rōmaji is also used when typing on the computer. Although Japanese keyboards can type with kana, many people use the Latin script to type out the sounds and characters in **Rōmaji**. When you're first learning the characters, **Rōmaji** will help you read the Japanese words.

Hiragana Characters Info（ひらがな）

Learning hiragana is a crucial part of your studies. Hiragana is a group of characters that represent sounds, similar to our alphabet. Each hiragana symbol corresponds to a sound or syllable for instance, ("か" for "ka," "ま" for "ma," "な" for "na"). Hiragana is often used for particles, verbs, and adjective endings, while kanji is for verb stems, adjectives, and nouns. However, hiragana can be utilized to write anything in Japanese.

Katakana Characters Info（カタカナ）

Just like hiragana, katakana is another type of character set used for writing sounds. Katakana is mainly used for foreign words that come from languages like English, German, French, and so on. While there are some exceptions, you'll often see katakana for foreign words. In Japan, there are many foreign words, especially from English. You'll find katakana on billboards, magazines, and more.

Kanji Characters Info（漢字）

In the Japanese writing system, there are thousands of kanji characters used regularly. Each kanji has its own meanings, and many of them can be pronounced in different ways depending on the situation. For example, the kanji 今日 can be read as "kyou," which means "today," or "konnichi," which means "recent days." These different readings are called "Onyomi," which comes from Chinese, and "Kunyomi," which are native Japanese readings. Most kanji have both types of readings, but some have more, and some have only one. In Japanese schools, students learn over 2,000 important kanji characters called "Jyouyou" or regularly used kanji.

Additional Info

- Uppercase and Lowercase

There are no upper and lower case letters in the Japanese writing system Emphasis can be done by including font styling, putting dots over letters, and putting them in quotes 「」『』.

- Question Marks

In Japanese writing, question marks are represented by particle か (ka?) or "？" (Full-width question mark). The use of "か？" is more traditional and used in informal writing like a conversation, while "？" is more modern and used in formal writing like an article or news.

Examples:

これは何ですか。　　　　　kore wa nan des ka.　　　　What is that?
あなたは食べましたか。　Anata wa tabe mashita ka.　Did you eat?

Particle か at the end indicates a question, which ends with the normal Japanese full stop (。).

Japanese Language Proficiency Test (JLPT)

The Japanese Language Proficiency Test (JLPT) is an internationally standardized exam that evaluates and certifies the proficiency of non-native speakers of Japanese. It is administered by the Japan Foundation and the Japan Educational Exchanges and Services.

The JLPT has three sections: vocabulary, grammar and reading, and listening. The vocabulary and grammar sections are multiple-choice, while the reading and listening sections consist of both multiple-choice and fill-in-the-blank questions.

The JLPT is widely recognized by Japanese language schools, companies, and government agencies as a reliable measure of Japanese language proficiency. Many people take the JLPT to improve their job prospects, study at a Japanese university, or simply challenge themselves and track their progress in learning Japanese.

To pass the JLPT, you need to have a solid understanding of hiragana, katakana, kanji, and grammar, and be able to read and write them accurately. The JLPT is offered at five levels, and the number of required kanji increases with each level.

- Here is an overview of the number of kanji required for each JLPT level:

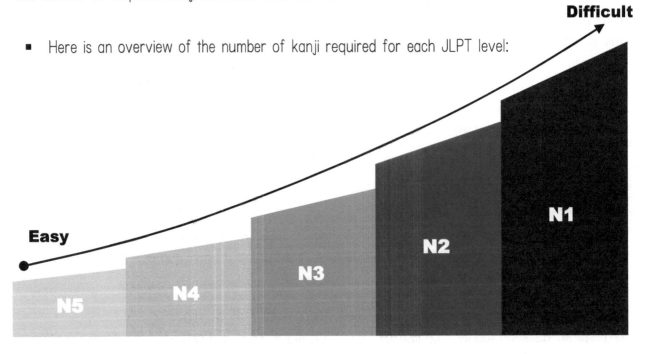

- N5 150 – 200 Hours + 300 Vocabulary and 100 of Kanji
- N4 250 – 300 Hours + 600 Vocabulary and 300 of Kanji
- N3 450 – 500 Hours + 1,500 Vocabulary and 800 of Kanji
- N2 600 – 800 Hours + 2,500 Vocabulary and 1,500 of Kanji
- N1 800 – 2150 Hours + 6,000 Vocabulary and 2,000 of Kanji

In Japanese, you'll come across two types of "tsu" characters: the regular "tsu" つ and the smaller version, known as small "tsu" っ. You can see this difference in both hiragana and katakana. For instance, "mittsu" みっつ means "three," and "nattsu" ナッツ means "nuts."

➤ So, what's the deal with small "tsu"? How does it work, and what's it called?

Small "tsu" (っ) is a little kana used in Japanese to show that the consonant before it is said twice as long. You might also hear it referred to as "sokuon" or "chiisai tsu," which means "small tsu." It helps make the consonant sound more emphasized. Small tsu (っ) is a small kana that is used in the Japanese language to indicate that the preceding consonant is pronounced in a geminated or "double" manner. It is also known as a sokuon or chiisai "tsu" 小さい「っ」.

Unlike most other kana characters, the small tsu doesn't stand for a whole sound in a syllable. Instead, it helps create a unique effect known as a "clogged sound" or a "double consonant." When you spot a small tsu before another kana in a word, it makes that kana's consonant sound twice as long. Some of these double consonants come with a quick pause at the start, almost like a tiny throat closure, making the sound distinct.

If you find a small tsu at the end of a word or sentence, it signals a quick pause in the sound, abruptly ending the word's pronunciation instead of gradually fading away.

Examples:

kekkon	Married	けっこん
motto	More	もっと
happa	Leaf	はっぱ
gakkou	School	がっこう

Hiragana
Example of Regular "tsu"

Hiragana
Example of Small "tsu"

hatto	Hat	ハット
nattsu	Nuts	ナッツ
poketto	Pocket	ポケット

Katakana
Example of Regular "tsu"

Katakana
Example of Small "tsu"

In Japanese, there are only 5 vowel sounds, and they are always pronounced consistently. Even if your grammar and vocabulary aren't perfect, if you speak clearly, Japanese people will understand you. Pronouncing Japanese is easier than English, as it has fewer vowels and consonants.

Normal Vowels →

あ a	as in Ah!	**Example:** あめ	ame	Rain
い i	as in See!	**Example:** いす	isu	Chair
う u	as in Moon!	**Example:** うさぎ	usagi	Rabbit
え e	as in Get!	**Example:** えんぴつ	enpitsu	Pencil
お o	as in Oh!	**Example:** おちゃ	ocha	Tea

Long Vowels (chouon 長音)

1. Long vowels in Japanese, they are pronounced for twice the duration of short vowels. ああ、いい、うう、ええ、おお、These words have longer sounds, and whether a vowel is short or long can actually change the word's meaning.

2. ああ long vowel ああ (aa) for two beats.
   Examples: お母さん okaasan おかあさん mother, お・か・あ・さ・ん Its written か・あ. don't read them separately — read them all together.

3. The sound "いい" is twice as long as "い". When a sound ends with "い" (i), you simply add another "い" after it. For example, "おじさん" (Uncle) becomes "おじいん" (Uncle) → おじいさん (Grandfather).

4. うう is twice the length of う. すうじ (Numbers) す・う・じ、すうじ

5. ええ oneesan お姉さん・おねえさん (older sister). For sounds ending in a え e sound add either a え or い. It might seem unclear, but as you learn new vocabulary words, memorize which pronunciation to use for each.

6. When a long vowel with an "o" sound (お) comes at the end of a word, you add an extra う (u) sound. For instance, "ohayou" (おはよう) means "good morning." However, some words have two "o" sounds together, like "ookii" (大きい・おおきい), meaning "big."

It's very important to master long vowels because the meaning of a word can change depending on whether the vowel is long or short.

Example:

おじさん (oji-san)
meaning (uncle)

おじいさん (o-jii-san)
meaning (grandfather)

Long Vowels in Katakana

This is much easier than hiragana. Instead of adding another vowel simply add a dash after it ー.

コーヒー	Coffee	ニュース	News
アパート	Apartment	メニュー	Menu
バター	Butter	サーモン	Salmon
ビール	Beer	サッカー	Soccer
カード	Card	テーブル	Table
スーパー	Supermarket	スイーツ	Sweets
デパート	Department	フォーム	Foam

In Japanese, you'll notice that some words appear identical, but the only distinction is that one has a long vowel while the other doesn't.

It's important to note that in some cases, you may also encounter a repetition of the same vowel character to represent a long vowel sound. For instance:

エ (e) → エエ (**ee**)

オ (o) → オオ (**oo**)

Note: If you pronounce a word incorrectly, it can completely change its meaning.

1. Hiragana（平仮名）

Hiragana is a phonetic alphabet that was developed in the ninth century to simplify writing. Nowadays, it is mainly used for native Japanese words. Hiragana is derived from a more complex Kanji and each hiragana represents a syllable. A total of 46 Hiragana are used in contemporary Japanese writing.

2. Katakana（片仮名）

Katakana, an alphabet like hiragana, includes 46 unique characters and uses dakuten and handakuten modifications to alter syllable pronunciation. Its primary function is transcribing foreign loanwords, and sometimes it replaces kanji or hiragana for emphasis. It originated in the ninth century, evolving from a complex kanji script.

3. Kanji（漢字）

Tategaki is a traditional Japanese writing style that is read from top to bottom and right to left. It is still employed in specific contexts, including traditional books, documents, poetry, street signs, menus, as well as personal communication like letters, postcards, and calligraphy.

▪ Traditionally: Tategaki（縦書き）

Tategaki is a traditional Japanese writing style that is read from top to bottom and right to left. It is still employed in specific contexts, including traditional books, documents, poetry, street signs, menus, as well as personal communication like letters, postcards, and calligraphy.

▪ Modern: Yokogaki（横書き）

Yokogaki is a popular Japanese writing style that reads from left to right and top to bottom, resembling English text. It is widely used in modern literature, newspapers, and various forms of writing. Introduced during the Meiji era, Yokogaki gained popularity due to its ease of reading for foreigners and its facilitation of foreign language learning for Japanese individuals.

**Tategaki
Vertical Writing**
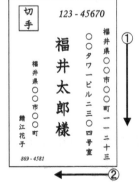

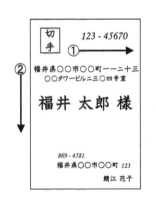
**Yokogaki
Horizontal Writing**

| Pronunciation | "a" as in <u>ah</u>! | 【Write the character in the boxes】 |

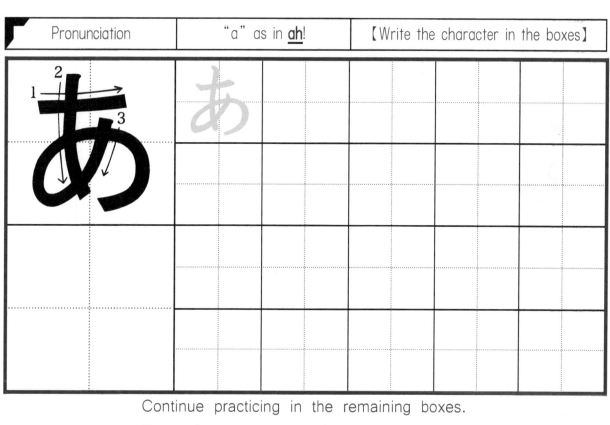

Continue practicing in the remaining boxes.

Remember to pay attention to stroke order.

🔊 Vocabulary – Write the character in the boxes below.

1. ai (Love) 2. ao (Blue) 3. aka (Red) 4. amai (Sweet)

5. aki (Autumn) 6. ame (Rain) 7. ashi (Leg) 8. ashita (Tomorrow)

Pronunciation	"i" as in <u>I</u>taly	【Write the character in the boxes】

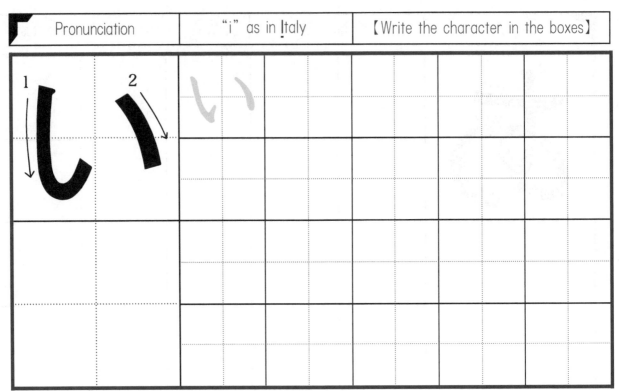

Continue practicing in the remaining boxes.
Remember to pay attention to stroke order.

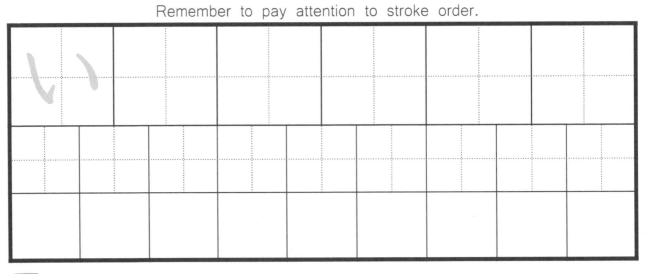

🔊 Vocabulary - Write the character in the boxes below.

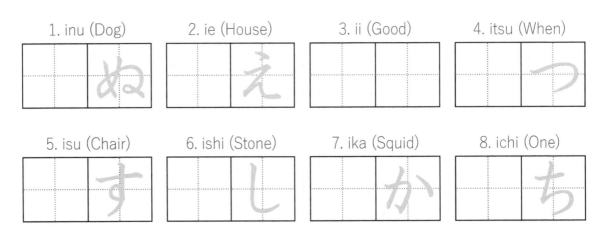

1. inu (Dog)　　2. ie (House)　　3. ii (Good)　　4. itsu (When)

5. isu (Chair)　　6. ishi (Stone)　　7. ika (Squid)　　8. ichi (One)

| Pronunciation | "u" as in s<u>oo</u>n | 【Write the character in the boxes】 |

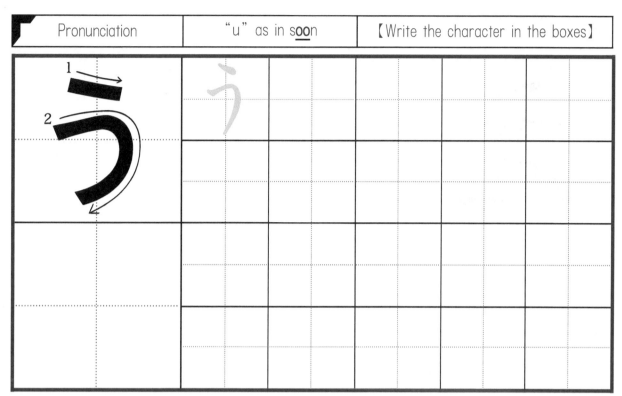

Continue practicing in the remaining boxes.

Remember to pay attention to stroke order.

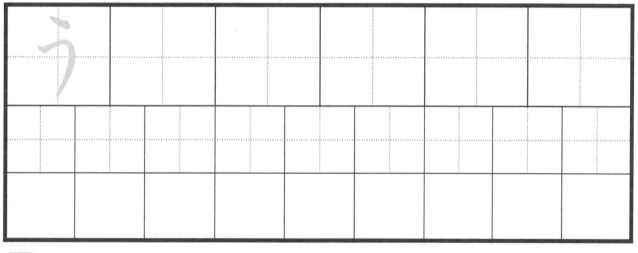

🔊 Vocabulary – Write the character in the boxes below.

1. umi(Sea) 2. ushi (Cow) 3. uta (Song) 4. usagi (Rabbit)

5. ue (Up) 6. uma (Horse) 7. uso (Lie) 8. ugoku (to move)

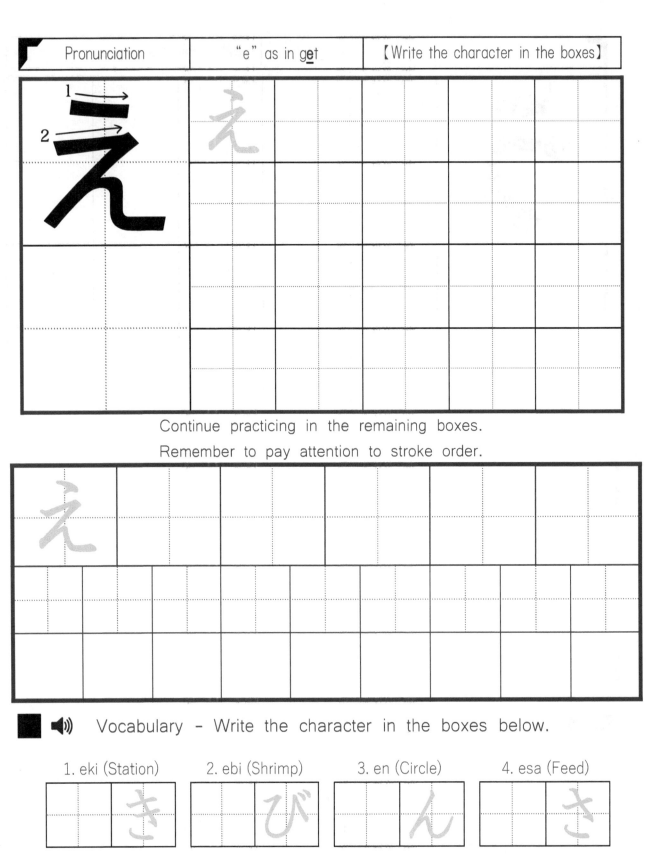

| Pronunciation | "e" as in g<u>e</u>t | 【Write the character in the boxes】 |

Continue practicing in the remaining boxes.

Remember to pay attention to stroke order.

■ 🔊 Vocabulary – Write the character in the boxes below.

1. eki (Station)　　2. ebi (Shrimp)　　3. en (Circle)　　4. esa (Feed)

き　　び　　ん　　さ

5. eiga (Movie)　　6. eigo (English)　　7. egao (Smile)

いが　　いご　　がお

| Pronunciation | "o" as in <u>o</u>ld | 【Write the character in the boxes】 |

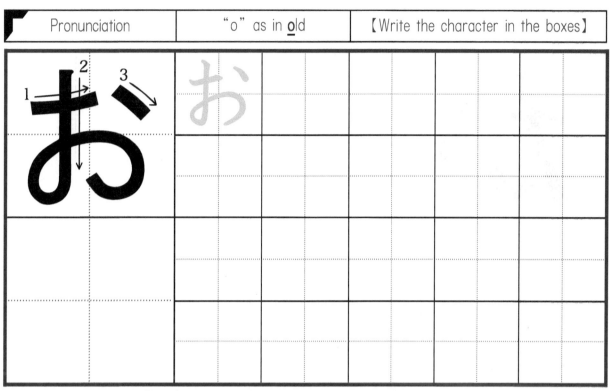

Continue practicing in the remaining boxes.
Remember to pay attention to stroke order.

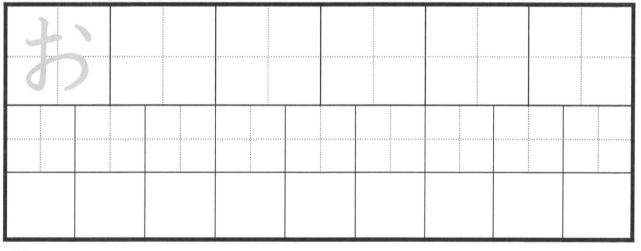

🔊 Vocabulary – Write the character in the boxes below.

1. oto (Sound) 2. oya (Parents) 3. oka (Hill) 4. oji (Uncle)

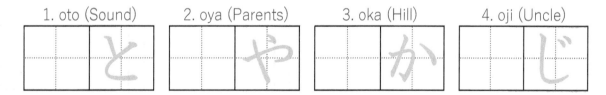

5. on'na (Woman) 6. otoko (Man) 7. otona (Adult)

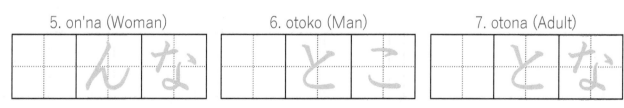

| Pronunciation | "ka" as in <u>car</u> | 【Write the character in the boxes】 |

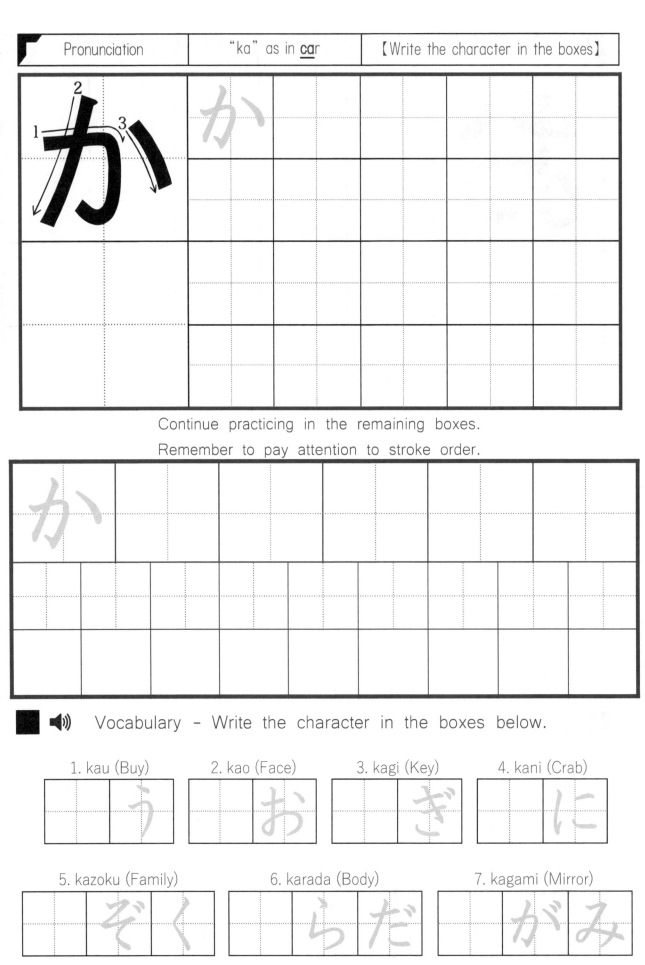

Continue practicing in the remaining boxes.

Remember to pay attention to stroke order.

🔊 Vocabulary - Write the character in the boxes below.

| 1. kau (Buy) | 2. kao (Face) | 3. kagi (Key) | 4. kani (Crab) |

| 5. kazoku (Family) | 6. karada (Body) | 7. kagami (Mirror) |

24

Pronunciation	"ki" as in <u>ke</u>y	【Write the character in the boxes】

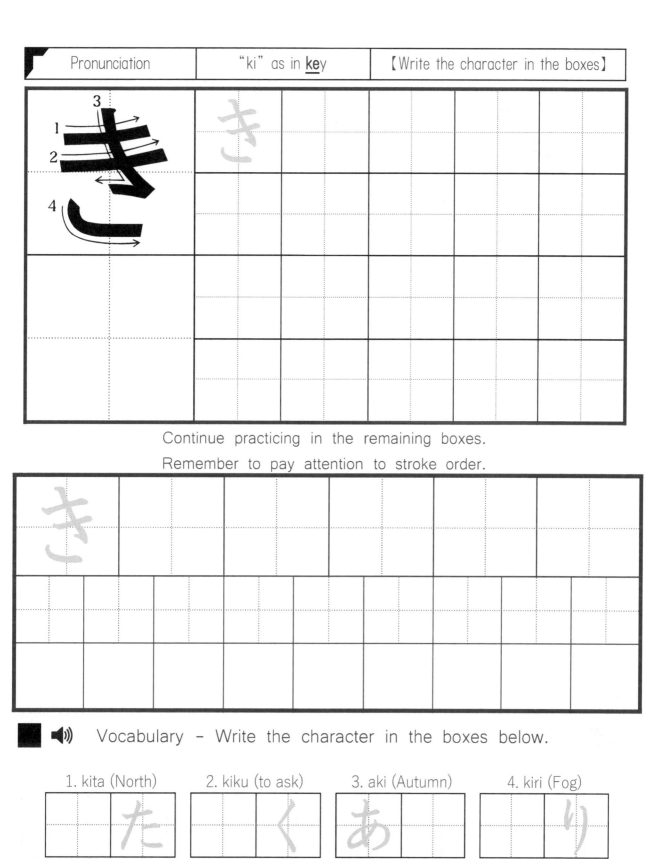

Continue practicing in the remaining boxes.

Remember to pay attention to stroke order.

🔊 Vocabulary – Write the character in the boxes below.

1. kita (North)	2. kiku (to ask)	3. aki (Autumn)	4. kiri (Fog)

5. kisetsu (Season)	6. kiiro (Yellow)	7. kikon (Married)

Pronunciation	"ku" as in <u>coo</u>l	【Write the character in the boxes】

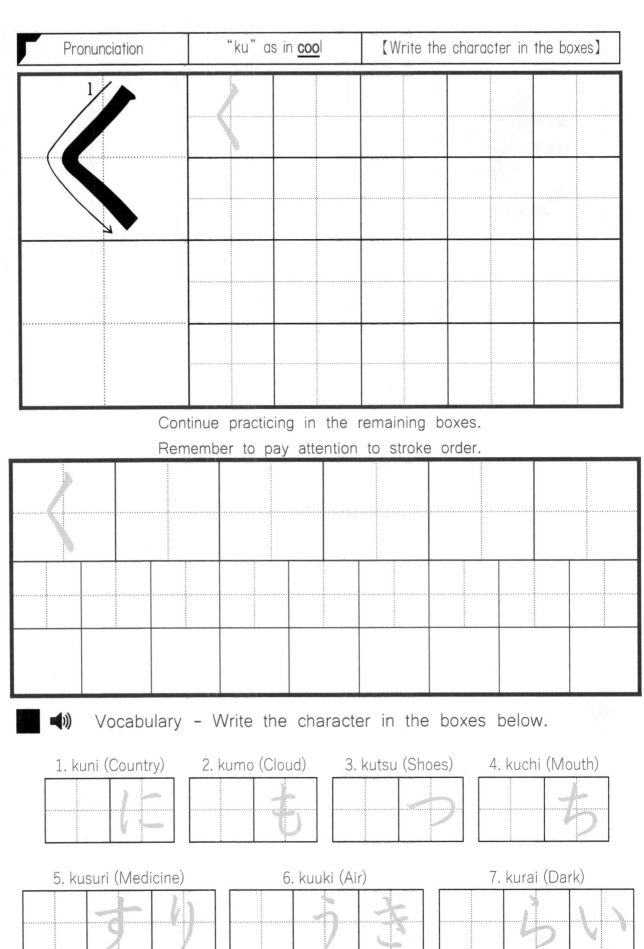

Continue practicing in the remaining boxes.

Remember to pay attention to stroke order.

Vocabulary - Write the character in the boxes below.

1. kuni (Country)   2. kumo (Cloud)   3. kutsu (Shoes)   4. kuchi (Mouth)

5. kusuri (Medicine)   6. kuuki (Air)   7. kurai (Dark)

Pronunciation	"ke" as in <u>ke</u>n (Name)	【Write the character in the boxes】

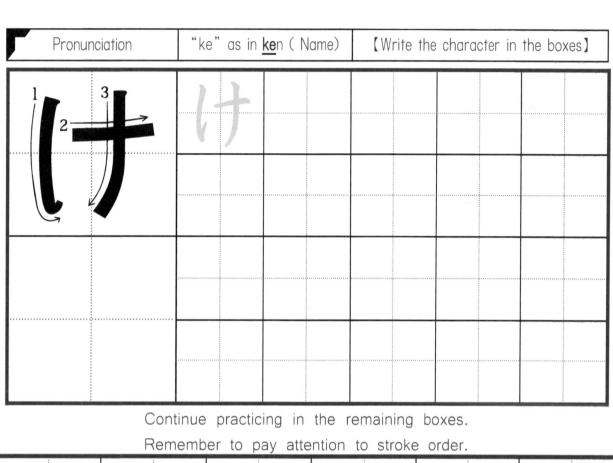

Continue practicing in the remaining boxes.

Remember to pay attention to stroke order.

Vocabulary - Write the character in the boxes below.

1. keihi (Expense)　　　　2. kega (Injury)　　　　3. keiken (Experience)

4. keshiki (Scenery)　　　　5. ken (Ticket)　　　　6. keisatsu (Police)

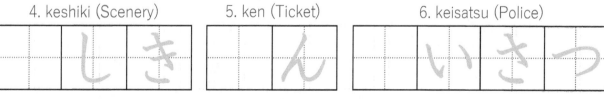

Pronunciation	"ko" as in <u>co</u>ke	【Write the character in the boxes】

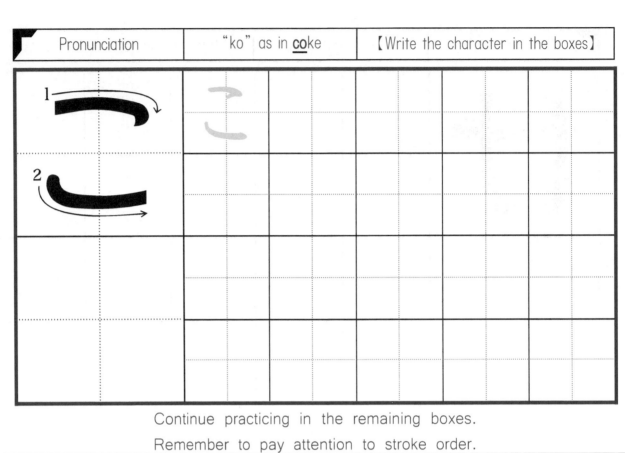

Continue practicing in the remaining boxes.

Remember to pay attention to stroke order.

Vocabulary - Write the character in the boxes below.

1. koe (Voice)

え

2. koya (Shed)

や

3. kore (This)

れ

4. koto (Thing)

と

5. kotoba (Word)

とば

6. kodomo (Children)

ども

7. kouza (Bank account)

うざ

Pronunciation	"sa" as in **sa**ndwich	【Write the character in the boxes】

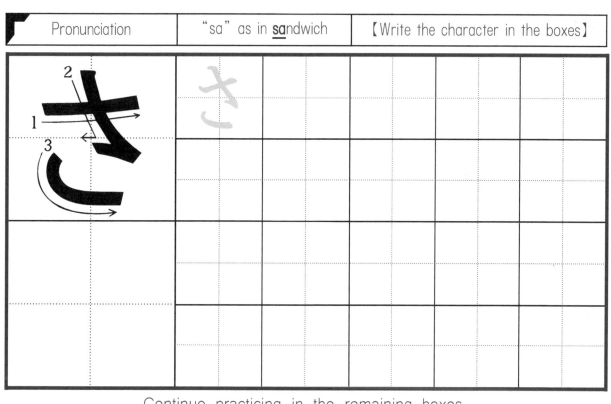

Continue practicing in the remaining boxes.

Remember to pay attention to stroke order.

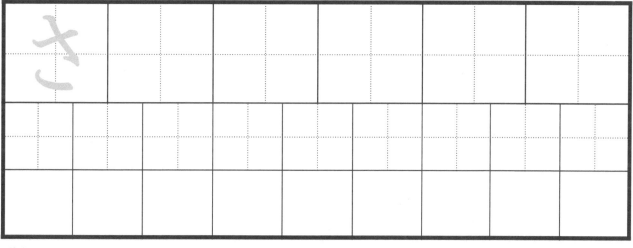

🔊 Vocabulary – Write the character in the boxes below.

1. sara (Plate)　　2. san (Three)　　3. saru (Monkey)　　4. sake (Liquor)

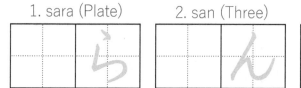

5. saigo (Last)　　　　6. sakana (Fish)　　　　7. saifu (Wallet)

| Pronunciation | "shi" as in **she** | 【Write the character in the boxes】 |

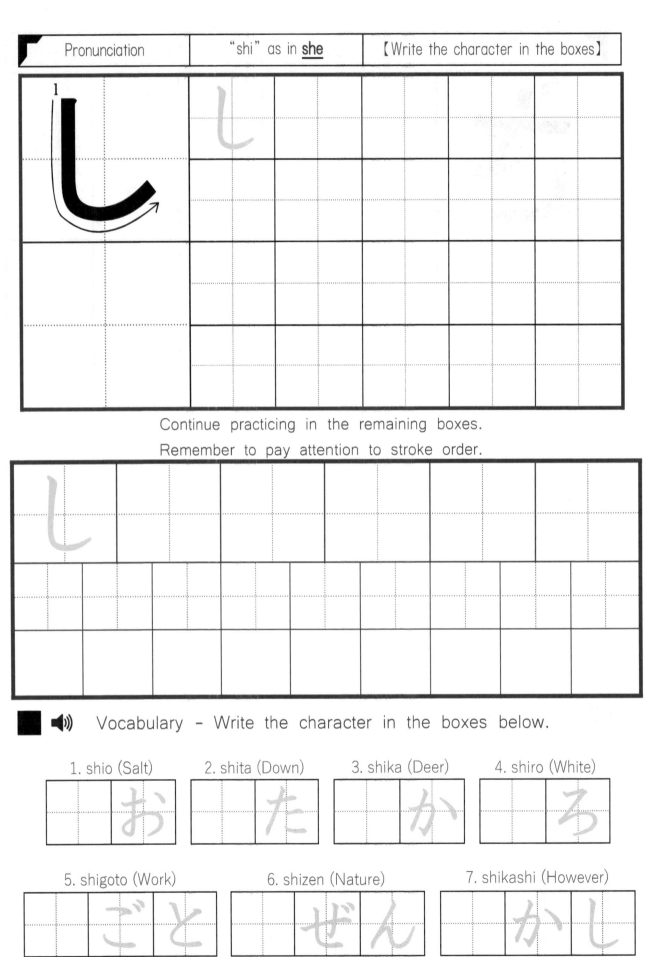

Continue practicing in the remaining boxes.

Remember to pay attention to stroke order.

🔊 Vocabulary – Write the character in the boxes below.

1. shio (Salt)   お

2. shita (Down)   た

3. shika (Deer)   か

4. shiro (White)   ろ

5. shigoto (Work)   ごと

6. shizen (Nature)   ぜん

7. shikashi (However)   かし

30

| Pronunciation | "su" as in **sue** | 【Write the character in the boxes】|

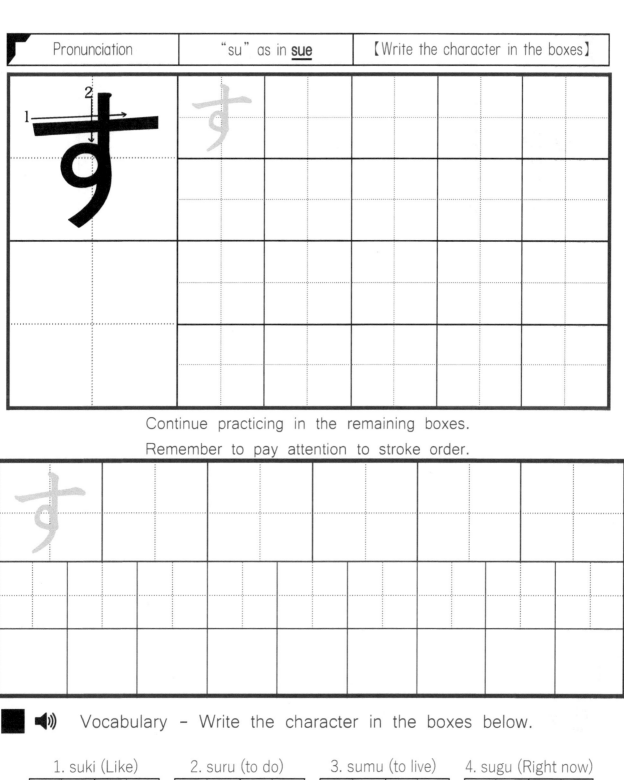

Continue practicing in the remaining boxes.
Remember to pay attention to stroke order.

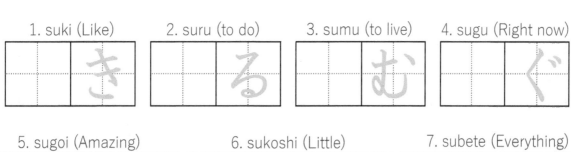

■ ◀)) Vocabulary – Write the character in the boxes below.

1. suki (Like)　　2. suru (to do)　　3. sumu (to live)　　4. sugu (Right now)

5. sugoi (Amazing)　　6. sukoshi (Little)　　7. subete (Everything)

Pronunciation	"se" as in <u>se</u>t	【Write the character in the boxes】

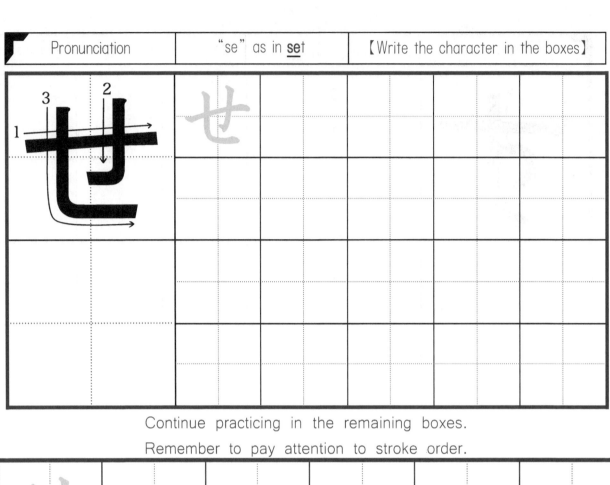

Continue practicing in the remaining boxes.

Remember to pay attention to stroke order.

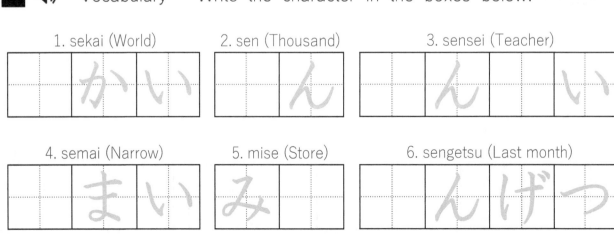

🔊 Vocabulary - Write the character in the boxes below.

1. sekai (World)

かい

2. sen (Thousand)

ん

3. sensei (Teacher)

ん　い

4. semai (Narrow)

まい

5. mise (Store)

み

6. sengetsu (Last month)

んげつ

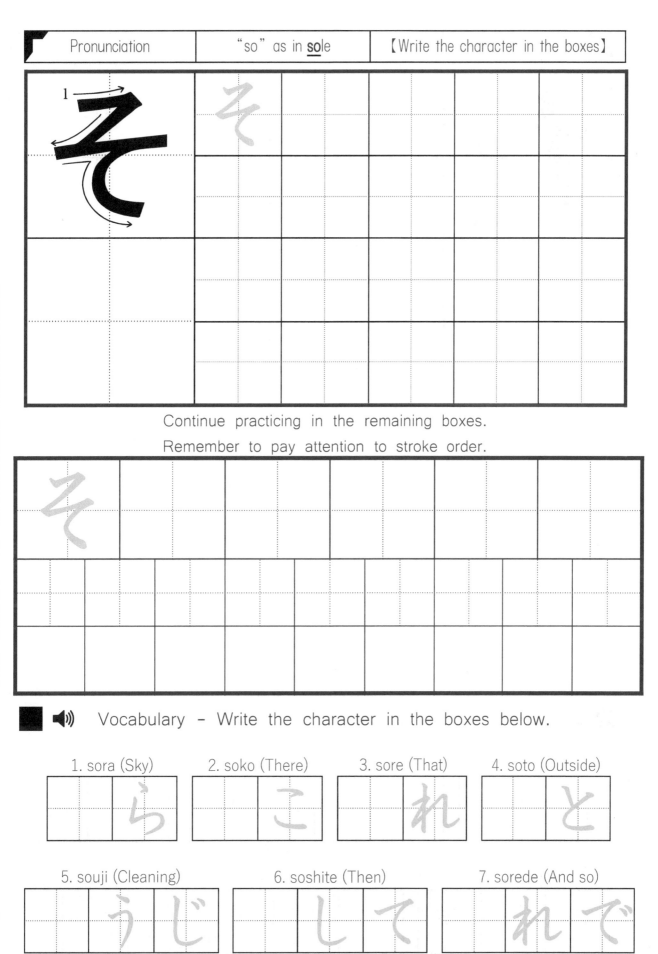

| Pronunciation | "so" as in <u>so</u>le | 【Write the character in the boxes】 |

Continue practicing in the remaining boxes.
Remember to pay attention to stroke order.

🔊 Vocabulary – Write the character in the boxes below.

1. sora (Sky)   2. soko (There)   3. sore (That)   4. soto (Outside)

5. souji (Cleaning)   6. soshite (Then)   7. sorede (And so)

33

Pronunciation	"ta" as in **ta**p	【Write the character in the boxes】

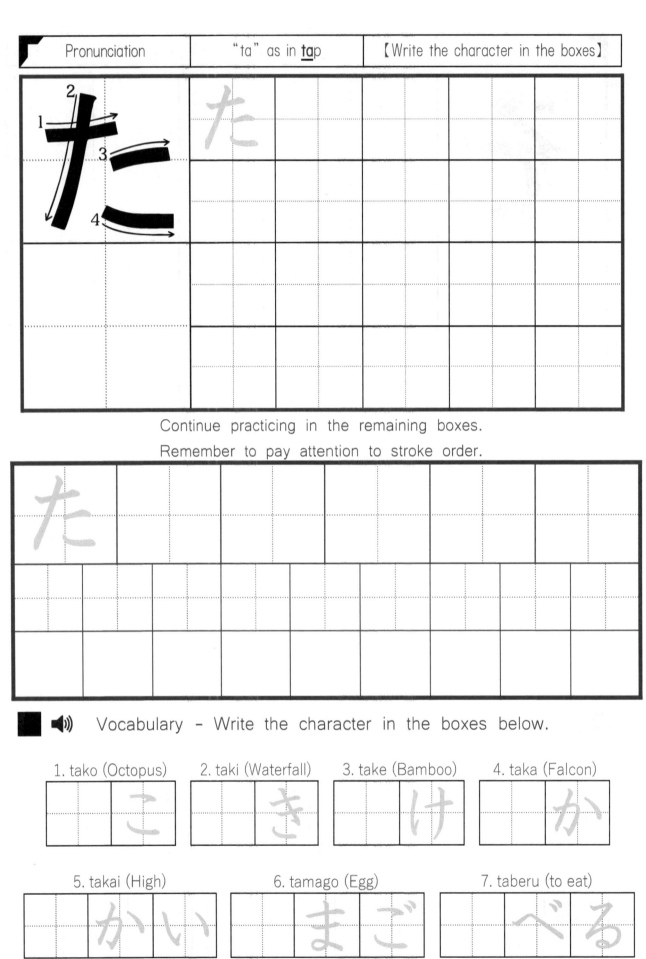

Continue practicing in the remaining boxes.

Remember to pay attention to stroke order.

🔊 Vocabulary – Write the character in the boxes below.

1. tako (Octopus)   2. taki (Waterfall)   3. take (Bamboo)   4. taka (Falcon)

5. takai (High)   6. tamago (Egg)   7. taberu (to eat)

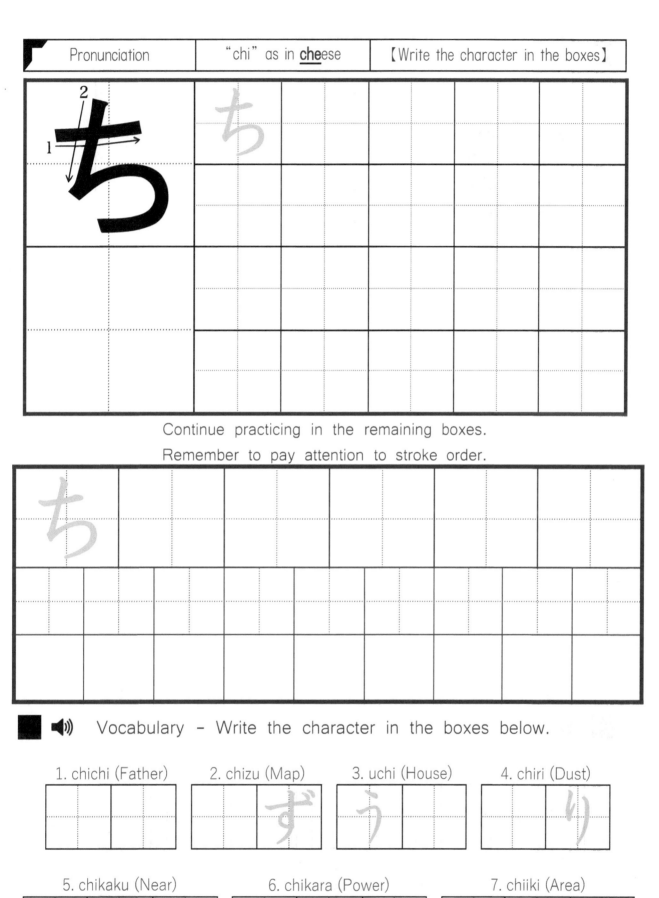

| Pronunciation | "chi" as in <u>che</u>ese | 【Write the character in the boxes】 |

Continue practicing in the remaining boxes.
Remember to pay attention to stroke order.

Vocabulary – Write the character in the boxes below.

1. chichi (Father)   2. chizu (Map)   3. uchi (House)   4. chiri (Dust)

5. chikaku (Near)   6. chikara (Power)   7. chiiki (Area)

35

| Pronunciation | "tsu" as in <u>tsu</u>nami | 【Write the character in the boxes】 |

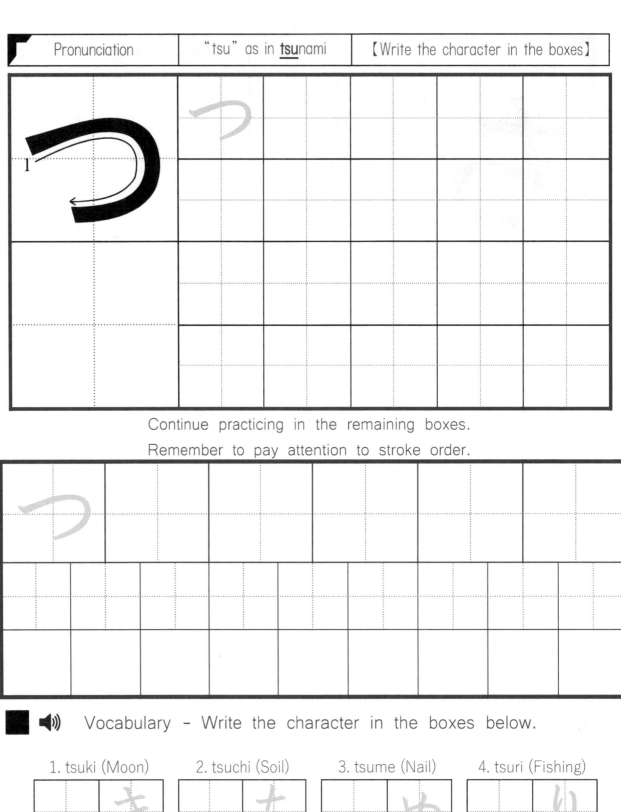

Continue practicing in the remaining boxes.

Remember to pay attention to stroke order.

🔊 Vocabulary - Write the character in the boxes below.

1. tsuki (Moon)　　き
2. tsuchi (Soil)　　ち
3. tsume (Nail)　　め
4. tsuri (Fishing)　　り

5. tsukau (to use)　　かう
6 tsukue (Desk)　　くえ
7. tsuyoi (Strong)　　よい

Pronunciation	"te" as in <u>te</u>mple	【Write the character in the boxes】

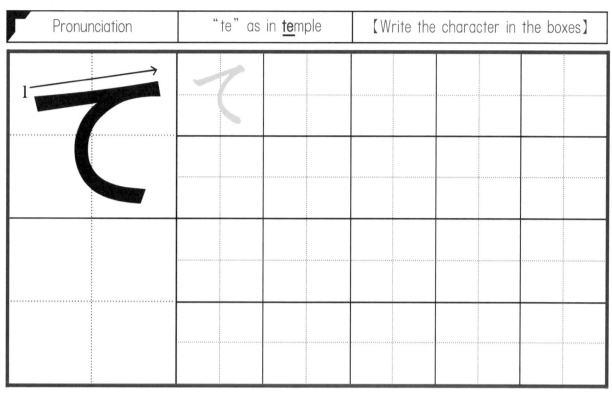

Continue practicing in the remaining boxes.
Remember to pay attention to stroke order.

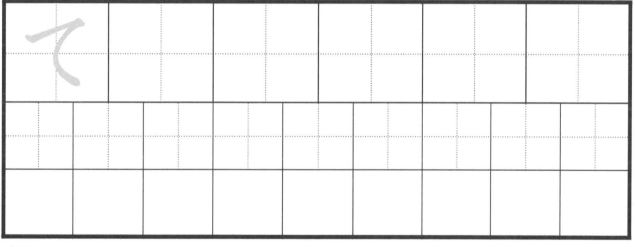

■ 🔊 Vocabulary – Write the character in the boxes below.

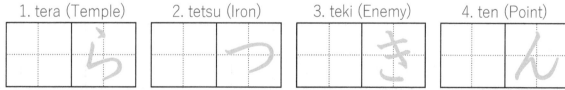

1. tera (Temple) 2. tetsu (Iron) 3. teki (Enemy) 4. ten (Point)

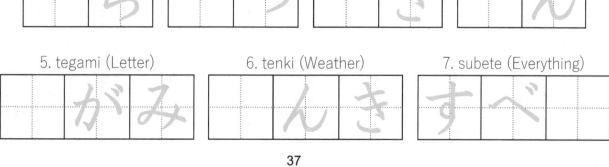

5. tegami (Letter) 6. tenki (Weather) 7. subete (Everything)

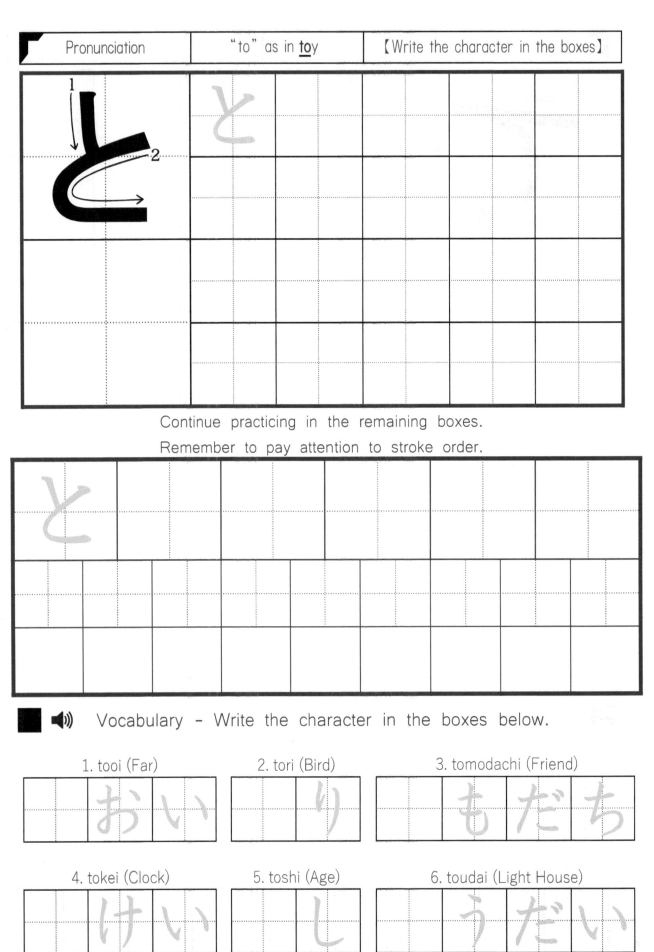

| Pronunciation | "to" as in <u>to</u>y | 【Write the character in the boxes】 |

Continue practicing in the remaining boxes.

Remember to pay attention to stroke order.

🔊 Vocabulary - Write the character in the boxes below.

1. tooi (Far)

2. tori (Bird)

3. tomodachi (Friend)

4. tokei (Clock)

5. toshi (Age)

6. toudai (Light House)

Pronunciation	"na" as in **na**p	【Write the character in the boxes】

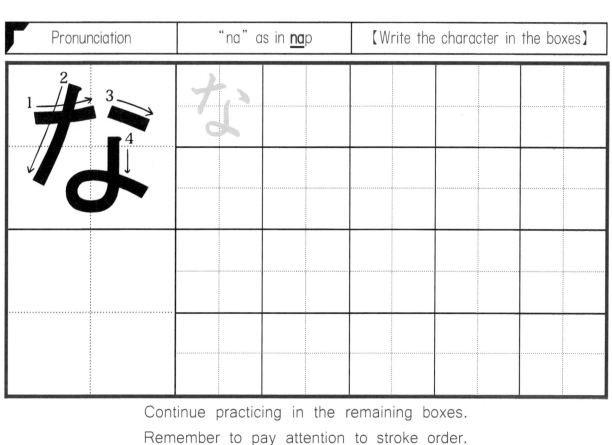

Continue practicing in the remaining boxes.
Remember to pay attention to stroke order.

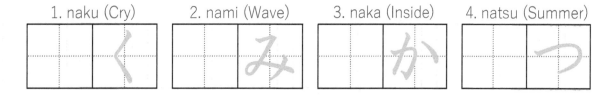

■ ◀)) Vocabulary – Write the character in the boxes below.

1. naku (Cry)　　2. nami (Wave)　　3. naka (Inside)　　4. natsu (Summer)

5. namae (Name)　　　6. nagai (Long)　　　7. naosu (to fix)

39

Pronunciation	"ni" as in <u>knee</u>	【Write the character in the boxes】

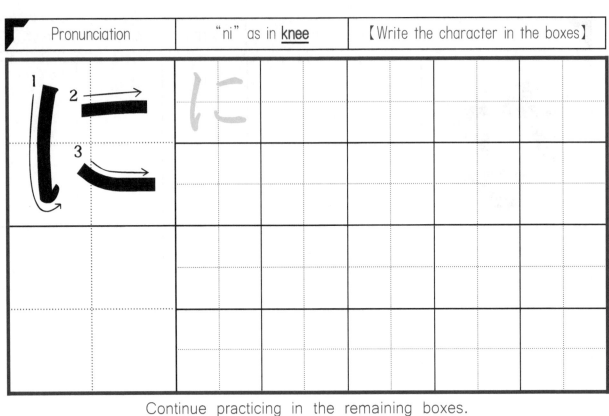

Continue practicing in the remaining boxes.

Remember to pay attention to stroke order.

 Vocabulary – Write the character in the boxes below.

1. nishi (West)   2. niku (Meat)   3. niwa (Garden)   4. niji (Rainbow)

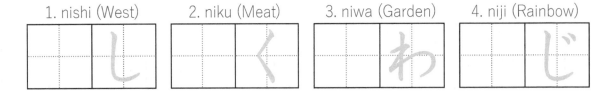

5. nigatsu (February)   6. nihon (Japan)   7. nioi (Smell)

| Pronunciation | "nu" as in **noo**dles | 【Write the character in the boxes】 |

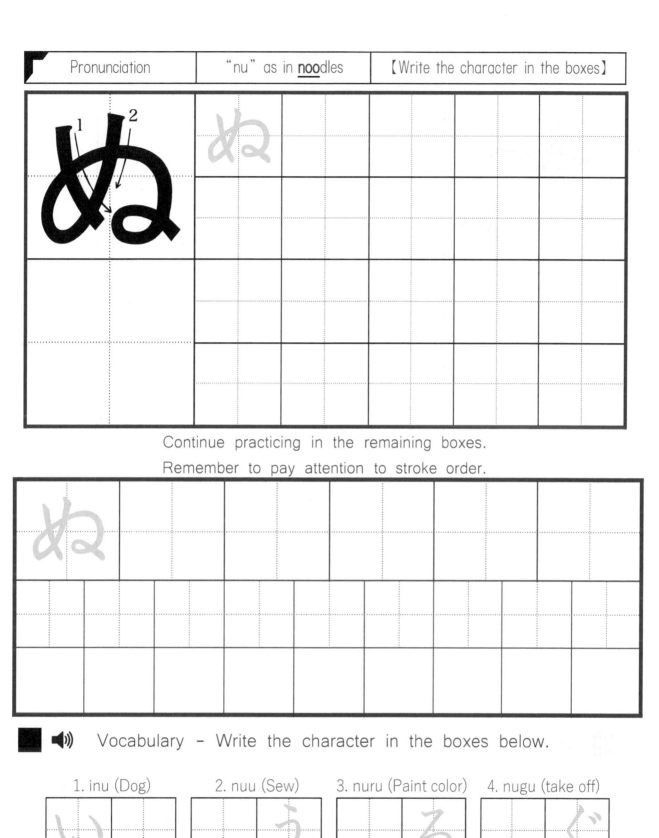

Continue practicing in the remaining boxes.
Remember to pay attention to stroke order.

🔊 Vocabulary – Write the character in the boxes below.

1. inu (Dog) 2. nuu (Sew) 3. nuru (Paint color) 4. nugu (take off)

5. nureru (Wet) 6. nusumu (to steal) 7. nurie (Coloring)

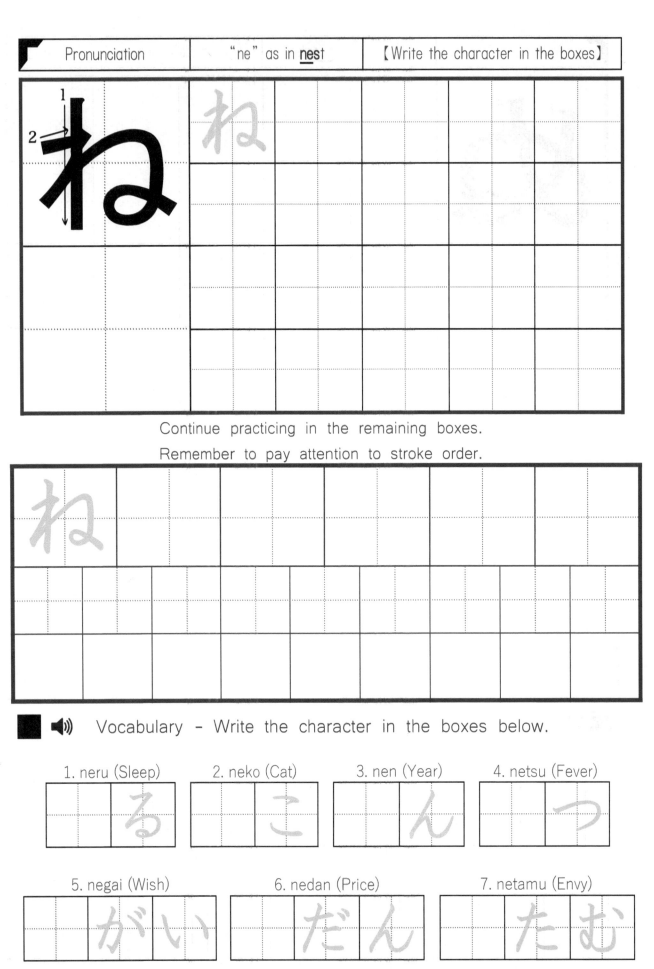

Continue practicing in the remaining boxes.

Remember to pay attention to stroke order.

THE BASIC 46 HIRAGANA CHARACTERS

🔊 Vocabulary - Write the character in the boxes below.

1. neru (Sleep)　　2. neko (Cat)　　3. nen (Year)　　4. netsu (Fever)

5. negai (Wish)　　6. nedan (Price)　　7. netamu (Envy)

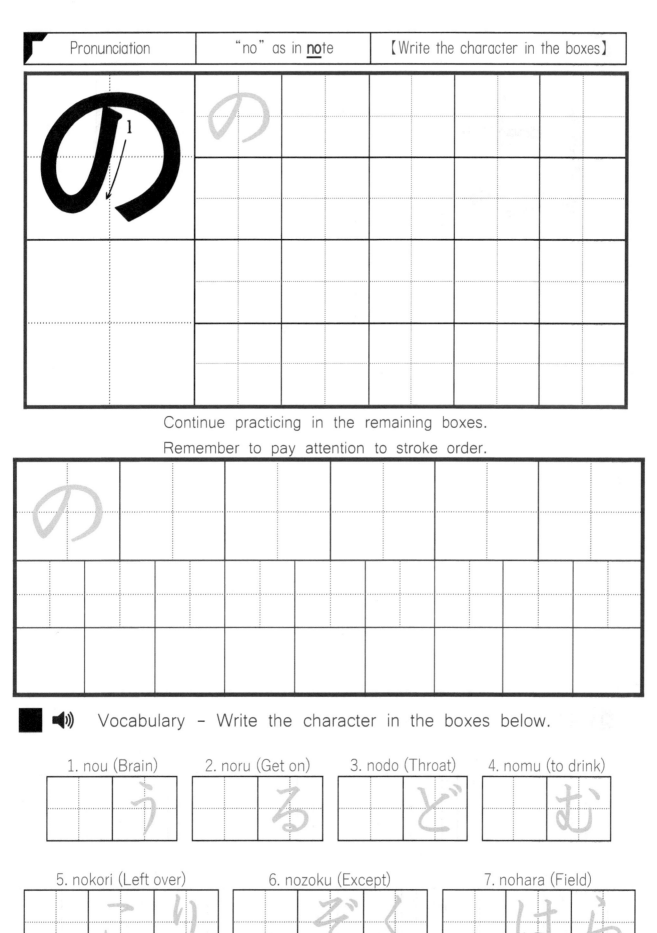

| Pronunciation | "no" as in **no**te | 【Write the character in the boxes】 |

Continue practicing in the remaining boxes.

Remember to pay attention to stroke order.

Vocabulary – Write the character in the boxes below.

1. nou (Brain)
2. noru (Get on)
3. nodo (Throat)
4. nomu (to drink)

5. nokori (Left over)
6. nozoku (Except)
7. nohara (Field)

Pronunciation	"ha" as in <u>ha</u>t	【Write the character in the boxes】

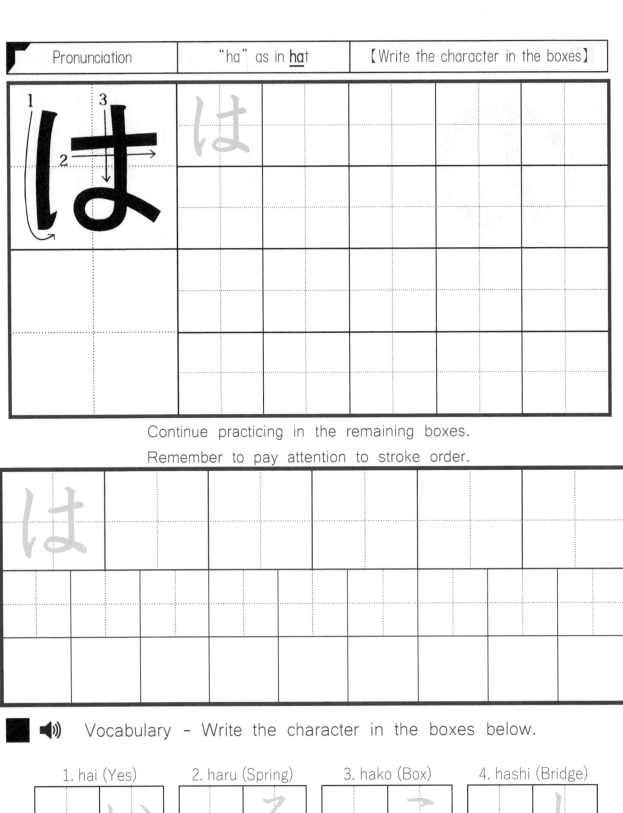

Continue practicing in the remaining boxes.

Remember to pay attention to stroke order.

■ 🔊 Vocabulary - Write the character in the boxes below.

1. hai (Yes)　　2. haru (Spring)　　3. hako (Box)　　4. hashi (Bridge)

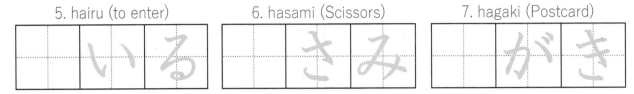

5. hairu (to enter)　　6. hasami (Scissors)　　7. hagaki (Postcard)

Pronunciation	"hi" as in yes <u>he</u> is!	【Write the character in the boxes】

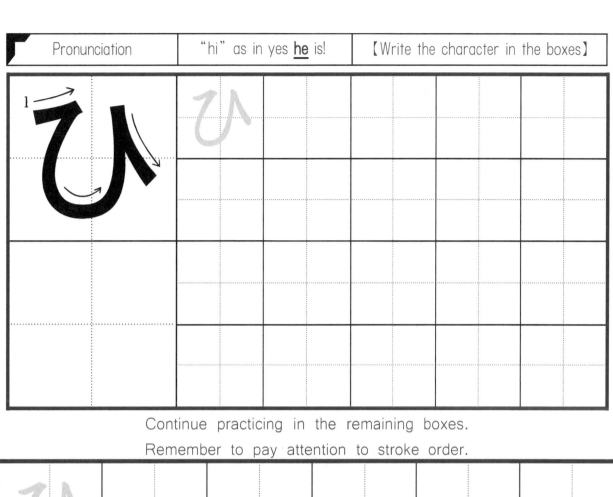

Continue practicing in the remaining boxes.

Remember to pay attention to stroke order.

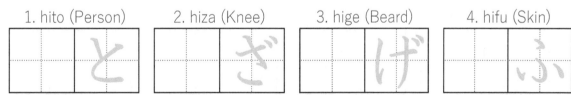

🔊 Vocabulary – Write the character in the boxes below.

1. hito (Person)　　2. hiza (Knee)　　3. hige (Beard)　　4. hifu (Skin)

5. higashi (East)　　6. hidari (Left side)　　7. himitsu (Secret)

| Pronunciation | "fu" as in <u>fu</u>ji mount | 【Write the character in the boxes】 |

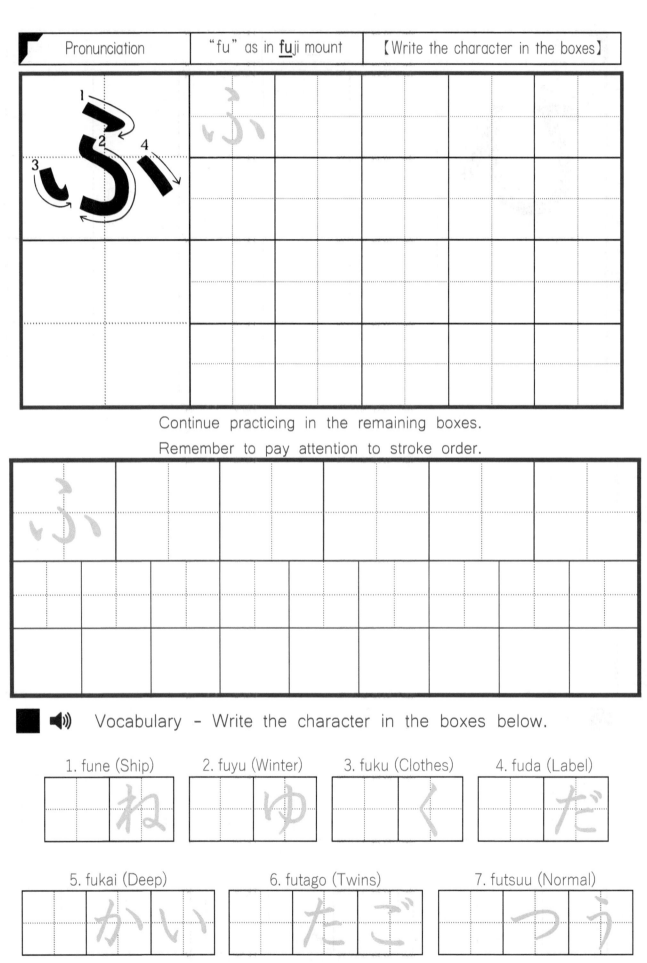

Continue practicing in the remaining boxes.

Remember to pay attention to stroke order.

🔊 Vocabulary - Write the character in the boxes below.

1. fune (Ship)

2. fuyu (Winter)

3. fuku (Clothes)

4. fuda (Label)

5. fukai (Deep)

6. futago (Twins)

7. futsuu (Normal)

| Pronunciation | "he" as in **her**! | 【Write the character in the boxes】 |

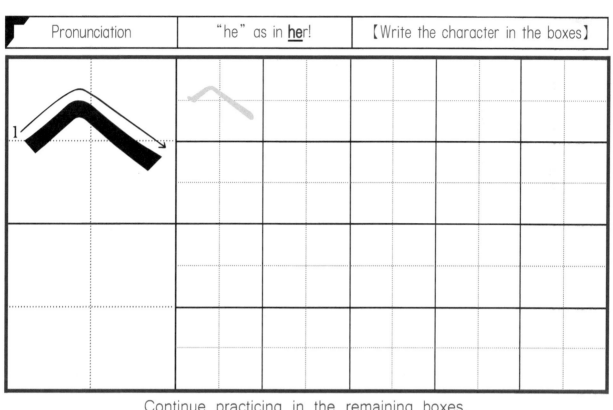

Continue practicing in the remaining boxes.
Remember to pay attention to stroke order.

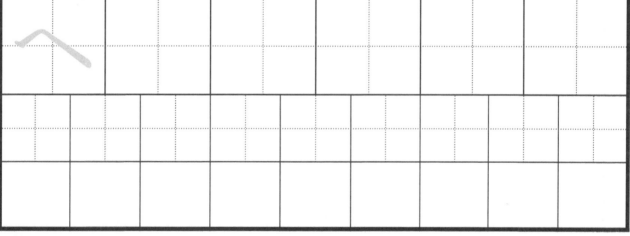

🔊 Vocabulary – Write the character in the boxes below.

1. hen (Strange)　2. hebi (Snake)　3. heya (Room)　4. heso (Navel)

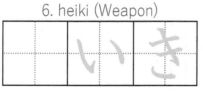

5. heiwa (Peace)　6. heiki (Weapon)　7. henka (Changing)

| Pronunciation | "ho" as in <u>ho</u>pe | 【Write the character in the boxes】 |

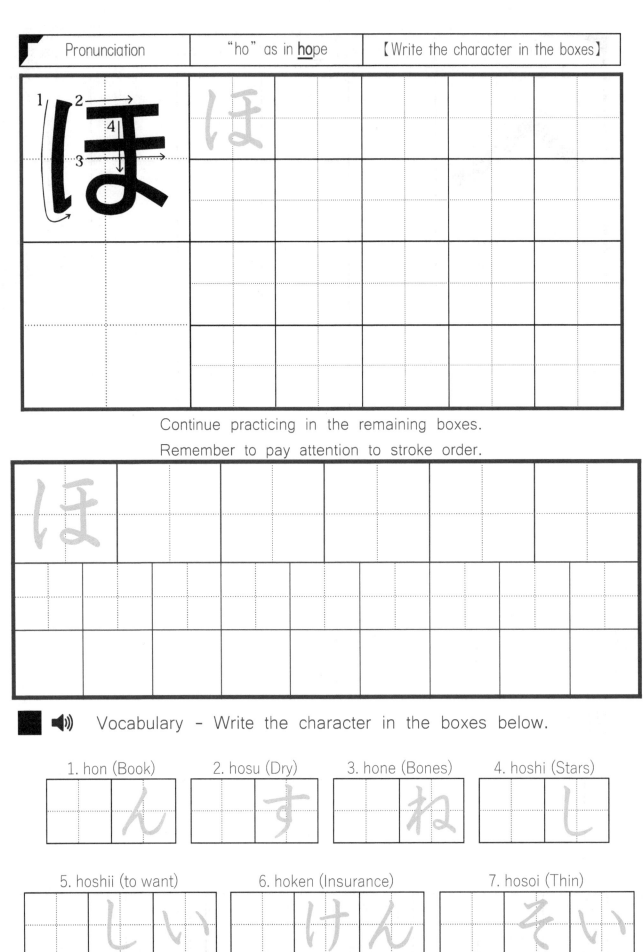

Continue practicing in the remaining boxes.
Remember to pay attention to stroke order.

Vocabulary - Write the character in the boxes below.

1. hon (Book)
2. hosu (Dry)
3. hone (Bones)
4. hoshi (Stars)

5. hoshii (to want)
6. hoken (Insurance)
7. hosoi (Thin)

| Pronunciation | "ma" as in <u>ma</u>t | 【Write the character in the boxes】 |

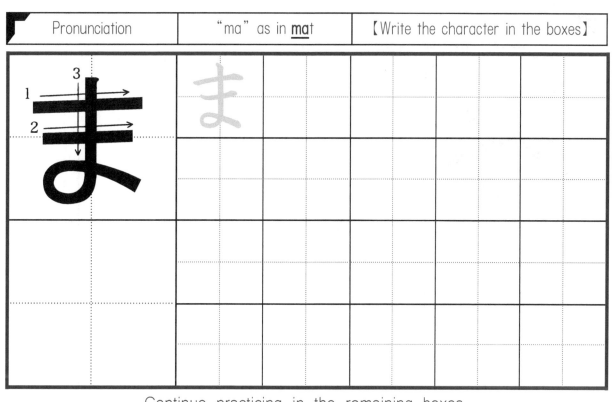

Continue practicing in the remaining boxes.

Remember to pay attention to stroke order.

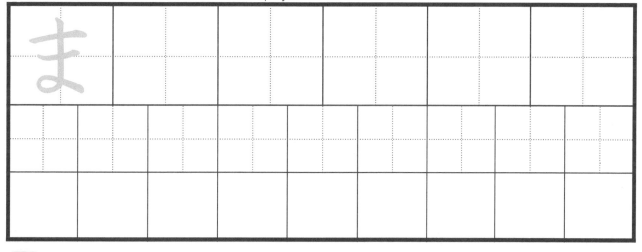

🔊 Vocabulary – Write the character in the boxes below.

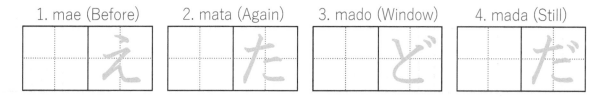

1. mae (Before)   2. mata (Again)   3. mado (Window)   4. mada (Still)

5. majime (Serious)   6. maguro (Tuna)   7. makura (Pillow)

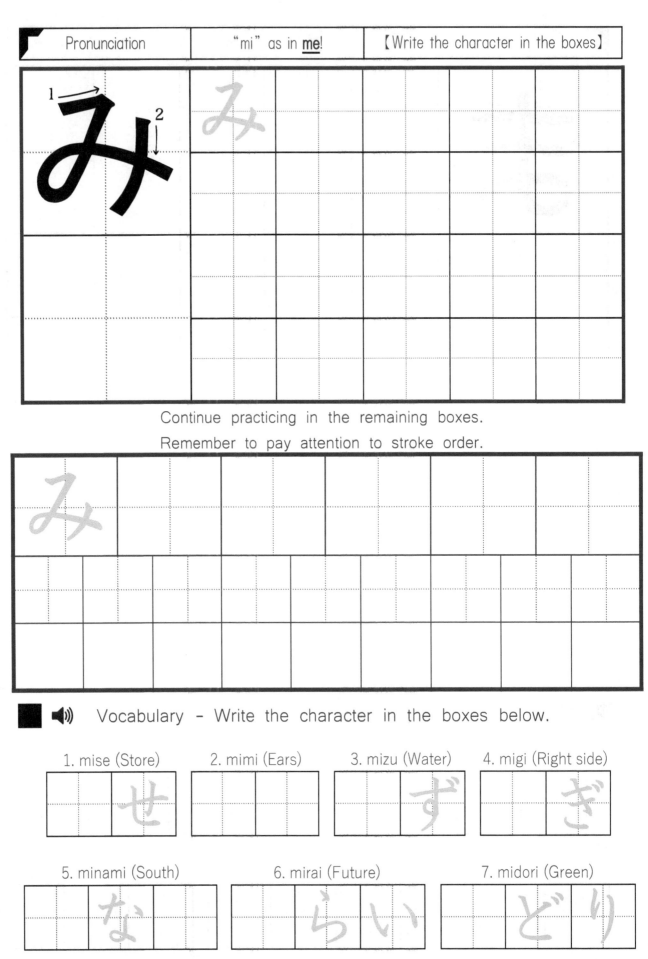

| Pronunciation | "mi" as in **me**! | 【Write the character in the boxes】 |

Continue practicing in the remaining boxes.

Remember to pay attention to stroke order.

Vocabulary - Write the character in the boxes below.

1. mise (Store)

2. mimi (Ears)

3. mizu (Water)

4. migi (Right side)

5. minami (South)

6. mirai (Future)

7. midori (Green)

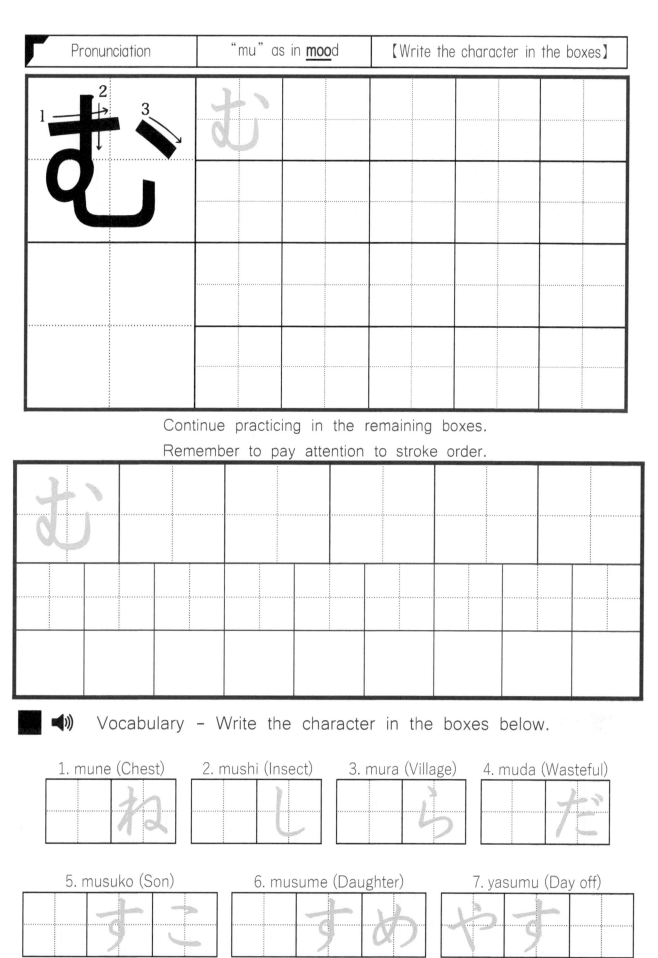

| Pronunciation | "mu" as in **moo**d | 【Write the character in the boxes】 |

Continue practicing in the remaining boxes.
Remember to pay attention to stroke order.

THE BASIC 46 HIRAGANA CHARACTERS

🔊 Vocabulary – Write the character in the boxes below.

1. mune (Chest)
2. mushi (Insect)
3. mura (Village)
4. muda (Wasteful)

5. musuko (Son)
6. musume (Daughter)
7. yasumu (Day off)

51

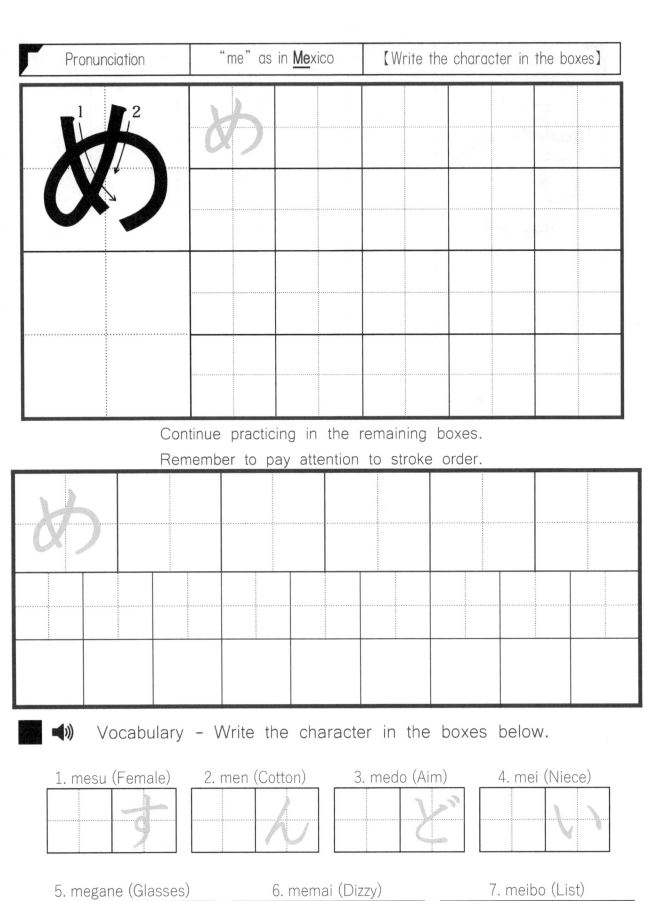

| Pronunciation | "me" as in **Me**xico | 【Write the character in the boxes】 |

Continue practicing in the remaining boxes.
Remember to pay attention to stroke order.

THE BASIC 46 HIRAGANA CHARACTERS

🔊 Vocabulary - Write the character in the boxes below.

1. mesu (Female) す

2. men (Cotton) ん

3. medo (Aim) ど

4. mei (Niece) い

5. megane (Glasses) がね

6. memai (Dizzy) まい

7. meibo (List) いぼ

| Pronunciation | "mo" as in **mo**re | 【Write the character in the boxes】 |

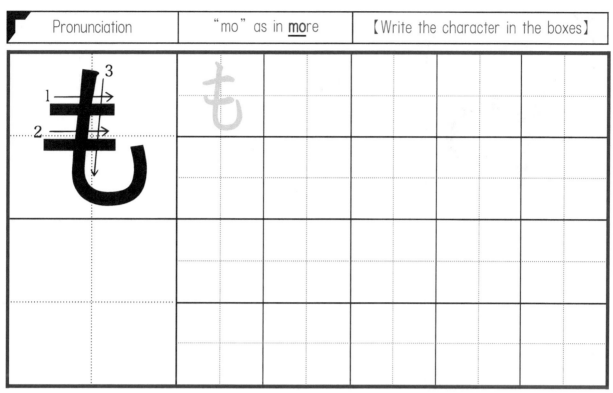

Continue practicing in the remaining boxes.
Remember to pay attention to stroke order.

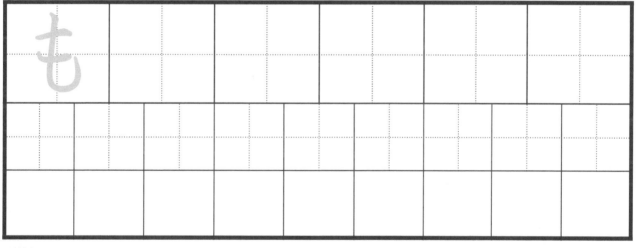

🔊 Vocabulary – Write the character in the boxes below.

1. mono (Thing)　　2. momo (Peach)　　3. mon (Gate)　　4. motsu (to hold)

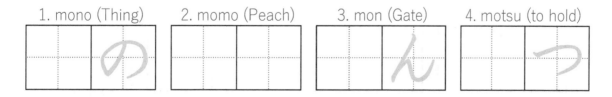

5. motto (More)　　6. moufu (Blanket)　　7. monku (Complaint)

| Pronunciation | "ya" as in **ya**cht | 【Write the character in the boxes】 |

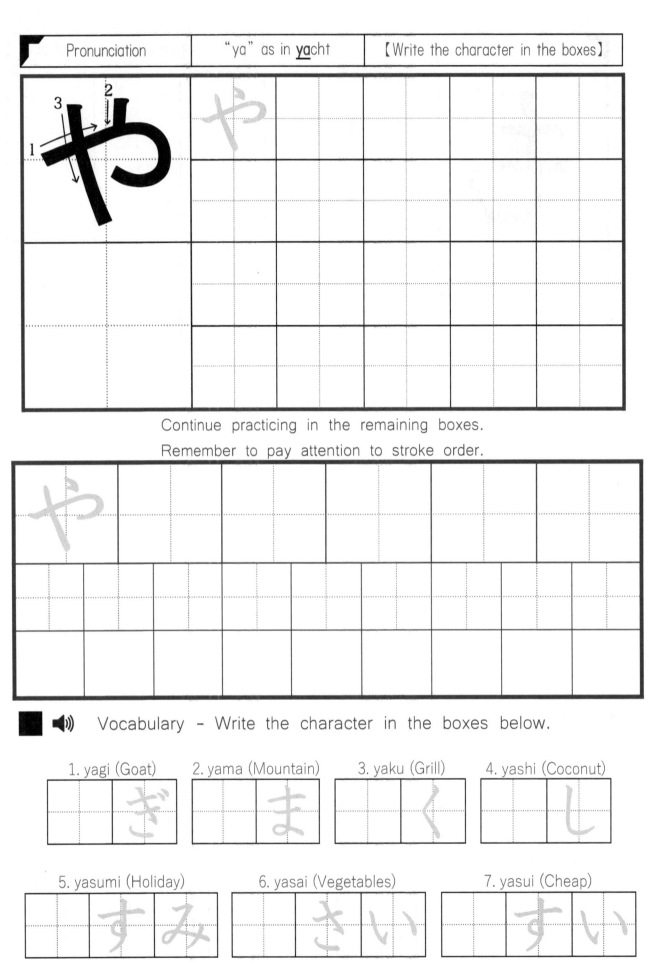

Continue practicing in the remaining boxes.

Remember to pay attention to stroke order.

🔊 Vocabulary - Write the character in the boxes below.

1. yagi (Goat)　　2. yama (Mountain)　　3. yaku (Grill)　　4. yashi (Coconut)

5. yasumi (Holiday)　　6. yasai (Vegetables)　　7. yasui (Cheap)

54

Pronunciation	"yu" as in **yew**	【Write the character in the boxes】

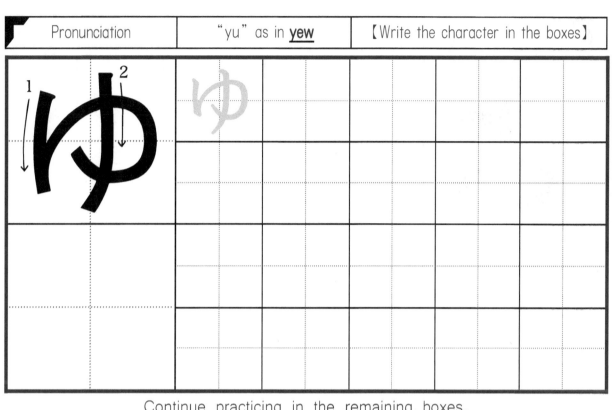

Continue practicing in the remaining boxes.
Remember to pay attention to stroke order.

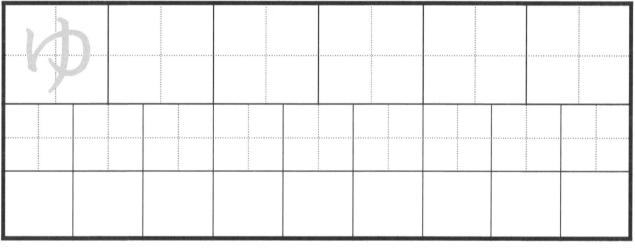

🔊 Vocabulary – Write the character in the boxes below.

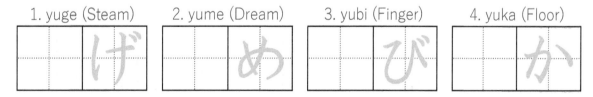

1. yuge (Steam)　　2. yume (Dream)　　3. yubi (Finger)　　4. yuka (Floor)

5. yubiwa (Ring)　　6. yuderu (to boile)　　7. yurai (Orgin)

Pronunciation	"yo" as in **yo**ga	【Write the character in the boxes】

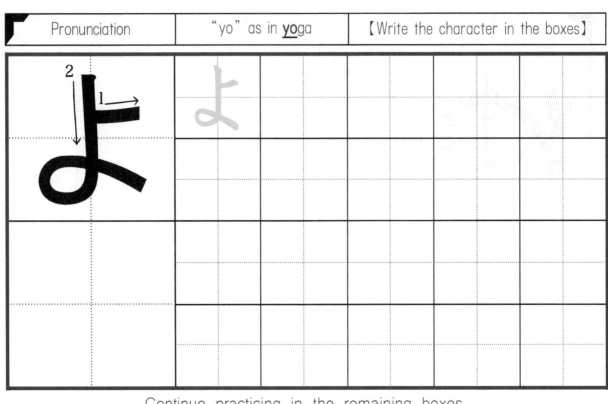

Continue practicing in the remaining boxes.

Remember to pay attention to stroke order.

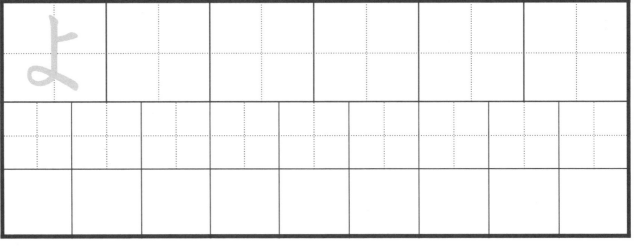

◀)) Vocabulary - Write the character in the boxes below.

1. yoi (Good)　　2. yoko (Beside)　　3. yomu (to read)　　4. yoru (Night)

い　　こ　　む　　る

5. yotei (Schedule)　　6. yowai (Weak)　　7. yonaka (Midnight)

てい　　わい　　なか

| Pronunciation | "ra" as in **ra**men | 【Write the character in the boxes】 |

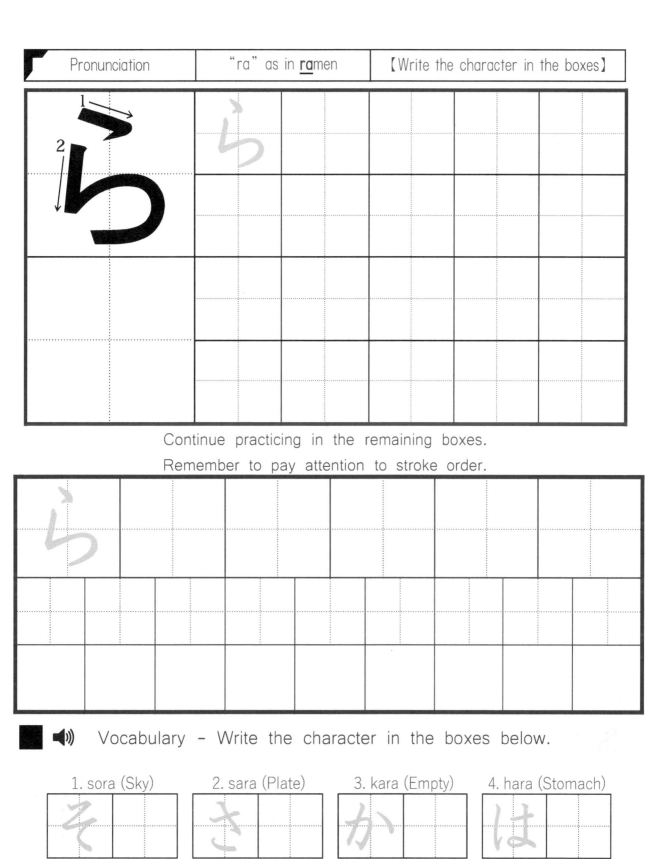

Continue practicing in the remaining boxes.

Remember to pay attention to stroke order.

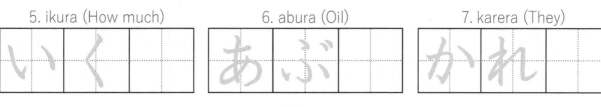

Vocabulary – Write the character in the boxes below.

1. sora (Sky)

2. sara (Plate)

3. kara (Empty)

4. hara (Stomach)

5. ikura (How much)

6. abura (Oil)

7. karera (They)

| Pronunciation | "ri" as in **ri**ng | 【Write the character in the boxes】 |

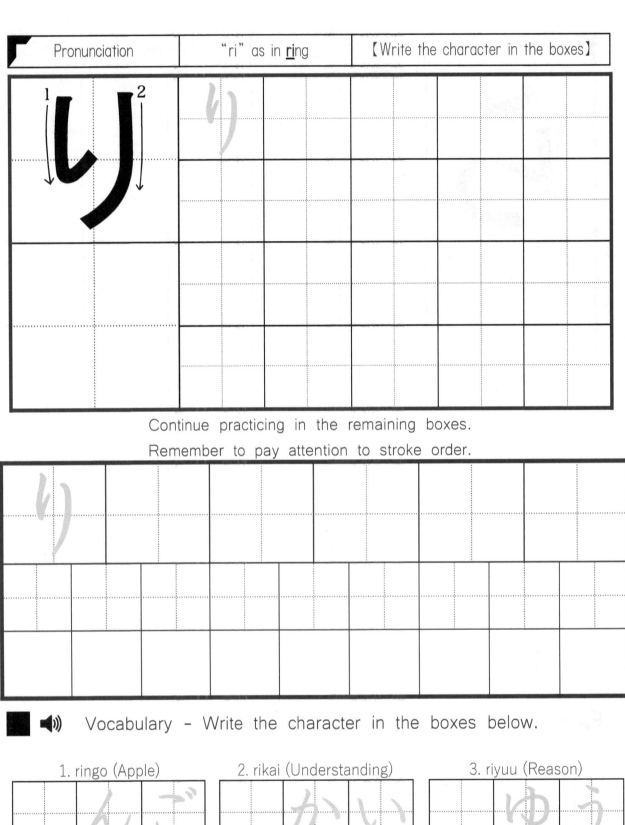

Continue practicing in the remaining boxes.

Remember to pay attention to stroke order.

Vocabulary - Write the character in the boxes below.

1. ringo (Apple)   2. rikai (Understanding)   3. riyuu (Reason)

4. kumori (Cloudy)   5. kusuri (Medicine)   6. odori (Dance)

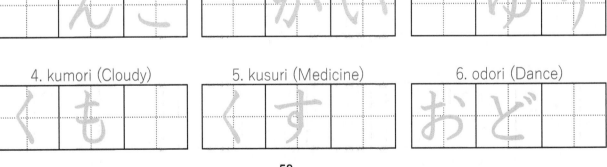

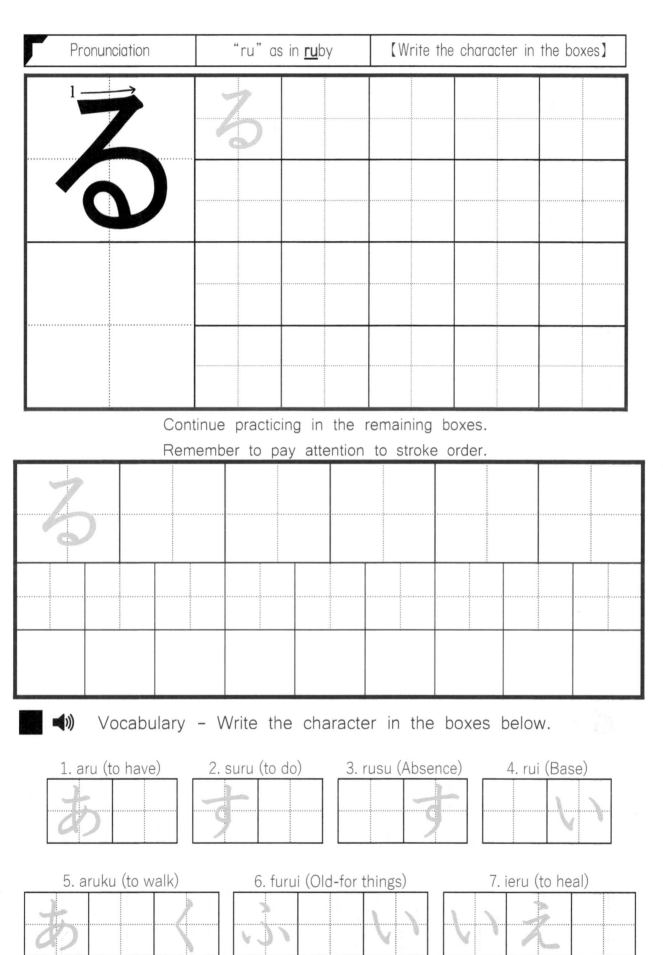

| Pronunciation | "ru" as in **ru**by | 【Write the character in the boxes】 |

Continue practicing in the remaining boxes.
Remember to pay attention to stroke order.

Vocabulary – Write the character in the boxes below.

1. aru (to have)
2. suru (to do)
3. rusu (Absence)
4. rui (Base)

5. aruku (to walk)
6. furui (Old-for things)
7. ieru (to heal)

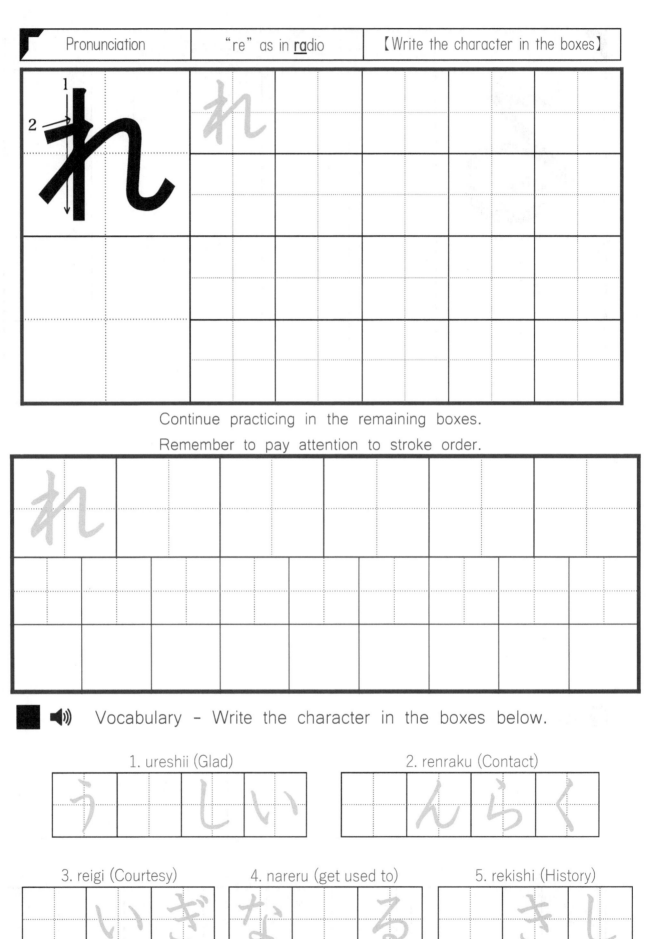

Continue practicing in the remaining boxes.

Remember to pay attention to stroke order.

🔊 Vocabulary - Write the character in the boxes below.

1. ureshii (Glad)

2. renraku (Contact)

3. reigi (Courtesy)

4. nareru (get used to)

5. rekishi (History)

| Pronunciation | "ro" as in **ro**pe | 【Write the character in the boxes】 |

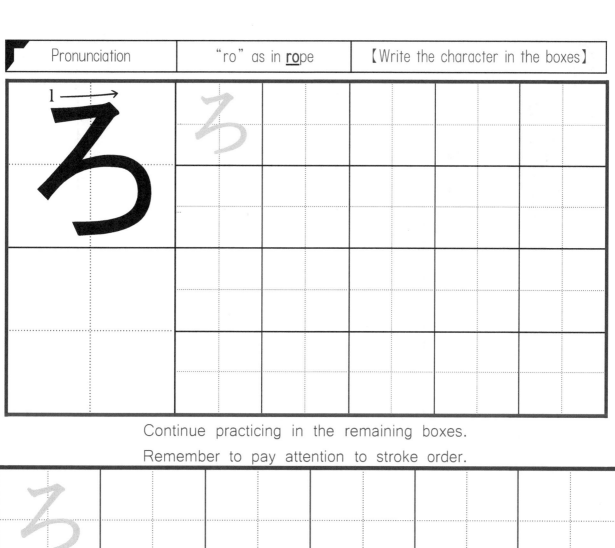

Continue practicing in the remaining boxes.

Remember to pay attention to stroke order.

🔊 Vocabulary – Write the character in the boxes below.

1. roba (Donkey) 2. iro (Color) 3. shiro (White) 4. roku (Six)

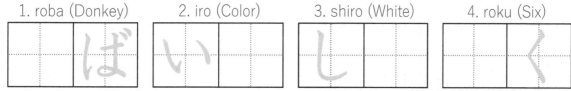

5. ushiro (Behind) 6. rokuji (6 o'clock) 7. kiiro (Yellow)

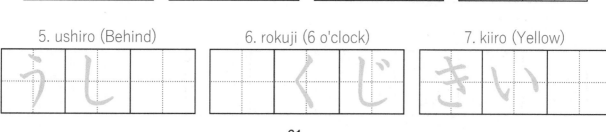

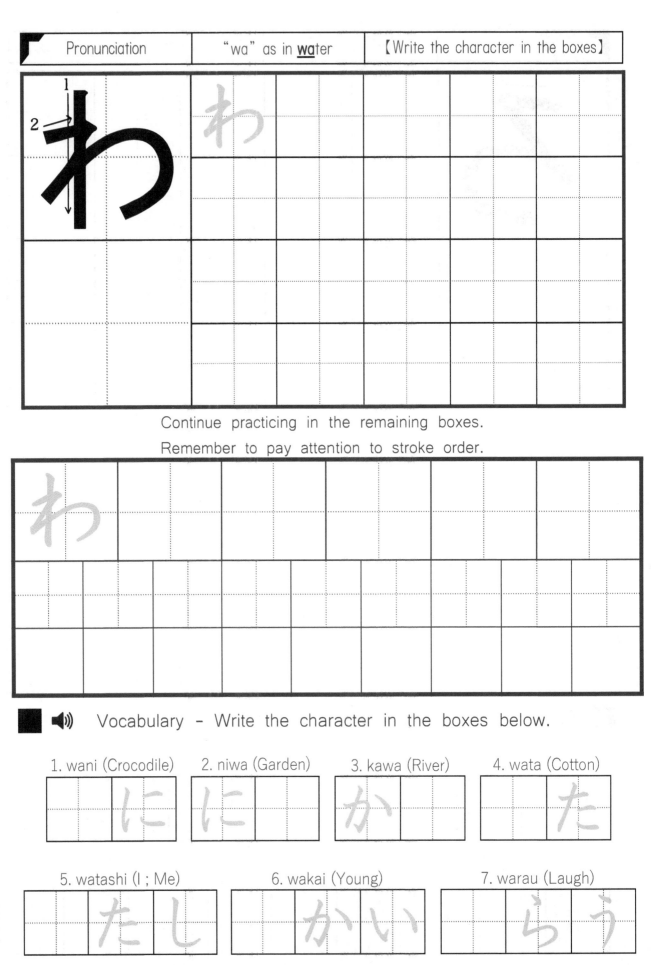

| Pronunciation | "wa" as in **wa**ter | 【Write the character in the boxes】 |

Continue practicing in the remaining boxes.

Remember to pay attention to stroke order.

🔊 Vocabulary – Write the character in the boxes below.

1. wani (Crocodile)

2. niwa (Garden)

3. kawa (River)

4. wata (Cotton)

5. watashi (I ; Me)

6. wakai (Young)

7. warau (Laugh)

Pronunciation	"wo" as in **wo**rry	【Write the character in the boxes】

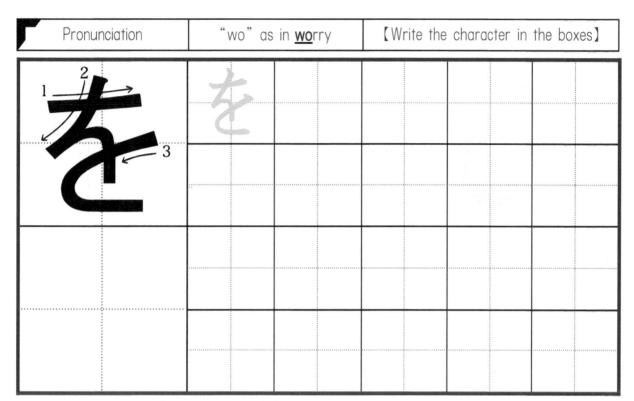

Continue practicing in the remaining boxes.

Remember to pay attention to stroke order.

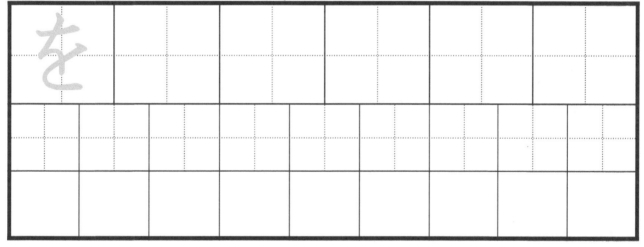

Note: The Japanese particle **WO (を)** marks the direct object of a Japanese sentence. Even though it is spelled with を in Hiragana, we need to pronounce the particle を as "o". The direct object is linked to the action of the verb. so we must use を to glue these words together.

Example sentences:

1. きょうは、さかな (**を**) たべました。　　(I ate fish today.)

2. にほんご (**を**) べんきょうしています。　　(I am studying Japanese.)

3. あした、やま (**を**) のぼります。　　　(Tomorrow, I will climb a mountain.)

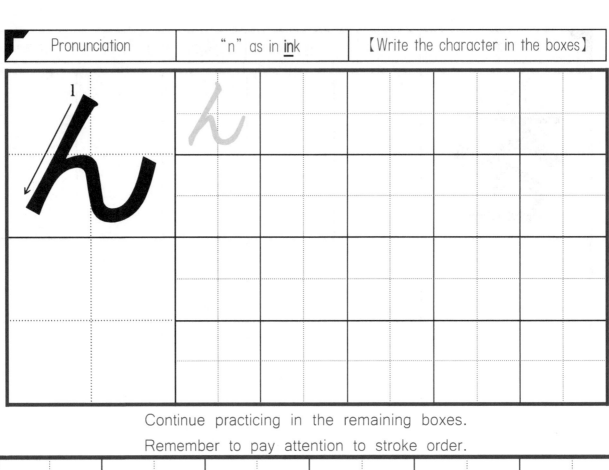

Continue practicing in the remaining boxes.

Remember to pay attention to stroke order.

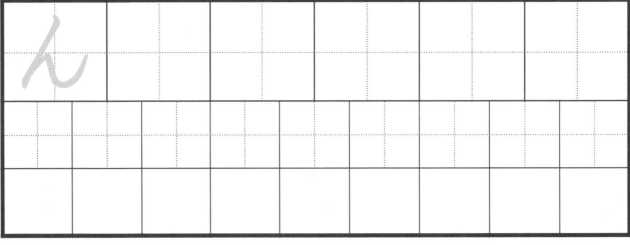

🔊 Vocabulary – Write the character in the boxes below.

1. densha (Train)
2. anzen (Safety)

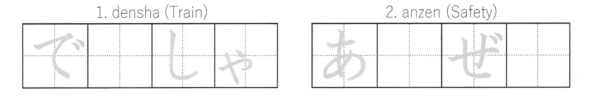

3. kaban (Bag)
4. gohan (Rice)
5. min'na (Everybody)

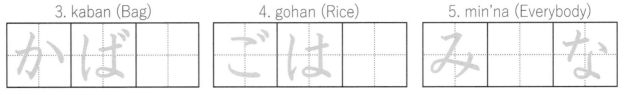

Both hiragana and katakana have two special groups of characters called
Dakuten and Handakuten.

Each character is a slightly altered version of a basic character.

❖ Additionally, Hiragana makes use of two diacritical marks.

<u>The first</u> diacritical mark is called a dakuten or ten-ten and looks like this ˝, two diagonal strokes placed on the top right corner of a character.

Its job is to change an unvoiced sound into its voiced counterpart. ⟨k⟩ changes to ⟨g⟩, ⟨sa⟩ changes to ⟨za⟩, ⟨t⟩ changes to ⟨d⟩ and ⟨h⟩ changes to ⟨b⟩.

<u>The second</u> diacritical mark is the handakuten or maru and looks like this ˚, a circle which is also placed on the top right corner of a character.

The handakuten is only used with Hiragana in the h- column and turns the consonant ⟨h⟩ into a ⟨p⟩.

You can see all the changes made by the dakuten and handakuten in the chart below.

Normal sound	with dakuten	with handakuten
は ha	ば ba	ぱ pa
ひ hi	び bi	ぴ pi
ふ hu	ぶ bu	ぷ pu
へ he	べ be	ぺ pe
ほ ho	ぼ bo	ぽ po

□˝ **dakuten**
□˚ **handakuten**

Dakuten

が **ga**	ぎ **gi**	ぐ **gu**	げ **ge**	ご **go**
ざ **za**	じ **zi(ji)**	ず **zu**	ぜ **ze**	ぞ **zo**
だ **da**	ぢ **di(ji)**	づ **du**	で **de**	ど **do**
ば **ba**	び **bi**	ぶ **bu**	べ **be**	ぼ **bo**

Handakuten

ぱ **pa**	ぴ **pi**	ぷ **pu**	ぺ **pe**	ぽ **po**

Note: "ji" and "zu" are usually written with じ and ず.

Pronunciation	"ga" as in **go**t	【Write the character in the boxes】

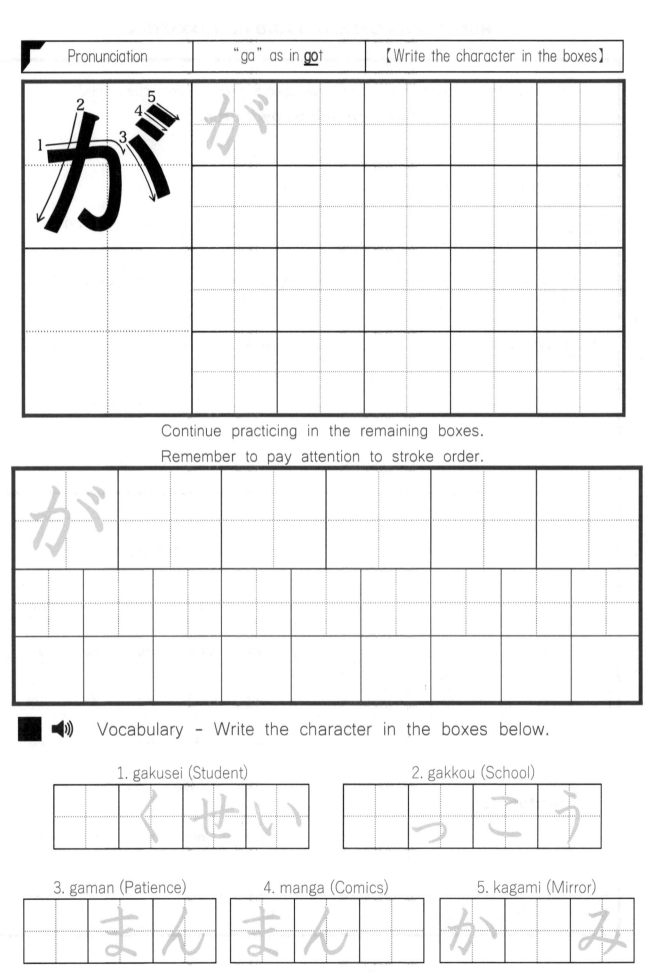

Continue practicing in the remaining boxes.

Remember to pay attention to stroke order.

🔊 Vocabulary - Write the character in the boxes below.

1. gakusei (Student)

く せ い

2. gakkou (School)

っ こ う

3. gaman (Patience)

ま ん

4. manga (Comics)

ま ん

5. kagami (Mirror)

か み

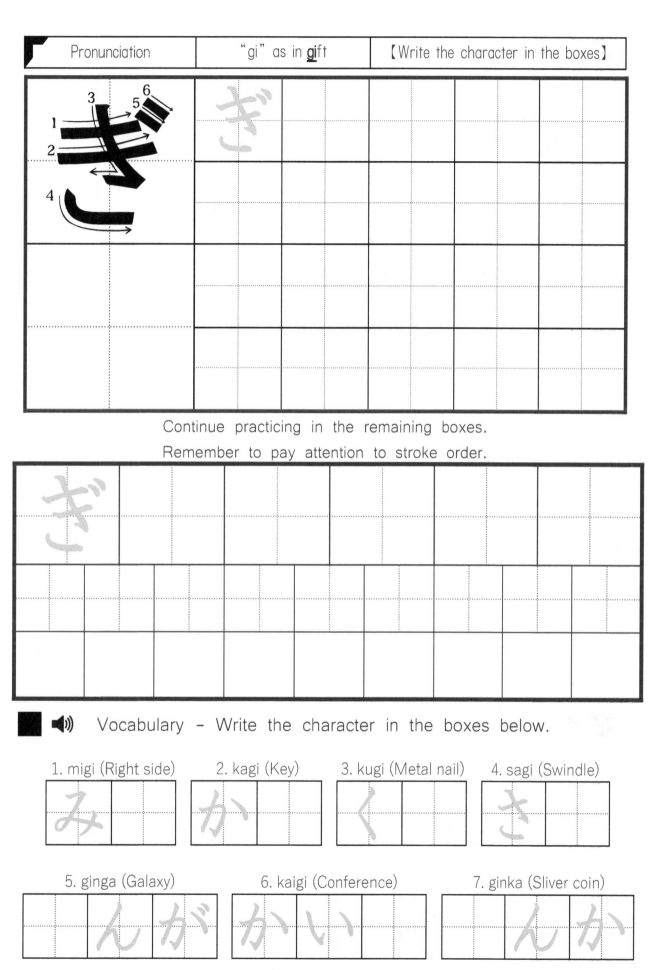

| Pronunciation | "gi" as in **gi**ft | 【Write the character in the boxes】 |

Continue practicing in the remaining boxes.
Remember to pay attention to stroke order.

🔊 Vocabulary – Write the character in the boxes below.

1. migi (Right side)　　2. kagi (Key)　　3. kugi (Metal nail)　　4. sagi (Swindle)

5. ginga (Galaxy)　　6. kaigi (Conference)　　7. ginka (Sliver coin)

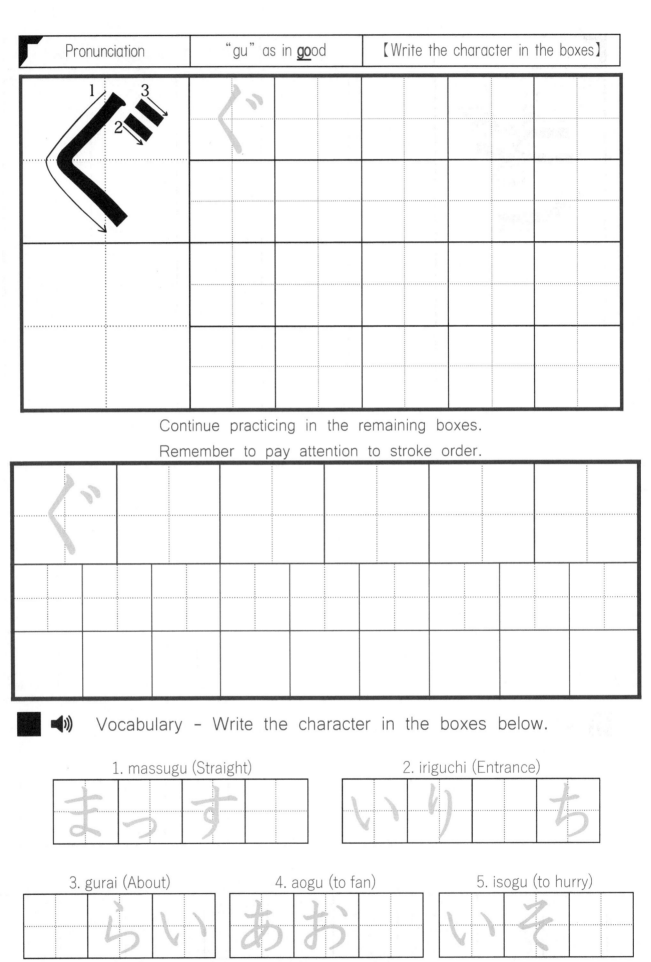

Pronunciation	"gu" as in **go**od	【Write the character in the boxes】

ぐ

Continue practicing in the remaining boxes.
Remember to pay attention to stroke order.

Vocabulary – Write the character in the boxes below.

1. massugu (Straight)

まっす

2. iriguchi (Entrance)

いり　　ち

3. gurai (About)

らい

4. aogu (to fan)

あお

5. isogu (to hurry)

いそ

68

Pronunciation	"ge" as in <u>ge</u>t	【Write the character in the boxes】

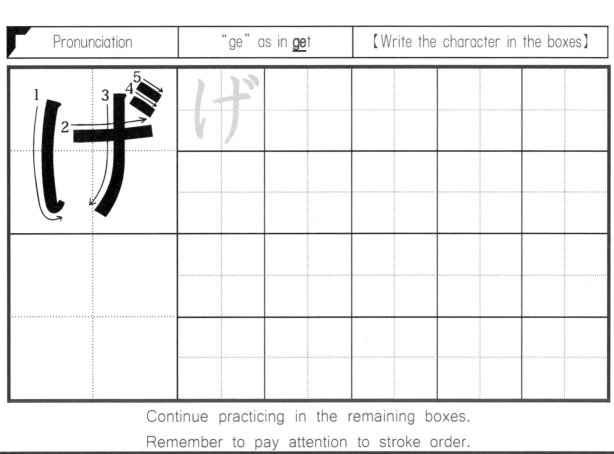

Continue practicing in the remaining boxes.

Remember to pay attention to stroke order.

Vocabulary – Write the character in the boxes below.

1. genkan (Entrance)

2. genkin (Cash)

3. genki (Fine; Healthy)

4. gengo (Language)

5. gendo (Limit)

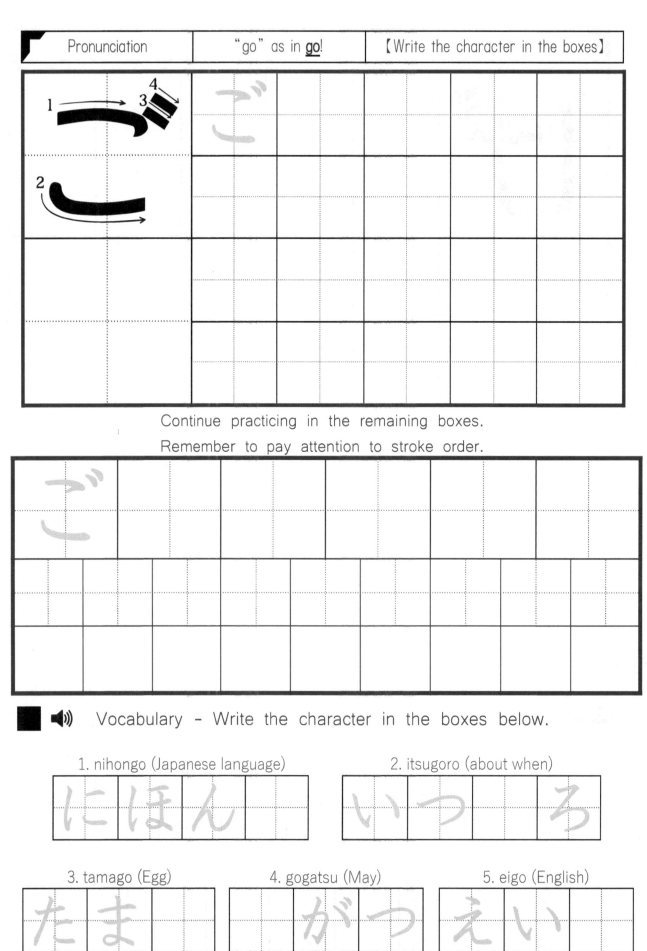

| Pronunciation | "go" as in **go**! | 【Write the character in the boxes】 |

Continue practicing in the remaining boxes.
Remember to pay attention to stroke order.

🔊 Vocabulary - Write the character in the boxes below.

1. nihongo (Japanese language)

にほん

2. itsugoro (about when)

いつ　　ろ

3. tamago (Egg)

たま

4. gogatsu (May)

がつ

5. eigo (English)

えい

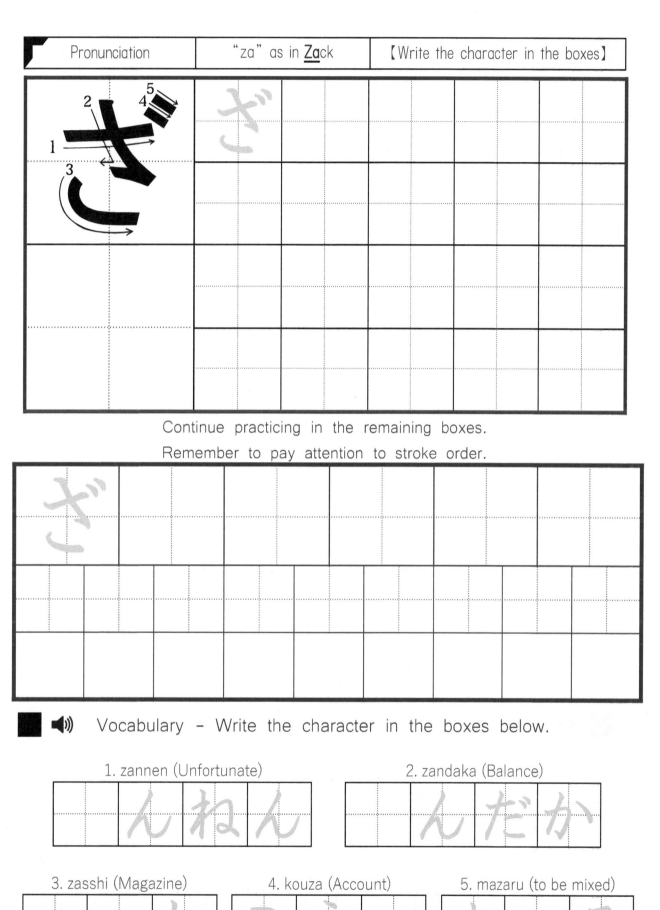

| Pronunciation | "za" as in **Za**ck | 【Write the character in the boxes】 |

Continue practicing in the remaining boxes.
Remember to pay attention to stroke order.

🔊 Vocabulary – Write the character in the boxes below.

1. zannen (Unfortunate)

2. zandaka (Balance)

3. zasshi (Magazine)

4. kouza (Account)

5. mazaru (to be mixed)

71

Pronunciation	"zi (ji)" as in Kan**ji**	【Write the character in the boxes】

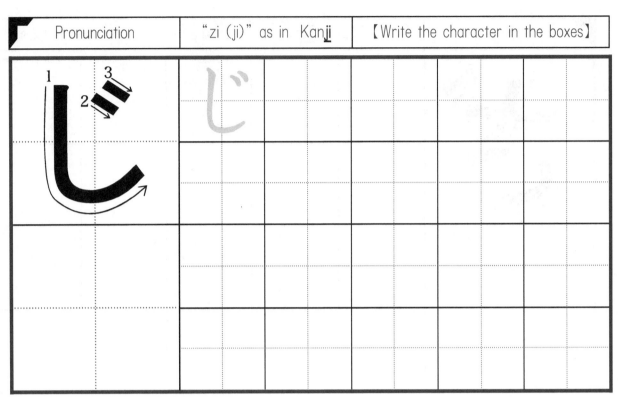

Continue practicing in the remaining boxes.

Remember to pay attention to stroke order.

  Vocabulary - Write the character in the boxes below.

Note: This Character written with tenten has one exception: じ is pronounced "ji."

1. jikan (Time)   2. jisho (Dictionary)   3. jishin (Earthquake)

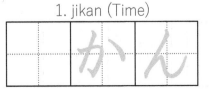

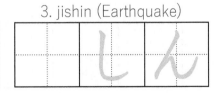

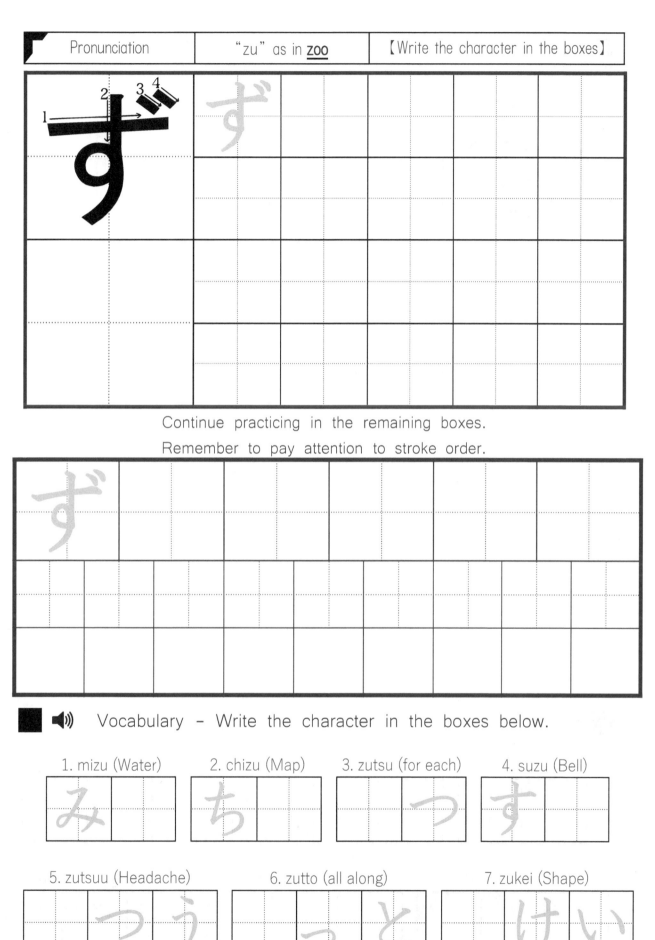

| Pronunciation | "zu" as in **ZOO** | 【Write the character in the boxes】 |

Continue practicing in the remaining boxes.

Remember to pay attention to stroke order.

🔊 Vocabulary - Write the character in the boxes below.

1. mizu (Water)

2. chizu (Map)

3. zutsu (for each)

4. suzu (Bell)

5. zutsuu (Headache)

6. zutto (all along)

7. zukei (Shape)

| Pronunciation | "ze" as in <u>zeh</u> | 【Write the character in the boxes】 |

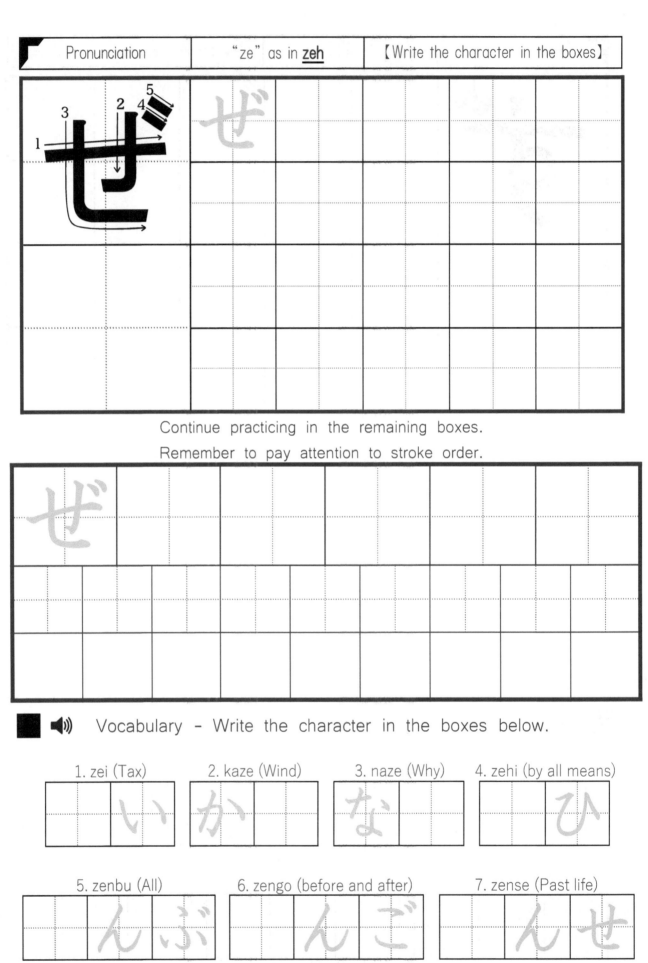

Continue practicing in the remaining boxes.
Remember to pay attention to stroke order.

Vocabulary - Write the character in the boxes below.

1. zei (Tax)　　2. kaze (Wind)　　3. naze (Why)　　4. zehi (by all means)

5. zenbu (All)　　6. zengo (before and after)　　7. zense (Past life)

74

| Pronunciation | "zo" as in **zo**ne | 【Write the character in the boxes】 |

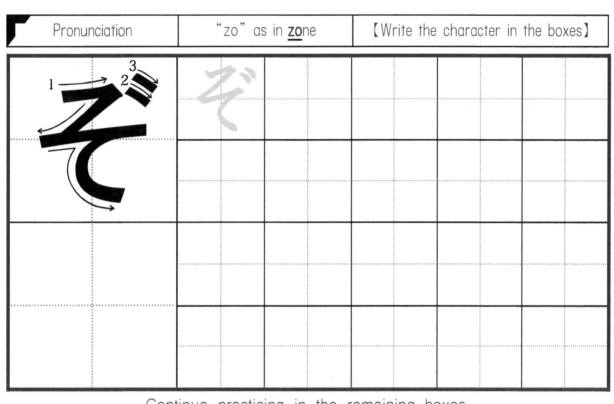

Continue practicing in the remaining boxes.
Remember to pay attention to stroke order.

🔊 Vocabulary – Write the character in the boxes below.

1. kazoeru (to count)

2. kanzou (Liver)

3. nozoku (Remove)   4. kazoku (Family)   5. douzo (Please; go a head)

| Pronunciation | "da" as in **da**nce | 【Write the character in the boxes】 |

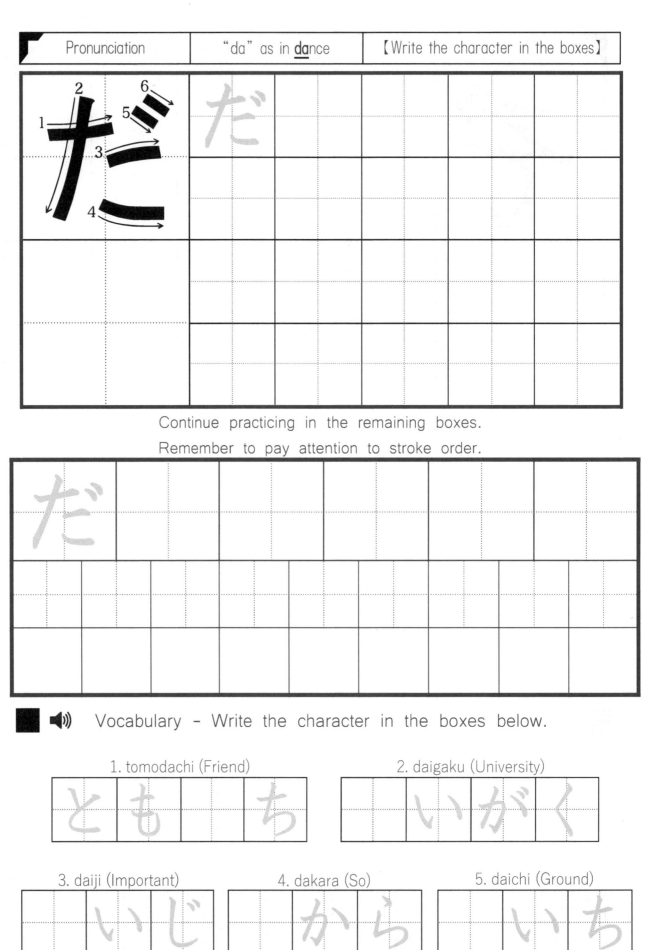

Continue practicing in the remaining boxes.
Remember to pay attention to stroke order.

🔊 Vocabulary - Write the character in the boxes below.

1. tomodachi (Friend)

と　も　　　　ち

2. daigaku (University)

　　い　が　く

3. daiji (Important)

　　い　じ

4. dakara (So)

か　ら

5. daichi (Ground)

　　い　ち

Pronunciation	"di"	【Write the character in the boxes】

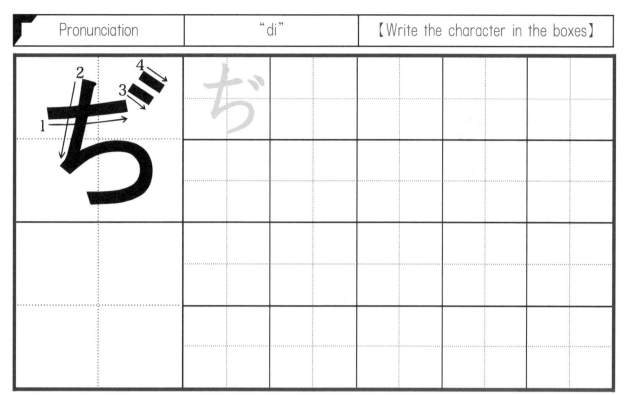

Continue practicing in the remaining boxes.

Remember to pay attention to stroke order.

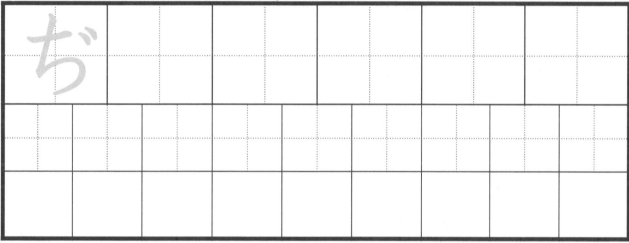

Note: Again, it's quite easy to understand that じ(ji) is derived from し (shi) and that ぢ (ji)is derived from チ (chi). Similar enough to the other pair, they are identical in sound and have changed compared to their original intended sound.

Original sound Modern Japanese sound.

じ	zi	dʑi/ ʑi
ぢ	di	dʑi/ ʑi

Example :（はなぢ）‐ (Nose blood) かのじょは、はなぢがでていました。 (She had a nosebleed).
じ and ぢ are now mainly used in a similar manner that represents the sound dʑi/ ʑi. If you are still confused about how it's pronounced, it sounds like the French J where it produces a softer sound where your teeth are technically closed and your tongue is technically raised to your upper palate.
If that's still confusing for you, try saying or listening to someone say je m'appelle in a French accent.
The initial "je" in the beginning is how "dz" in じ and ぢ should be pronounced as.

| Pronunciation | "du" | 【Write the character in the boxes】 |

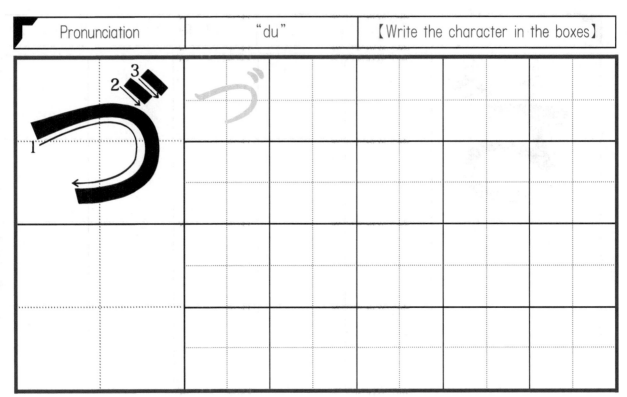

Continue practicing in the remaining boxes.

Remember to pay attention to stroke order.

Note: づ have irregular pronunciations; also, to write this character, type it as if they were pronounced according to the pattern: du = づ) In modern Japanese, the hiragana letter has exactly the same pronunciation as the hiragana letter, that is, 'zu' or 'dzu'. When the kana scripts were reformed after the Second World War, were almost completely replaced by -- but not quite.

There are still a few words that preserve as it originally was. Mostly has been retained where a word is etymologically derived by voicing.

🔊 **Example** : I. (つづく) (continue)   **Example** : 2. (みちづれ)(together or with)

Example Sentence : このつづきはあしたやりましょう。   かれをみちづれにしないでください。
(Kono tsuduki wa ashita yarimashou.)   (Kare wo michidure ni shinaide kudasai.)
(Let's continue this tomorrow.)   (Don't take him with you.)

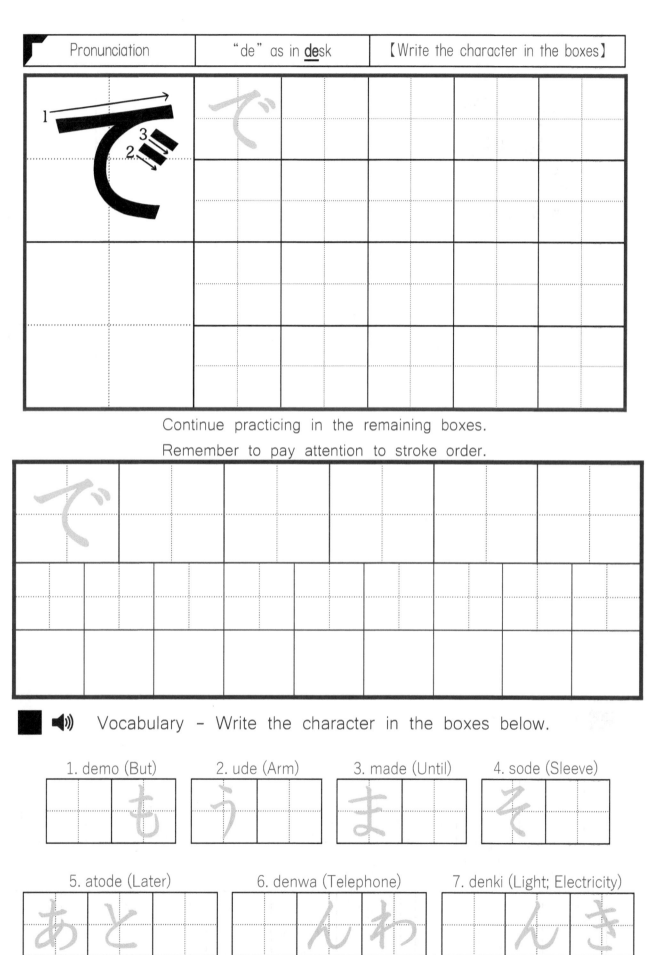

| Pronunciation | "de" as in **de**sk | 【Write the character in the boxes】 |

Continue practicing in the remaining boxes.
Remember to pay attention to stroke order.

🔊 Vocabulary - Write the character in the boxes below.

1. demo (But) 2. ude (Arm) 3. made (Until) 4. sode (Sleeve)

5. atode (Later) 6. denwa (Telephone) 7. denki (Light; Electricity)

Pronunciation	"do" as in **do**or	【Write the character in the boxes】

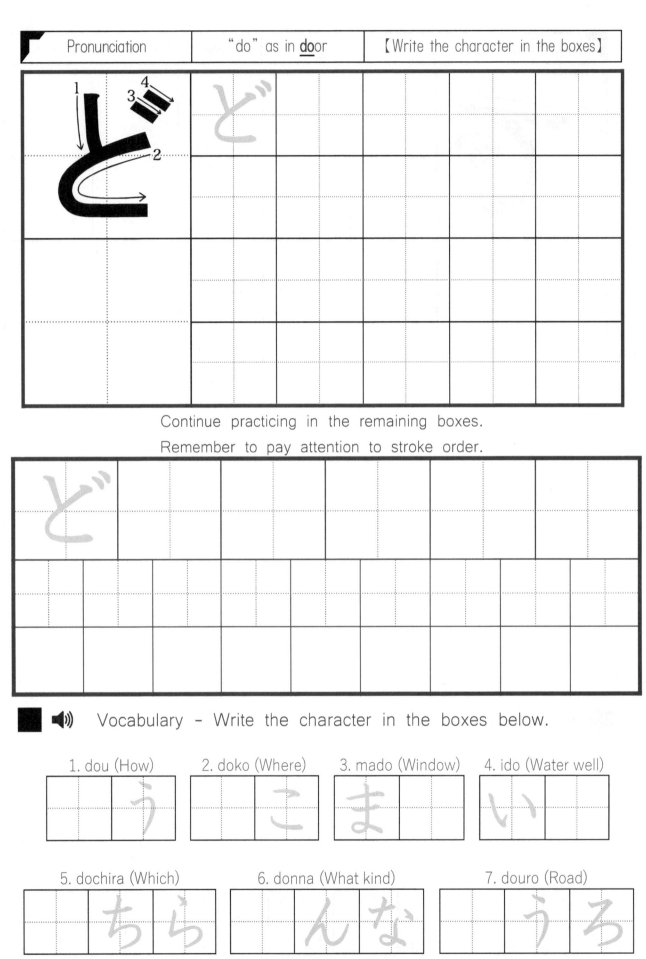

Continue practicing in the remaining boxes.

Remember to pay attention to stroke order.

Vocabulary – Write the character in the boxes below.

1. dou (How)

2. doko (Where)

3. mado (Window)

4. ido (Water well)

5. dochira (Which)

6. donna (What kind)

7. douro (Road)

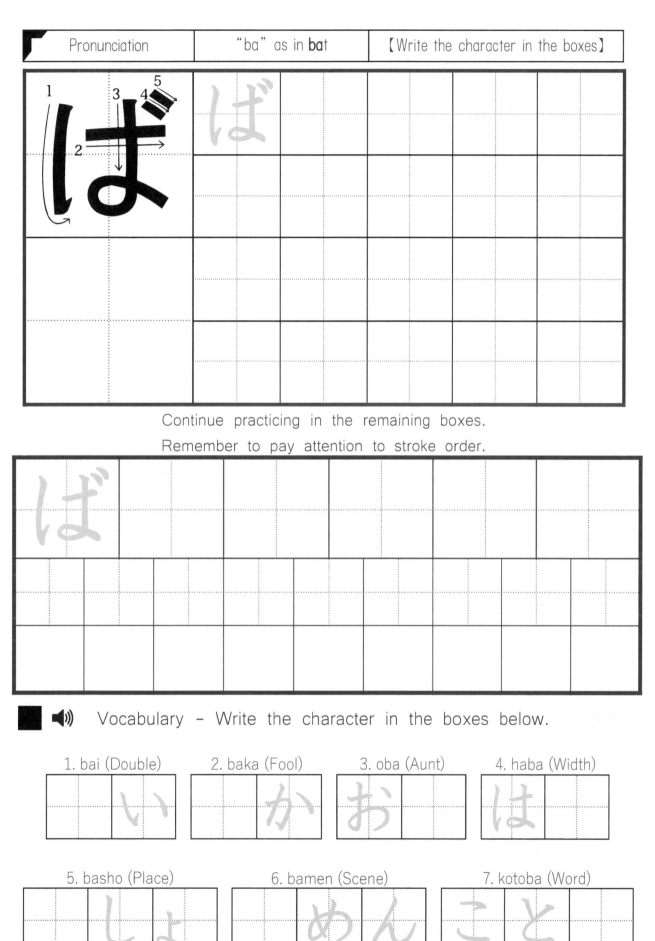

| Pronunciation | "ba" as in **ba**t | 【Write the character in the boxes】 |

Continue practicing in the remaining boxes.
Remember to pay attention to stroke order.

🔊 Vocabulary - Write the character in the boxes below.

1. bai (Double) 2. baka (Fool) 3. oba (Aunt) 4. haba (Width)

5. basho (Place) 6. bamen (Scene) 7. kotoba (Word)

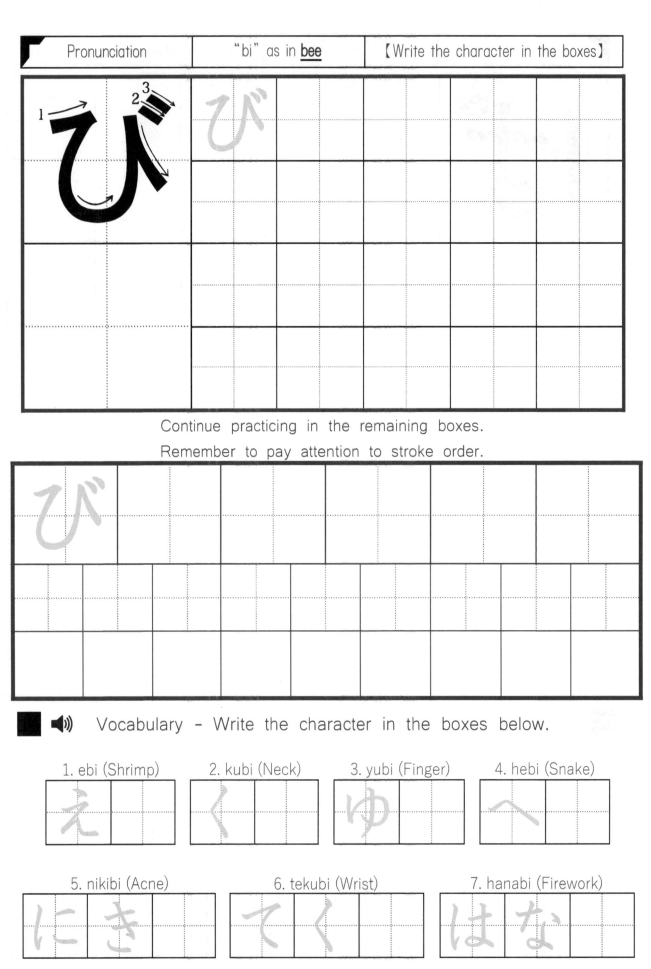

| Pronunciation | "bi" as in **bee** | 【Write the character in the boxes】 |

Continue practicing in the remaining boxes.

Remember to pay attention to stroke order.

HIRAGANA - DAKUTEN AND HANDAKUTEN

🔊 Vocabulary - Write the character in the boxes below.

1. ebi (Shrimp)

2. kubi (Neck)

3. yubi (Finger)

4. hebi (Snake)

5. nikibi (Acne)

6. tekubi (Wrist)

7. hanabi (Firework)

82

Pronunciation	"bu" as in **bo**om	【Write the character in the boxes】

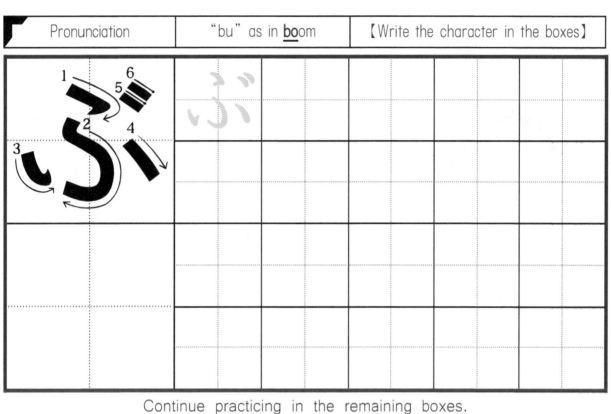

Continue practicing in the remaining boxes.
Remember to pay attention to stroke order.

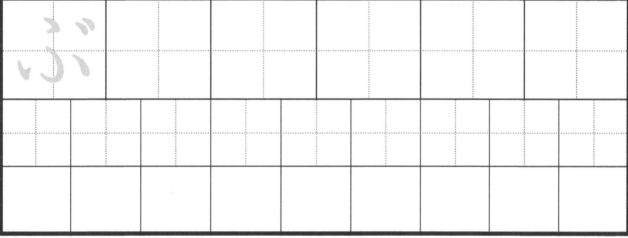

◼ ◀)) Vocabulary – Write the character in the boxes below.

1. jibun (Self)   2. erabu (to choose)   3. bunka (Culture)

4. zenbu (Entire)   5. asobu (to play)   6. hakobu (to carry)

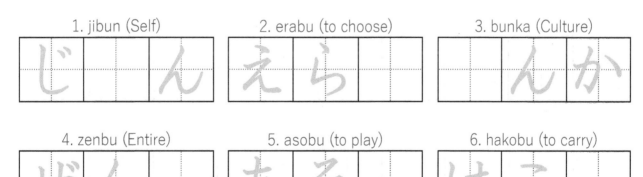

83

| Pronunciation | "be" as in <u>Be</u>n | 【Write the character in the boxes】 |

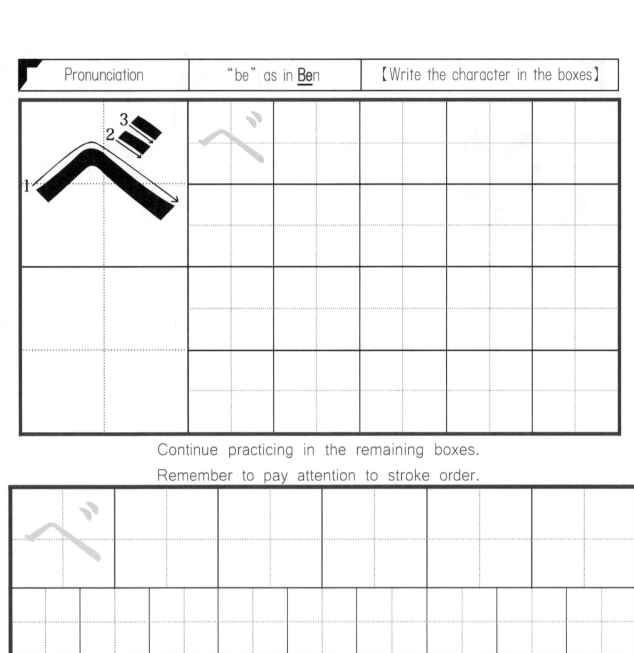

Continue practicing in the remaining boxes.

Remember to pay attention to stroke order.

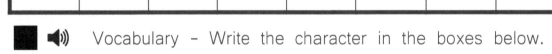

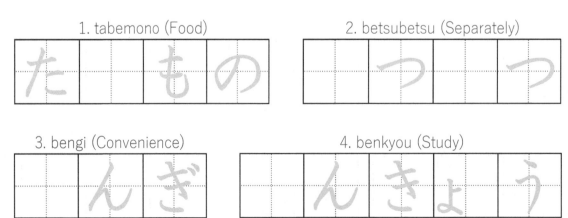 Vocabulary - Write the character in the boxes below.

1. tabemono (Food)

2. betsubetsu (Separately)

3. bengi (Convenience)

4. benkyou (Study)

Pronunciation	"bo" as in <u>bo</u>y	【Write the character in the boxes】

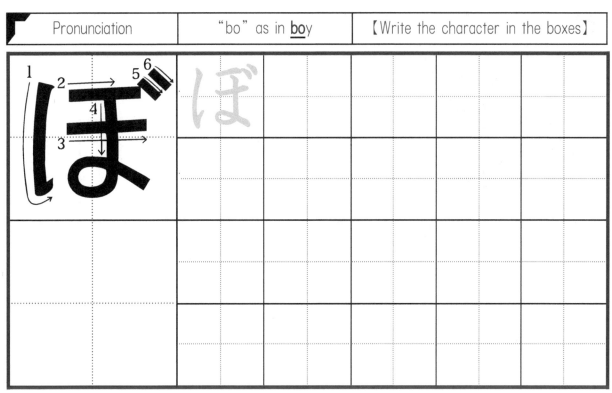

Continue practicing in the remaining boxes.

Remember to pay attention to stroke order.

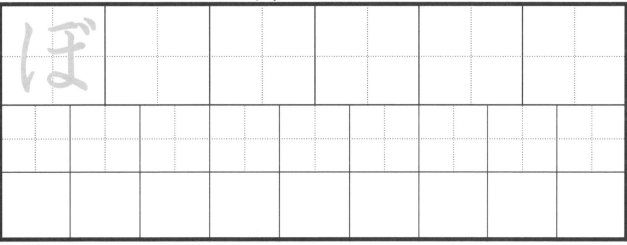

🔊 Vocabulary - Write the character in the boxes below.

1. bouryoku (Violence)

2. boushi (Hat)

3. kibou (Hope)

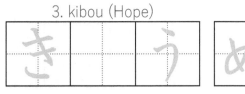

4. meibo (List)

5. ekubo (Dimple)

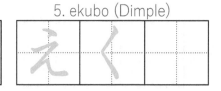

Pronunciation	"pa" as in <u>pa</u>ckage	【Write the character in the boxes】

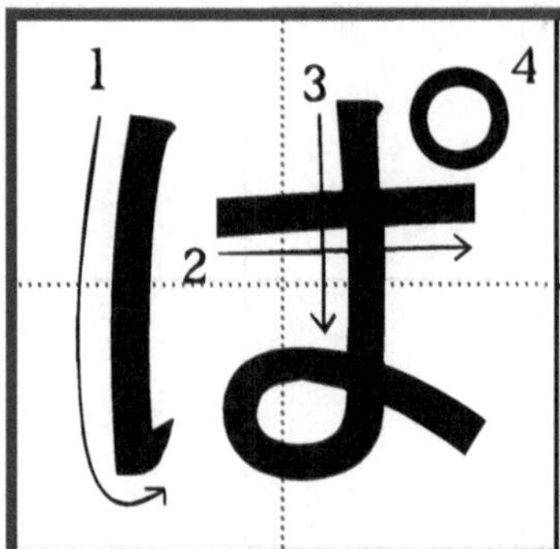

ぱ

Continue practicing in the remaining boxes.
Remember to pay attention to stroke order.

ぱ

Vocabulary - Write the character in the boxes below.

1. yappari (Finally; Absolutely)
やっ り

2. ippai (Full)
いっ い

3. happa (Leaves)
はっ

4. rippa (Splendid)
りっ

5. rappa (Trumpet)
らっ

Pronunciation	"pi" as in **pee**	【Write the character in the boxes】

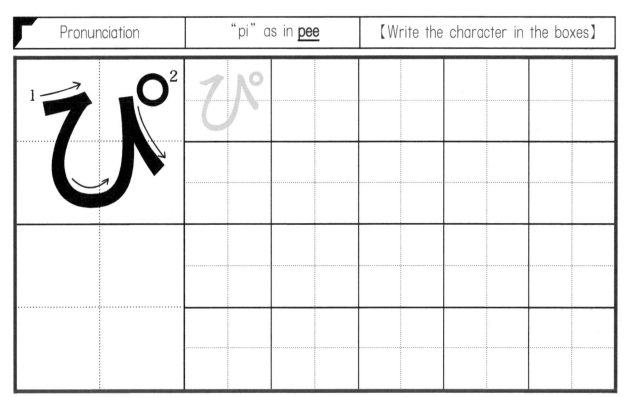

Continue practicing in the remaining boxes.
Remember to pay attention to stroke order.

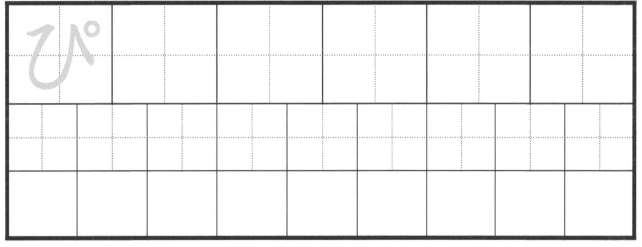

🔊 Vocabulary - Write the character in the boxes below.

1. enpitsu (Pencil)

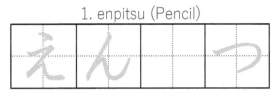

2. beppin (Pretty girl)

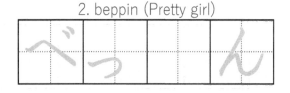

3. pikapika (Shiny)

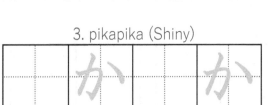

4. tanpin (One item)

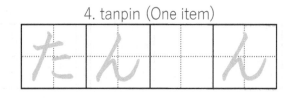

| Pronunciation | "pu" as in **poo**r | 【Write the character in the boxes】 |

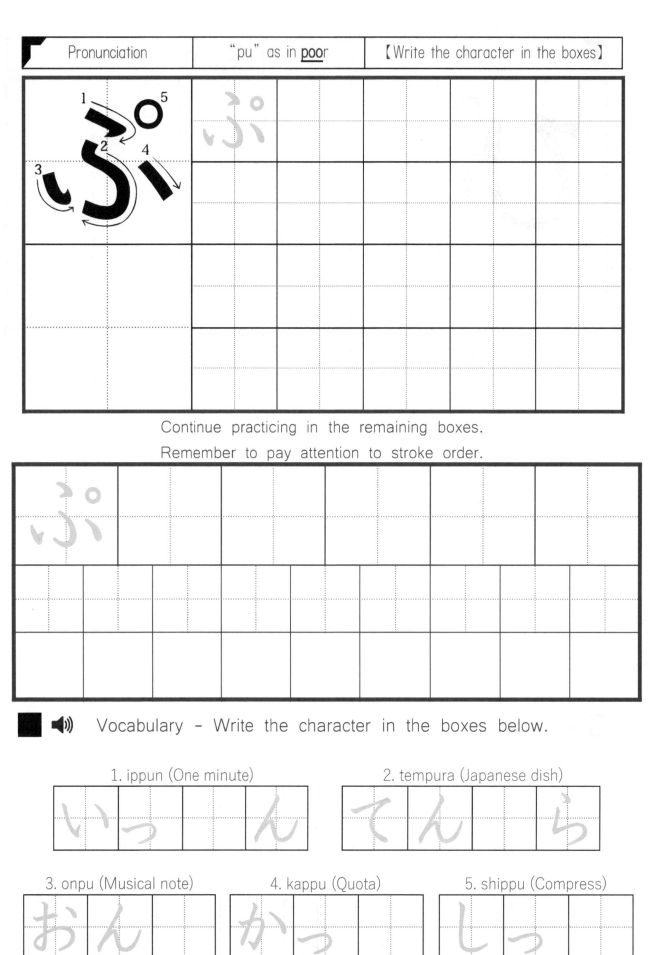

Continue practicing in the remaining boxes.

Remember to pay attention to stroke order.

🔊 Vocabulary - Write the character in the boxes below.

1. ippun (One minute)

い っ ん

2. tempura (Japanese dish)

て ん ら

3. onpu (Musical note)

お ん

4. kappu (Quota)

か っ

5. shippu (Compress)

し っ

88

Pronunciation	"pe" as in **pay**	【Write the character in the boxes】

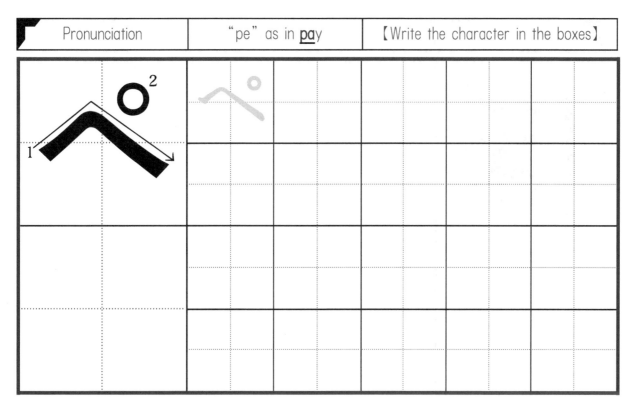

Continue practicing in the remaining boxes.

Remember to pay attention to stroke order.

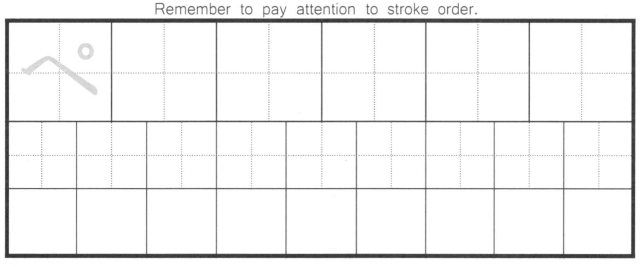

■ 🔊 Vocabulary - Write the character in the boxes below.

1. ippen (Once)

2. kanpeki (Perfect)

3. perapera (Fluent)

4. keppeki (Fastidiousness)

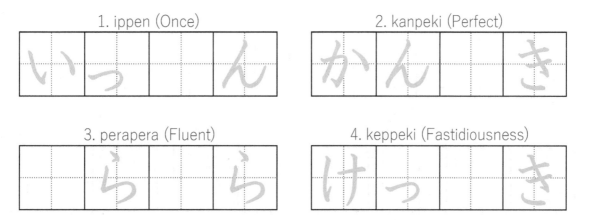

| Pronunciation | "po" as in <u>po</u>int | 【Write the character in the boxes】 |

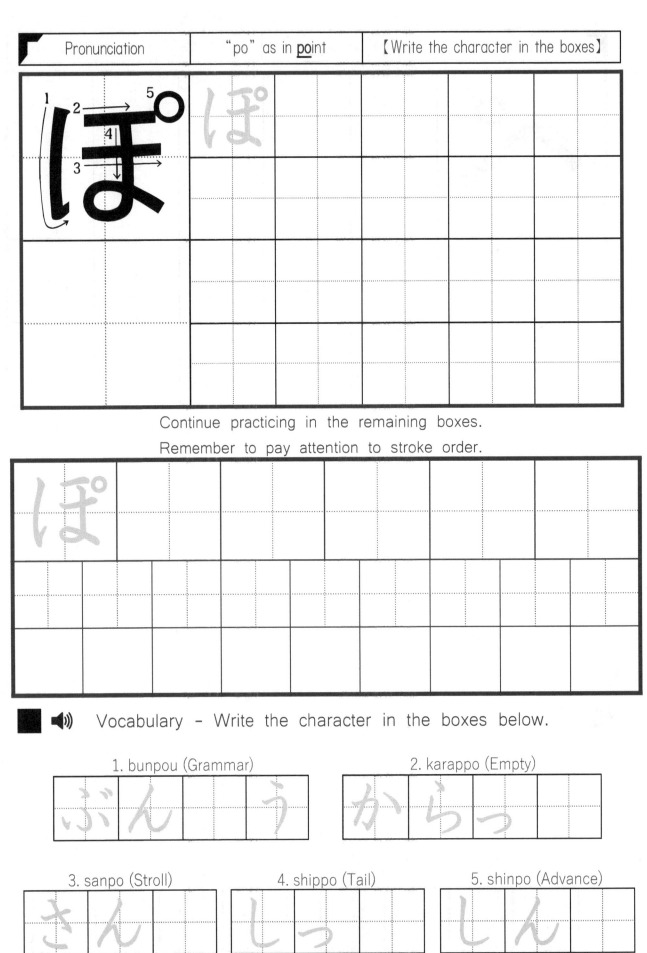

Continue practicing in the remaining boxes.

Remember to pay attention to stroke order.

Vocabulary - Write the character in the boxes below.

1. bunpou (Grammar)

ぶ ん う

2. karappo (Empty)

か ら っ

3. sanpo (Stroll)

さ ん

4. shippo (Tail)

し っ

5. shinpo (Advance)

し ん

90

Additional Sounds Youon Hiragana Rules

Which is Combination two sounds, the pronunciation will change When combined in this way <u>"ya," "yu" and "yo"</u> are written in half-size characters

きゃ **kya**	きゅ **kyu**	きょ **kyo**
しゃ **sha(sya)**	しゅ **shu(syu)**	しょ **sho(syo)**
ちゃ **cha(tya)**	ちゅ **chu(tyu)**	ちょ **cho(tyo)**
にゃ **nya**	にゅ **nyu**	にょ **nyo**
ひゃ **hya**	ひゅ **hyu**	ひょ **hyo**

みゃ **mya**	みゅ **myu**	みょ **myo**
りゃ **rya**	りゅ **ryu**	りょ **ryo**

ぎゃ **gya**	ぎゅ **gyu**	ぎょ **gyo**
じゃ **zya(ja)**	じゅ **zyu(ju)**	じょ **zyo(jo)**

びゃ **bya**	びゅ **byu**	びょ **byo**
ぴゃ **pya**	ぴゅ **pyu**	ぴょ **pyo**

Note: "ja," "ju" and "jo" are usually written with じゃ, じゅ and じょ.

✓ **Review** ☐**Awesome!** ☐**Excellent!** ☐**Good!** ☐**Average!** ☐**Poor!**

Note:

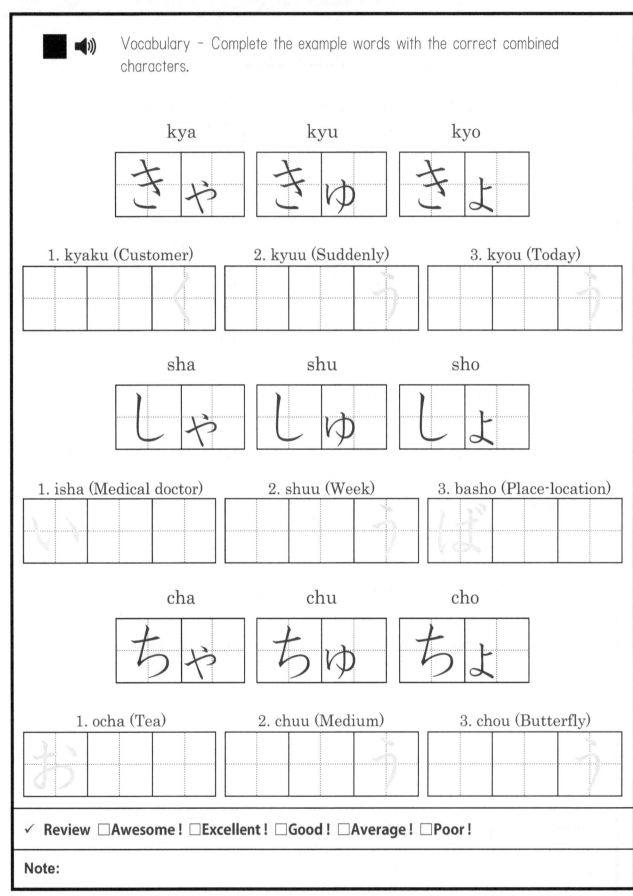

Vocabulary – Complete the example words with the correct combined characters.

kya   kyu   kyo

きゃ   きゅ   きょ

1. kyaku (Customer)   2. kyuu (Suddenly)   3. kyou (Today)

sha   shu   sho

しゃ   しゅ   しょ

1. isha (Medical doctor)   2. shuu (Week)   3. basho (Place-location)

cha   chu   cho

ちゃ   ちゅ   ちょ

1. ocha (Tea)   2. chuu (Medium)   3. chou (Butterfly)

✓ **Review** ☐**Awesome !** ☐**Excellent !** ☐**Good !** ☐**Average !** ☐**Poor !**

Note:

HIRAGANA - ADDITIONAL SOUNDS YOUON

Vocabulary – Complete the example words with the correct combined characters.

nya   nyu   nyo

 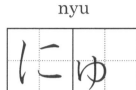 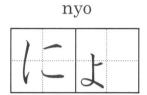

1. Kon'nyaku (Japanese dish)

2. tounyuu (Soy milk)

3. nyou kensa (Urine test)

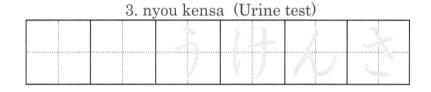

hya   hyu   hyo

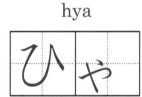  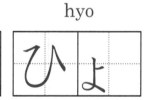

1. hyuku (Hundred)   2. hyuu (A whistling sound)   3. hyou (Leopard)

✓ **Review** □**Awesome!** □**Excellent!** □**Good!** □**Average!** □**Poor!**

Note:

Vocabulary – Complete the example words with the correct combined characters.

HIRAGANA - ADDITIONAL SOUNDS YOUON

mya	myu	myo

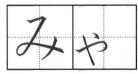  

1. myaku (Pulse)　　　　　2. myouji (Family name)

rya	ryu	ryo

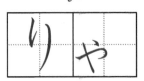 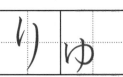 

1. ryaku (Abbreviation)　　　2. ryuu (Dragon)

3. ryokou (Travel)

✓ **Review** □**Awesome!** □**Excellent!** □**Good!** □**Average!** □**Poor!**

Note: *The character combination "myu" is only used in uncommon words not included here.*

Vocabulary – Complete the example words with the correct combined characters.

gya　　　　　gyu　　　　　gyo

1. gyaku (Reverse)　　　　　　　2. gyuuniku (Beef)

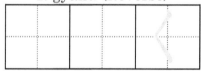 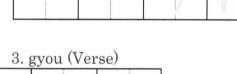

3. gyou (Verse)

ja　　　　　ju　　　　　jo

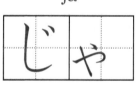 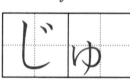 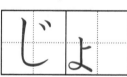

1. jari (Gravel)　　　2. jutsu (Way/Art)　　　3. joi (Female Doctor)

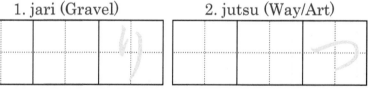 

4. jama (Hindrances)　　　5. juu (Ten)　　　6. kujo (Extermination)

✓ **Review** □**Awesome!** □**Excellent!** □**Good!** □**Average!** □**Poor!**

Note: *There is character combination "je" but is only used in Katakana

HIRAGANA - ADDITIONAL SOUNDS YOUON

🔊 Vocabulary – Complete the example words with the correct combined characters.

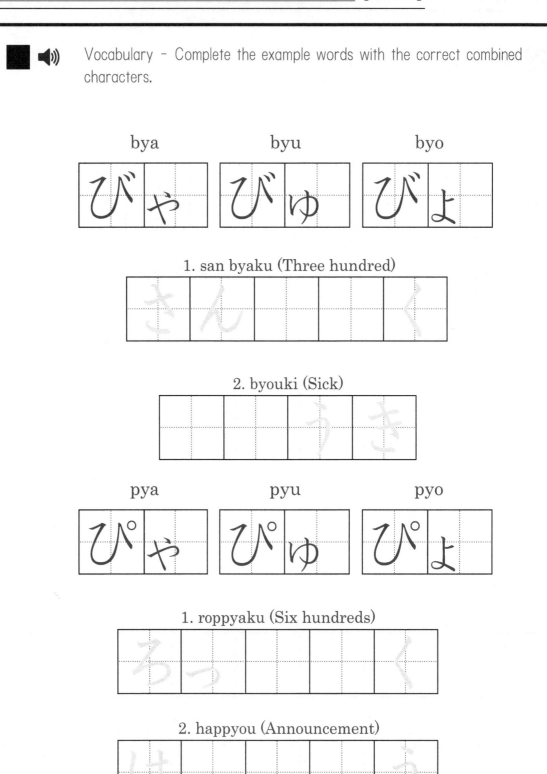

bya   byu   byo

びゃ   びゅ   びょ

1. san byaku (Three hundred)

さん　　　　　く

2. byouki (Sick)

うき

pya   pyu   pyo

ぴゃ   ぴゅ   ぴょ

1. roppyaku (Six hundreds)

ろっ　　　　　く

2. happyou (Announcement)

はっ　　　　　う

✓ **Review** □**Awesome!** □**Excellent!** □**Good!** □**Average!** □**Poor!**

Note: *The character combination "byu" is only used in uncommon words not included here, and puy used in katakana.

HIRAGANA EXERCISES

A LINE あ い う え お & K LINE か き く け こ

Activity 1

You should now be able to read and write the characters below.

A.   Try reading them aloud, repeat them until the sounds come fluently.

B.   Write them in romaji.

え	い	う	お	あ	く	こ	か	け	き

Activity 2

A.   Match the hiragana character to the katakana character with the same sound.

B.   Write the following words into hiragana.

お	エ		き	カ
え	ウ		こ	ク
あ	イ		か	キ
う	オ		け	コ
い	ア		く	ケ

Rain		Umbrella	
House		North	
Sea		Car	
Station		Bamboo	
Sound		Here	

Activity 3

A.   Read these words, and write their romaji and meaning.

あか   --------- ---------   いち   --------- ---------

あし   --------- ---------   かぞく   --------- ---------

いぬ   --------- ---------   きょう   --------- ---------

うえ   --------- ---------   くすり   --------- ---------

なまえ   --------- ---------   けいさつ   --------- ---------

おんな   --------- ---------   ことば   --------- ---------

A LINE あ い う え お **& K LINE** か き く け こ

Activity 3

B.   Read the following words in hiragana, and pick out the ones which mean "Today" and "Name." Then write all the words out in romaji.

くだもの	きょう	かいわ	おんな
なまえ	うれしい	いいえ	あいさつ

Activity 4

A.   Fill in each space with the appropriate Hiragana to make words.

1. ____たい   (Pain)   6. ____らい   (About)

2. ____とな   (Adult)   7. ____こん   (Married)

3. ____れしい   (Happy)   8. ____ども   (Children)

4. ____いご   (English)   9. ____いひ   (Expense)

5. ____した   (Tomorrow)   10. ____いわ   (Conversation)

う	え	い	お	あ	く	か	こ	け	き

B.   Write the following words in Hiragana.

1. kurai   (Dark)   _____   6. umi   (Sea)   _____

2. keisatsu (Police)   _____   7. akarui   (Bright)   _____

3. keshiki   (Scenery)   _____   8. isha   (Doctor)   _____

4. koukou   (High school) _____   9. arigatou (Thank You)   _____

5. urusai   (Noisy)   _____   10. kotae   (Answer)   _____

A LINE あ い う え お & K LINE か き く け こ

Activity 5

A. Read the following words in hiragana, and pick out the ones which mean "Tomorrow" and "Always." Then write all the words out in romaji.

こども	いつも	うみ	えいご
おとこ	あした	くつ	けが
あせ	いそぐ	おや	からい

B. Circle the English and Japanese romaji words, and then circle the same words in hiragana.

Next time	When	Lie	Adult	From now on
Experience	Chair	(Red)	Yellow	Autumn
Conversation	Today	Air	Movie	Mouth
Delicious	Face	Desk	Happy	Police

aki	itsu	kao	keisatsu	(aka)
keiken	kondo	uso	otona	kyou
isu	kuuki	tsukue	kiiro	korekara
kaiwa	oishii	ureshii	eiga	kuchi

(あか)きいろけいけんうそいつえいがかおかいわけいさつくうき
きょうあきうれしいこんどいすおいしいおとなつくえこれからくち

A LINE　あ　い　う　え　お　&　K LINE　か　き　く　け　こ

Activity 6

A.　Circle the correct Hiragana words for the Romaji.

1	ookii	(Big)	a.	おあきい	b.	おおけい	c.	おおきい
2	ginkou	(Bank)	a.	ぎんこう	b.	げんこう	c.	ぎんこう
3	kibishii	(Strict)	a.	きべいし	b.	きびしい	c.	けびしい
4	iku	(to go)	a.	いこ	b.	いく	c.	いこお
5	ichiban	(The first)	a.	いちぱん	b.	いちあん	c.	いちばん
6	kaisha	(Company)	a.	かいしゃ	b.	かいし	c.	かえしゃ

B.　Find the Japanese equivalents of the words listed below in the puzzle. They are lined horizontally. *If you don't know what they mean, we recommend that you review writing practice pages.

1. あいさつ
2. いそがしい
3. うるさい
4. えらぶ
5. えんぴつ
6. くうこう
7. こうえん
8. こうじょう
9. おかあさん
10. おかしい
11. かいもの
12. かわいい
13. きかい
14. けいけん
15. こうざ

こ	う	じ	ょ	う	る	さ	い
お	か	し	い	け	い	け	ん
か	い	も	の	こ	う	え	ん
か	わ	い	い	え	ん	ぴ	つ
え	ら	ぶ	く	う	こ	う	ざ
い	い	あ	い	さ	つ	こ	よ
も	い	そ	が	し	い	ん	が
お	か	あ	さ	ん	き	か	い

C.　Extend your range of vocabulary quite a bit. Try reading and memorizing the Kanji for these words.(Important Kanji for beginners level).

1. あした　（明日）- Tomorrow
2. きょう　（今日）- Today
3. あめ　（雨）- Rain
4. かいもの　（買い物）- Shopping
5. なに　（何）- What
6. ひゃく　（百）- Hundred

S LINE さ し す せ そ & T LINE た ち つ て と

Activity 1

A.   Write the following romaji into hiragana.

Romaji	Hiragana	Meaning	Romaji	Hiragana	Meaning
sugoi		Amazing	soto		Outside
sensei		Teacher	souji		Cleaning
shima		Island	sore		That
sakana		Fish	sora		Sky
shigoto		Work	soshite		Then
sukoshi		Little	tanoshii		Fun
sengetsu		Last month	takai		High

Activity 2

A.   Circle the hiragana characters for sa, shi, tsu, te, and to.

B.   Find the words in hiragana that mean the same as the English words.

C.   Read the following words, and write their romaji and meaning.

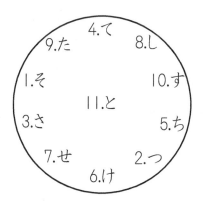

Temple ( )	Eat ( )	Egg ( )	Very ( )
Perhaps ( )	Small ( )	Near ( )	Strong ( )

1. たまご	2. つよい	3. たぶん	4. ちいさい
5. とても	6. ちかく	7. てら	8. たべる

さら   _____ _____   しろ   _____ _____

さい   _____ _____   つき   _____ _____

すこし _____ _____   すべて _____ _____

さむい _____ _____   せまい _____ _____

HIRAGANA EXERCISES ACTIVITY

S LINE さ し す せ そ & T LINE た ち つ て と

Activity 3

A.   Try reading them aloud, repeat them until the sounds come fluently.

B.   Write them in romaji.

せ	さ	そ	す	し	て	ち	た	と	つ

C.   Test yourself — check that you have learned the S & T lines of Hiragana well
     by filling in the missing kana.

さ				そ		ち			と

Activity 4

A.   With the 'S' & 'T' line you can extend your range of vocabulary quite a bit.
     Try reading these words and filling the missing with the appropriate Hiragana .

しお		Salt		【uchi】	House
	【saifu】	Wallet		【kimochi】	Feeling
	【tokei】	Clock		【shimeru】	To close
さいあく		The worst		【tsukareta】	Tired

B.   These are common girl's names in Japan. How would you write them?

Saori   Shizuka   Tsukasa   Chiaki

_____   _____   _____   _____

C.   Rewrite the following words in the correct order.

【seito】	Student	といせ	
【tsukue】	Desk	えつく	
【tegami】	Letter	みてが	
【deguchi】	Exit	ちでぐ	

S LINE さ し す せ そ **& T LINE** た ち つ て と

Activity 5

A. Match the hiragana character to the katakana character with the same sound.

て	シ		と	セ
し	ス		ち	サ
た	テ		そ	チ
す	タ		せ	ト
つ	ツ		さ	ソ

B. Write the following romaji into hiragana.

san _____ 【Three】   chiiki _____ 【Area】

mise _____ 【Store】   sorede _____ 【And so】

shichi _____ 【Seven】   tomaru _____ 【to stop】

tegami _____ 【Letter】   taki _____ 【Waterfall】

kyouto _____ 【Kyoto】   tsuku _____ 【to arrive】

subete _____ 【Everything】   tokuni _____ 【Especially】

C. Write the missing characters for the below words.

| I. Street | 2. Wrist | 3. Then | 4. Correctly | 5. Last month |
| 6. Very | 7. Cleaning | 8. Nature | 9. Menstruation | |

___おり 【　】　　　　___ゃんと 【　】　　　　___うじ 【　】

___くび 【　】　　　　___んげつ 【　】　　　　___ぜん 【　】

___して 【　】　　　　___ても 【　】　　　　___いり 【 9 】

S LINE さ し す せ そ & T LINE た ち つ て と

Activity 6

A.   Complete the following table using the words from the writing practice pages.

English	Romaji	Hiragana
	toshi	
Plate		
	tabun	
		しあい
Egg		

B.   Try to memorize those kanji and write the romaji for hiragana.
      (**Important Kanji for beginners level**).The first one has been done as an example.

1.	さかな	（魚）	Fish	1.	Ex. sakana
2.	たべる	（食べる）	Eat	2.	
3.	すこし	（少し）	little	3.	
4.	すき	（好き）	Like	4.	
5.	せんえん	（千円）	1,000 yen	5.	
6.	てんき	（天気）	Weather	6.	

C.   Extend your range of vocabulary quite a bit, Circle the correct Hiragana words
      for the Romaji. (Here are some words not mentioned in the practice pages).

1.	shashin	Picture	a.	しあしん	b.	しゃしん	c.	しゃね
2.	tokidoki	Sometimes	a.	とけどけ	b.	ときとき	c.	ときどき
3.	chikara	Power	a.	ちから	b.	しから	c.	ちかり
4.	tadaima	I'm home	a.	ただえま	b.	ただま	c.	ただいま
5.	tomodachi	Friend	a.	ともだし	b.	ともだち	c.	とまだち
6.	taishikan	Embassy	a.	たいしかん	b.	たしかん	c.	たちかん

<u>N LINE</u> な に ぬ ね の & <u>H LINE</u> は ひ ふ へ ほ

Activity 1

A.   Practice reading the following aloud, repeat them until the sounds come fluently.

ね な ぬ の に へ ひ は ふ ほ ね な ぬ の に へ

B.   Write the hiragana for this romaji in the boxes

nu	hu	ni	he	no	ha	ne	hi	na	ho

C.   Write the hiragana for this romaji in the boxes.

Name		Dog		Drink	
Summer		take off		get on	
Meat		Sleep		Other	
Japan		Age		Cat	

D.   Match the following hiragana with their meaning.

1. ながい   2. にかい   3. おかね   4. はさみ   5. ひがし

Money   Scissors   Long   Twice   East

◆━━━━━━━━━━━━━━━━━━━━━━━━━━━━━━━━━━━━◆

1. ふつう   2. へいじつ   3. ほけん   4. ふく   5. はじめ

Insurance   Clothes   Beginning   Weekday   Normal

N LINE な に ぬ ね の & H LINE は ひ ふ へ ほ

Activity 2

A. Match the hiragana character to the katakana character with the same sound.

ぬ	ナ	ふ	ヒ
の	ネ	は	ヘ
な	ニ	ほ	ハ
ね	ヌ	ひ	ホ
に	ノ	へ	フ

B. Write the following hiragana into romaji.

1. あなた _____   7. はしる _____   13. にほん _____

2. におい _____   8. ひだり _____   14. ぬりえ _____

3. ぬらす _____   9. ふくろ _____   15. ぬすむ _____

4. ねだん _____   10. へんか _____   16. ねがい _____

5. のこり _____   11. ほしい _____   17. のこす _____

6. はいる _____   12. ほとんど_____   18. ひみつ _____

C. Test yourself – check that you have learned the first 5 lines of Hiragana well by filling in the missing kana.

あ _ う _ お   _ _ く _ こ

さ _ す _ そ   た _ つ _ と

_ に _ _ の   _ ひ _ _ ほ

N LINE な に ぬ ね の & H LINE は ひ ふ へ ほ

Activity 3

A.   Write the hiragana letters that correspond to the katakana letters.

ネ	ナ	ノ	ニ	ヌ	ホ	フ	ハ	ヘ	ヒ
ね									

B.   Write the missing characters to make the word.

1. (Name)

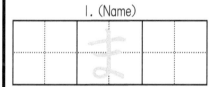

2. (Japan)

3. (Smell)

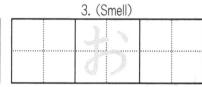

4. (Money)

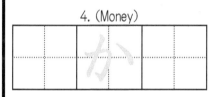

5. (Shopping)

6. (Spring)

7. (Hundred)

8. (Deep)

9. (Thin)

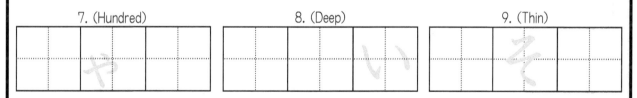

C.   Complete the following table using the words from the writing practice pages.

English	Romaji	Hiragana
	nigatsu	
Summer		
	jinushi	
Peace		へいわ
East		

HIRAGANA EXERCISES ACTIVITY

N LINE な に ぬ ね の & H LINE は ひ ふ へ ほ

Activity 4

A.   Circle the correct Hiragana words for the Romaji.For an extra challenge try reading the Japanese words by covering the romaji.

1.	haru	【Spring】	a. はる	b. はろ	c. はり
2.	haisha	【Dentist】	a. はしゃ	b. はいし	c. はいしゃ
3.	haizara	【Ashtray】	a. はいざり	b. はいぜら	c. はいざら
4.	furusato	【Hometown】	a. ふろさと	b. ふるさと	c. ふさと
5.	ane	【Older sister】	a. あぬ	b. あね	c. あの
6.	ani	【Older brother】	a. あね	b. あにい	c. あに

B.   Find the words in hiragana that mean the same as the English words.

C.   Circle the hiragana characters for nu, ne, hi, he, ha and ho.

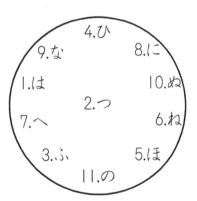

West ( )	Brain ( )	Inside ( )	Vomit ( )
Snake ( )	Fever ( )	Sunset ( )	Winter ( )

1. なか	2. にし	3. ねつ	4. のう
5. ひぐれ	6. ふゆ	7. へび	8. はく

D.   Try to memorize those kanji (Important Kanji for beginners level).

1.	にほん (nihon)	**日本**	Japan	
2.	にがつ (nigatsu)	**二月**	February	
3.	ふつか (futsuka)	**二日**	2nd day	
4.	のむ (nomu)	**飲む**	Drink	
5.	みせ (mise)	**店**	Store	
6.	はは (haha)	**母**	Mother	

M LINE　ま み む め も　&　Y LINE　や ゆ よ

Activity 1

A.　Try reading them aloud, repeat them until the sounds come fluently.

B.　Write them in romaji.

め	み	も	ま	む	ゆ	や	よ	み	む

C.　Match the hiragana character to the katakana character with the same sound.

む	モ		ゆ	ヨ
み	マ		や	ユ
め	ム		よ	ヤ
も	ミ		も	メ
ま	メ		め	モ

D.　Write the following romaji into hiragana.

■　For an extra challenge try to cover the romaji.

yasashii _____ 【Kind】　　　musuko _____ 【Son】

minami _____ 【South】　　　yowai _____ 【Weak】

megane _____ 【Glesse】　　　moufu _____ 【Blanket】

monku _____ 【Complaint】　　yuugata _____ 【Evening】

musume _____ 【Daughter】　　yotei _____ 【Schedule】

mainichi _____ 【Every day】　　yasai _____ 【Vegetables】

M LINE ま み む め も & Y LINE や ゆ よ
Activity 2

A.   Read below hiragana words, and write their romaji and meaning.

Hiragana	Romaji	Meaning	Hiragana	Romaji	Meaning
つめ			みぎ		
もうふ			ゆ		
やっと			やま		
ゆびわ			もの		
みらい			まじめ		
むいか			よなか		
まいつき			やすみ		

B.   Circle the correct Hiragana words for the Romaji.

1.   memai   【Dizzy】   a. みまい   b. めまい   c. ぬまい

2.   mata   【Again】   a. まだ   b. まて   c. また

3.   mune   【Chest】   a. むね   b. むに   c. もね

4.   yume   【Dream】   a. やめ   b. ゆめ   c. ゆみ

5.   mado   【Window】   a. まと   b. まどう   c. まど

6.   mikka   【 3rd day】   a. めっか   b. みっか   c. みか

D.   Write the hiragana for these given names.

Mayumi   Yumi   Yoriko   Yasuhiko

_____   _____   _____   _____

Yuriko   Mei   Aya   Mika

_____   _____   _____   _____

M LINE ま み む め も & Y LINE や ゆ よ

Activity 3

A.   Fill in each space with the appropriate Hiragana to make words.

1. _____ え	(Before)	6. _____ く	(Grill)
2. _____ み	(Ears)	7. _____ でる	(Boile)
3. _____ し	(Insect)	8. _____ む	(Read)
4. _____ ど	(Aim)	9. _____ る	(Night)
5. _____ ぐる	(to dive)	10. _____ ぎ	(Goat)

も	め	よ	や	み	ゆ	ま	む

B.   Find the words in hiragana that mean the same as the English words.

C.   Circle the hiragana characters for や, ゆ, よ, も, ま and む.

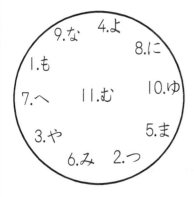

Water ( )	Beside ( )	Beautiful ( )	Someday ( )
Car ( )	Open ( )	Hold ( )	Long time ( )

1. いつか	2. あける	3. みず	4. むかし
5. きれい	6. もつ	7. よこ	8. くるま

D.   Write the hiragana for these surnames names.

Yamamoto   Yamaha   Yamashita   Fujiyama

_____   _____   _____   _____

❖ As you can see there are lots of names with **Yama.** This means mountain in Japanese and its wide use in names reflects the many mountains in Japan.

HIRAGANA EXERCISES ACTIVITY

M LINE ま み む め も & Y LINE や ゆ よ

Activity 4

A. Match the following hiragana with their meaning.

1. また	2. まだ	3. みえ	4. めい	5. もの

Thing	Again	Niece	Vanity	Still

◆————————————————————————————————◆

1. ゆうしょく	2. やくそく	3. むかし	4. ゆめ	5. よきん

long ago	Dreams	Promise	Deposit	Dinner

B. Write the hiragana letters that correspond to the katakana letters.

ム	モ	マ	メ	ミ	ヨ	ユ	ヤ

C. Try to memorize those kanji (Important Kanji for beginners level).

1. みず (mizu)   水   Water   4. くるま (kuruma)   車   Car

2. きょう (kyou)   今日   Today   5. やま (yama)   山   Mountain

3. こども (kodomo)   子供   Child   6. みて (miru)   見る   to see ; Look

D. Reading Practice

やすい   よこはま   はやい   おはよう   やまもと   にちようび   やさしい

R LINE　らりるれろ　&　W LINE　わをん

Activity 1

A.　Match the hiragana character to the katakana character with the same sound.

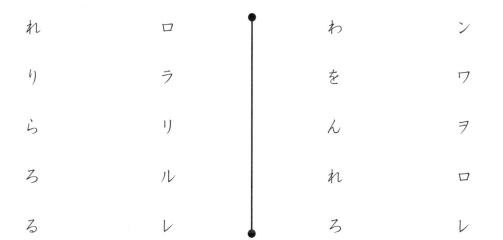

れ	ロ	わ	ン
り	ラ	を	ワ
ら	リ	ん	ヲ
ろ	ル	れ	ロ
る	レ	ろ	レ

B.　Match the following hiragana with their meaning.

1. いつから　　2. りゆう　　3. する　　4. おしゃれ　　5. いろ

Color　　　　To do　　　　Stylish　　　　Reason　　　　From when

◆──◆

1. わがまま　　2. われる　　3. わすれる　　4. ろば　　5. くもり

to forget　　　Cloudy　　　Selfish　　　Donkey　　　Broke

C.　Test yourself – Check that you have learned the R & W lines of Hiragana well.

ら				ろ	わ		

R LINE らりるれろ & W LINE わをん

Activity 2

A.   Write the following romaji into hiragana and their meaning.

Romaji	Hiragana	Meaning	Romaji	Hiragana	Meaning
kusuri			ureshii		
raishuu			renraku		
raigetsu			iroiro		
ringo			ushiro		
aruku			wakai		
furui			watashi		

B.   Read these words, and write their romaji and meaning.

はら _____ _____   ごはん _____ _____

ろく _____ _____   きいろ _____ _____

れきし _____ _____   わかる _____ _____

あける _____ _____   でんしゃ _____ _____

いりぐち _____ _____   あんぜん _____ _____

C.   Complete the following table using the words from the writing practice pages.

English	Romaji	Hiragana
	sara	
Candle		
	ringo	
	watashi	
		こんにちは

R LINE らりるれろ & W LINE わをん

Activity 3

A.   Circle the correct romaji for the hiragana words and write their meaning.

	Hiragana	Meaning	Choose the correct answer romaji				
1.	らいげつ		a.	reigetsu	b.	raigetsu	c.	raigitsu
2.	くもり		a.	kumore	b.	kumiri	c.	kumori
3.	ふるい		a.	furui	b.	furu	c.	furuii
4.	れんらく		a.	renrako	b.	renraku	c.	rinraku
5.	ろくじ		a.	rokoji	b.	rokuje	c.	rokuji
6.	われる		a.	wareru	b.	wararu	c.	warero

B.   Write the missing characters to make the word.

1. (From when)

2. (Entrance)

3. (Exception)

4. (About when)

C.   Rewrite the following words in the correct order.

1	【genki】	Good ; Fine	げきん	
2	【kaban】	Bag	ばんか	
3	【densha】	Electric train	でんゃし	
4	【min'na】	Everybody	なみん	

HIRAGANA EXERCISES ACTIVITY

R LINE らりるれろ & W LINE わ を ん

Activity 4

• There are no hiragana symbols for wi, wu, or we.

• を is the particle o or wo. It is only used after a word, to mark the object of the sentence. Check practice page for wo.

• ん is the only syllable which does not contain a vowel sound. It can be used at the end or in the middle of a word.

を Example:

にほんごをべんきょうします。

Nihongo **wo** benkyou shimasu.

I study Japanese.

B.   Practice reading the following words aloud, then rewrite them.

こんにちは	【Hello】	
こわい	【Scary】	
あさごはん	【Breakfast】	
わかりました	【Understood】	
かいわ	【Conversation】	
わかりません	【I do not understand】	

C.   Try to memorize those kanji (Important Kanji for beginners level).

1.	き （木）	Tree	
2.	ふるい （古）	Old (Things)	
3.	ろく （六）	Six	
4.	でんしゃ（電車）	Electric train	

DAKUTEN AND HANDAKUTEN

K line (ka ki ku ke ko)	+	ten ten " is	G line	ga gi	gu ge go
S line (sa shi su se so)	+	ten ten " is	Z line	za zi⟨ji⟩	zu ze zo
T line (ta chi tsu te to)	+	ten ten " is	D line	da di⟨ji⟩	du de do
H line (ha hi fu he ho)	+	ten ten " is	B line	ba bi	bu be bo
H line (ha hi fu he ho)	+	maru O is	P line	pa pi	pu pe po

Activity 1 Test yourself by writing the correct hiragana:

Ga		Za		Do		Go		Pe	
Da		Zi(ji)		Gi		Zo		Po	
Pa		De		Gu		Ba		Ge	
Zu		Bi		Be		Pi		Di(ji)	
Ze		Bu		Pu		Du		Bo	

Activity 2 Practice reading the following words aloud. and write their meanings.

がくせい		かぎ		わかりました	
がっこう		いりぐち		げつようび	
ぎんこう		およぐ		ごみ	
ぎゅうにく		げんきん		ごかい	

Activity 3 Now write the following romaji into hiragana.

gatsu _ _ _ _ _ _ _ pan _ _ _ _ _ _ _ jishin _ _ _ _ _ _ _ denchi _ _ _ _ _ _ _ terebi _ _ _ _ _ _ _

kagami _ _ _ _ _ _ _ guai _ _ _ _ _ _ _ zubon _ _ _ _ _ _ _ doyoubi _ _ _ _ _ _ bunka _ _ _ _ _ _ _

demo _ _ _ _ _ _ _ genki _ _ _ _ _ _ _ zenbu _ _ _ _ _ _ _ basho _ _ _ _ _ _ _ kibou _ _ _ _ _ _ _

migi _ _ _ _ _ _ _ kouza _ _ _ _ _ _ _ daiji _ _ _ _ _ _ _ byouin _ _ _ _ _ _ _ kabe _ _ _ _ _ _ _

kanpeki _ _ _ _ _ _ benkyou _ _ _ _ _ _ enpitsu _ _ _ _ _ _ _ ippai _ _ _ _ _ _ _ ippun _ _ _ _ _ _ _

Dakuten And Handakuten Hiragana Rules

Activity 4 Match the hiragana character to their pronunciation in romaji.

ぜ   ぎ   ぞ   ご   じ   が   ず   ぐ   ざ   げ

ga   zu   gu   za   ge   ze   gi   zo   go   zi (ji)

Activity 4 Write the **hiragana** character to the below katakana characters with the same sound.

g-line	ガ	ギ	グ	ゲ	ゴ
z-line	ザ	ジ	ズ	ゼ	ゾ
d-line	ダ	ヂ	ツ	デ	ド
b-line	バ	ビ	ブ	ベ	ボ
p-line	パ	ピ	プ	ペ	ポ

HIRAGANA EXERCISES ACTIVITY

っ - Small Tsu つ Hiragana Rules

The normal tsu つ, and the small tsu っ, which is smaller. You can notice this in hiragana in words like mittsu みっつ, "three," and in katakana in words like nattsu ナッツyou can create a double consonant (non-vowel) letter.

When reading out a word with a small つ you don't say the つ but instead leave a small pause or gap.

Let's look at some examples:

Kekkon   -   Married   （けっこん）

Motto   -   More   （もっと）

Happa   -   Leaf   （はっぱ）

Gakkou   -   School   （がっこう）

kitte   -   Stamp   （きって）

> がんばって ください。
> You will be able to read this!
> It means 'Do your best'.

Activity 1 Now try some yourself:

				つ	
yokka	4th Day				
matte	Wait				
zutto	By far				
otto	Husband				
kippu	Ticket				
mikka	3th Day				
nikki	Diary				
zasshi	Magazine				
Itte	Say it				

Example of regular "**tsu**"

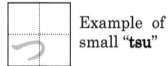

Example of small "**tsu**"

Activity 2 try writing the following classroom instructions:

1. Please stand up.   (tatte kudasai)   _____ 。

2. Please have a seat.   (suwatte kudasai)   _____ 。

3. Please say   (itte kudasai)   _____ 。

HIRAGANA EXERCISES ACTIVITY

Additional Sounds Youon Hiragana Rules (COMBINED CHARACTERS)

When you write these combinations you must always write や、ゆ or よ smaller than the character with which they are combined.

Activity 1 Practice writing them in the boxes below.

き	kya		kyu		kyo	
ぎ	gya		gyu		gyo	
し	sha		shu		sho	
じ	ja		ju		jo	
ち	cha		chu		cho	
に	nya		nyu		nyo	
ひ	hya		hyu		hyo	
び	bya		byu		byo	
み	mya		myu		myo	
り	rya		ryu		ryo	

✓ **Review** ☐**Awesome!** ☐**Excellent!** ☐**Good!** ☐**Average!** ☐**Poor!**

Note:

HIRAGANA EXERCISES ACTIVITY

Additional Sounds Youon Hiragana Rules (COMBINED CHARACTERS)

Activity 2

Try writing the following words using the special hiragana rules we have learned so far. For an extra challenge try to write the words by covering the Hiragana.

English	Hiragana	Rewrite here
Travel	りょこう	
Cooking	りょうり	
Study	べんきょう	
Train	でんしゃ	
Kyoto	きょうと	
Beef	ぎゅうにく	
Doctor	いしゃ	
Cucumber	きゅうり	
Japan	にほん	
Milk	ぎゅうにゅう	
Three hundred	さんびゃく	
Butterfly	ちょう	
Sick	びょうき	
Guest	きゃく	
Bike	じてんしゃ	
Middle school	ちゅうがっこう	
Photo	しゃしん	

✓ **Review** ☐**Awesome!** ☐**Excellent!** ☐**Good!** ☐**Average!** ☐**Poor!**

Note:

HIRAGANA EXERCISES ACTIVITY

Additional Sounds Youon Hiragana Rules (<u>COMBINED CHARACTERS</u>)

Activity 3

Circle the correct Hiragana (Youon) for the Romaji.

1. GYA

- びゃ
- ぎゃ
- じゃ
- ぎゅ

2. GYU

- ぎょ
- じゅ
- ぴょ
- ぎゅ

3. GYO

- ぎょ
- びょ
- ぴょ
- じょ

4. BYO

- ぎょ
- みょ
- じょ
- びょ

5. JA

- びゃ
- ぎゃ
- じゃ
- ぴゃ

6. BYA

- じゃ
- みゃ
- びゃ
- ぎゃ

7. PYO

- ひょ
- ぎゃ
- ぴょ
- ぴゃ

8. PYU

- ぴゅ
- みょ
- ぴょ
- びょ

✓ **Review** ☐**Awesome!** ☐**Excellent!** ☐**Good!** ☐**Average!** ☐**Poor!**

Note:

The Rules in Katakana

Japanese has a lot of foreign words, especially English.
Most Japanese billboards and magazines, sports, guitar, and piano are full of Katakana.
In modern Japanese, katakana is most often used for the transcription of words from foreign languages or loanwords.

Katakana in used in the following ways:

(1)   For words of foreign origin
(2)   For onomatopoeia
(3)   For the names of some animals and insects

The rules in Katakana

1.   Long vowels are represented by a dash " ー "

Ex. 1. Cookie = クッキー   2. taxi= タクシー

2.   Double consonants (kk, pp, ss, tt ,etc.) are represented by small tsu, ッ.

The ー Character

In katakana, the character ー (similar to but not the same as the kanji character 一, meaning "one") is used to show that the previous vowel should be spoken longer than usual. So the word ギター ("gita-")
is pronounced gitaa, with a long a. In romaji, this can either be shown by adding a dash (-) to replace ー, or by adding the same vowel again, so コーヒー (Coffee) can be written as either "ko-hi-" or
"koohii". Note that ー is only used in katakana, not hiragana.

✓ **Review** ☐**Awesome！** ☐**Excellent！** ☐**Good！** ☐**Average！** ☐**Poor！**

Note:

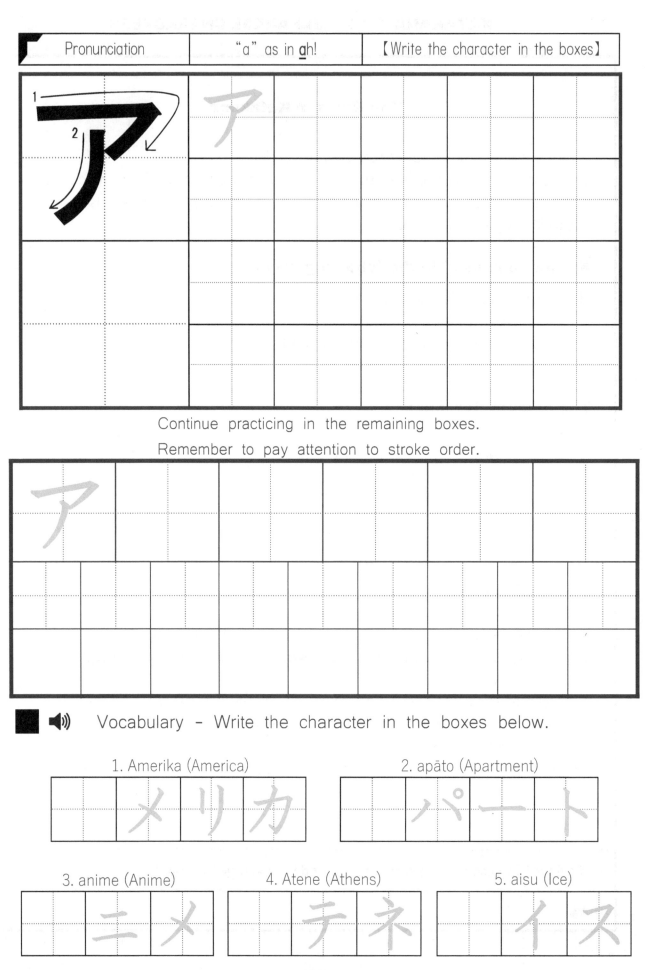

| Pronunciation | "a" as in <u>a</u>h! | 【Write the character in the boxes】 |

Continue practicing in the remaining boxes.

Remember to pay attention to stroke order.

Vocabulary – Write the character in the boxes below.

1. Amerika (America)

メリカ

2. apāto (Apartment)

パート

3. anime (Anime)

ニメ

4. Atene (Athens)

テネ

5. aisu (Ice)

イス

Pronunciation	"i" as in Italy	【Write the character in the boxes】

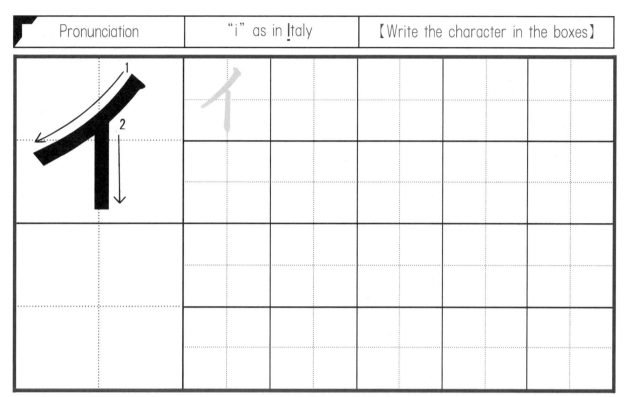

Continue practicing in the remaining boxes.
Remember to pay attention to stroke order.

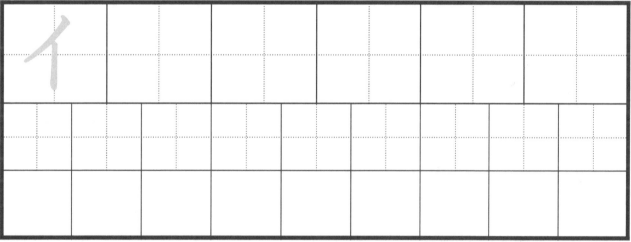

🔊 Vocabulary – Write the character in the boxes below.

1. Itaria (Italy)

2. aidea (Idea)

3. toire (Toilet)

4. taiya (Tire)

5. wain (Wine)

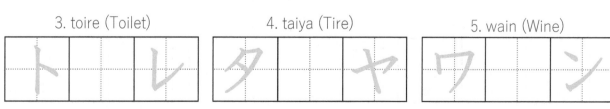

| Pronunciation | "u" as in s<u>oo</u>n | 【Write the character in the boxes】 |

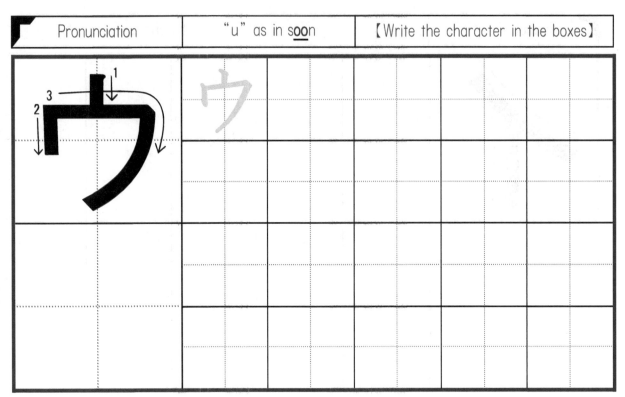

Continue practicing in the remaining boxes.

Remember to pay attention to stroke order.

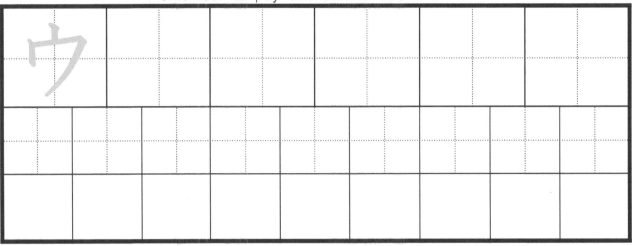

Vocabulary – Write the character in the boxes below.

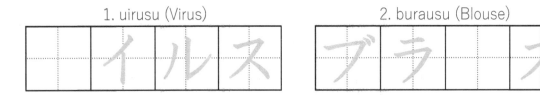

1. uirusu (Virus)　　　　　2. burausu (Blouse)

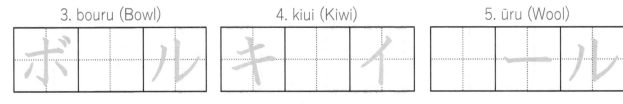

3. bouru (Bowl)　　　4. kiui (Kiwi)　　　5. ūru (Wool)

126

Pronunciation	"e" as in g<u>e</u>t	【Write the character in the boxes】

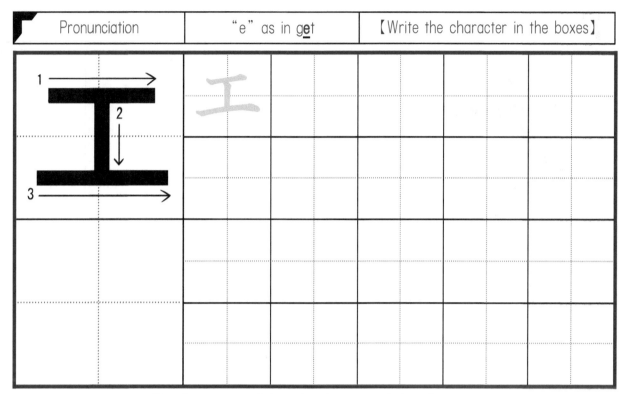

Continue practicing in the remaining boxes.
Remember to pay attention to stroke order.

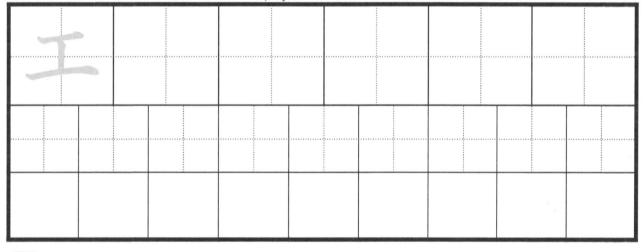

🔊 Vocabulary – Write the character in the boxes below.

1. enerugī (Energy)

2. ereganto (Elegant)

3. erebētā (Elevator)

| Pronunciation | "o" as in <u>o</u>ld | 【Write the character in the boxes】 |

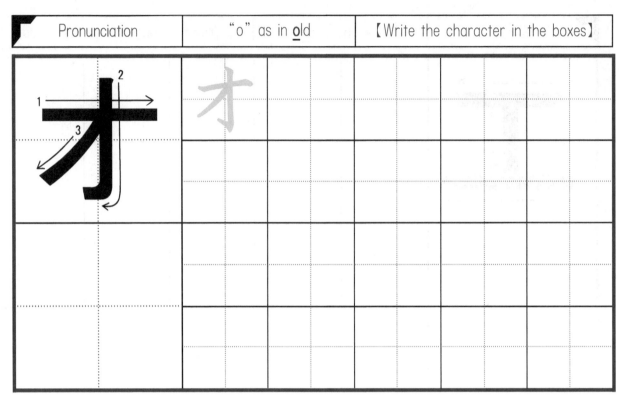

Continue practicing in the remaining boxes.

Remember to pay attention to stroke order.

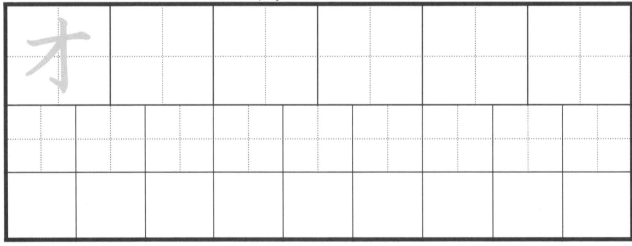

🔊 Vocabulary - Write the character in the boxes below.

1. orenji (Orange)   2. orību (Olive)

3. oiru (Oil)   4. taoru (Towel)   5. opera (Opera)

128

Pronunciation	"ka" as in <u>car</u>	【Write the character in the boxes】

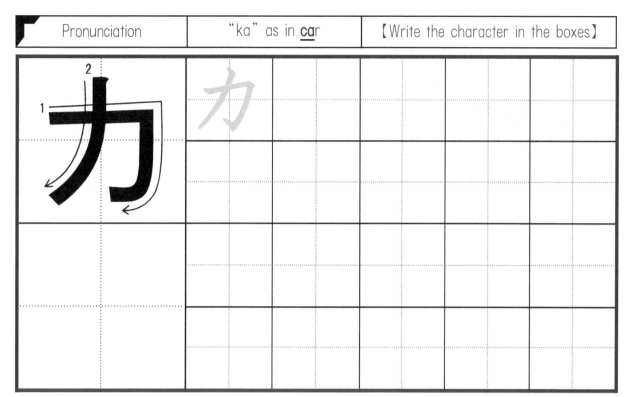

Continue practicing in the remaining boxes.
Remember to pay attention to stroke order.

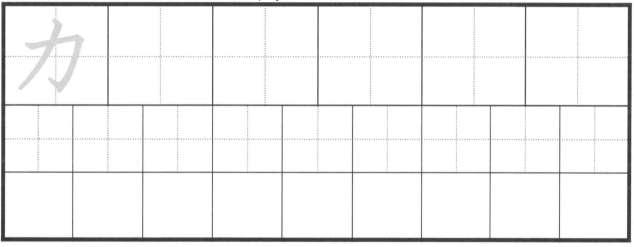

■ 🔊 Vocabulary – Write the character in the boxes below.

1. karaoke (Karaoke)

2. katakana (Characters)

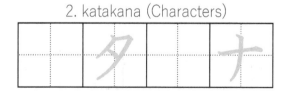

3. Kanada (Canada)   4. kamera (Camera)   5. karē (Curry)

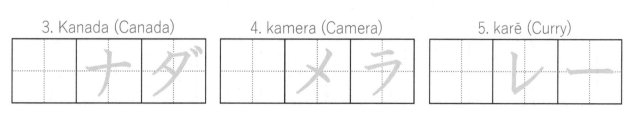

| Pronunciation | "ki" as in **ke**y | 【Write the character in the boxes】 |

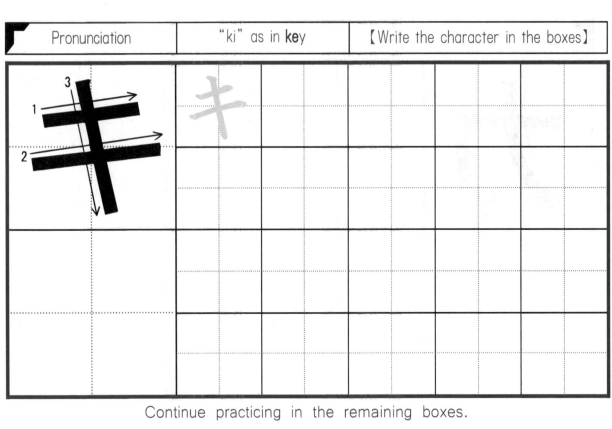

Continue practicing in the remaining boxes.

Remember to pay attention to stroke order.

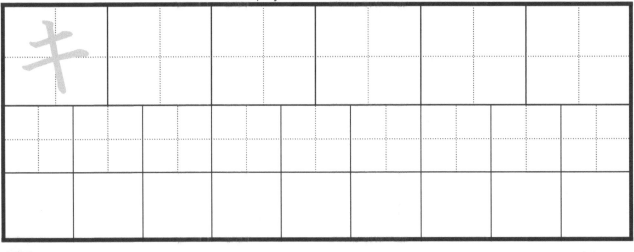

 Vocabulary – Write the character in the boxes below.

1. Mekishiko (Mexico)

メ　シコ

2. kitchin (Kitchen)

ッチン

3. kēki (Cake)

ケー

4. sukī (Skiing)

スー

5. chikin (Chicken)

チ　ン

130

| Pronunciation | "ku" as in <u>coo</u>l | 【Write the character in the boxes】 |

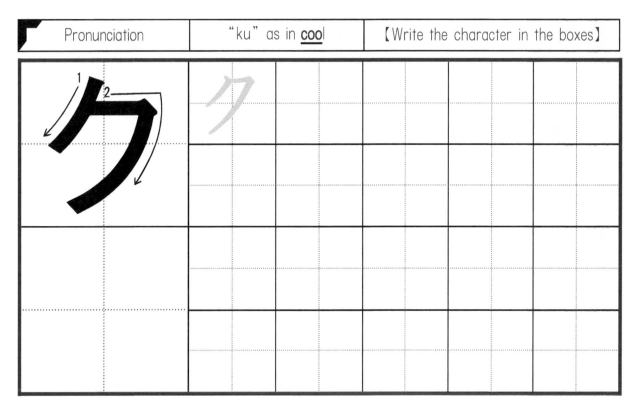

Continue practicing in the remaining boxes.
Remember to pay attention to stroke order.

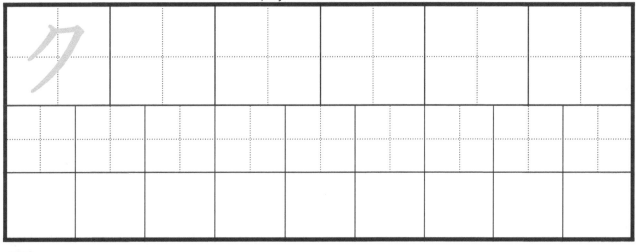

■ 🔊 Vocabulary – Write the character in the boxes below.

1. kukkī (Cookie)　　　　　　　2. fōku (Fork)

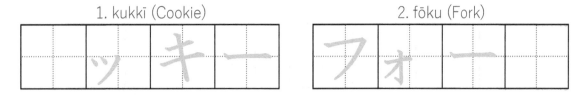

3. kurasu (Class)　　4. miruku (Milk)　　5. pinku (Pink)

131

| Pronunciation | "ke" as in **ke**n (Name) | 【Write the character in the boxes】 |

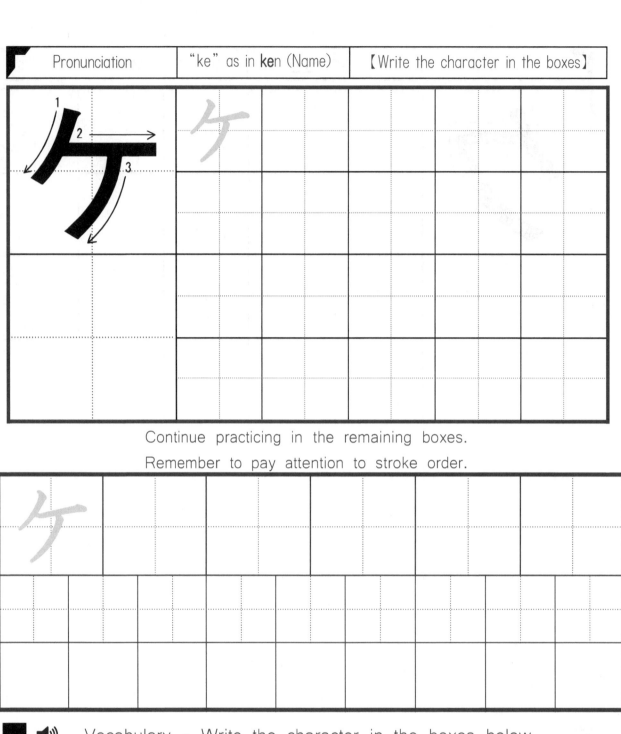

Continue practicing in the remaining boxes.

Remember to pay attention to stroke order.

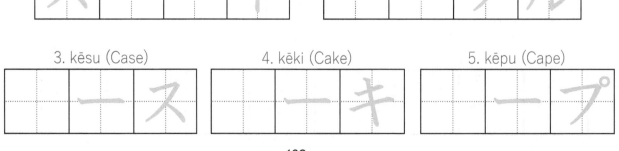

Vocabulary – Write the character in the boxes below.

1. sukēto (Skate)

2. kēburu (Cable)

3. kēsu (Case)

4. kēki (Cake)

5. kēpu (Cape)

| Pronunciation | "ko" as in <u>co</u>ke | 【Write the character in the boxes】 |

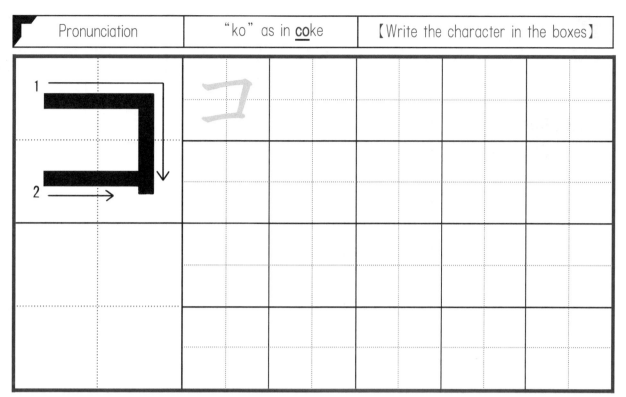

Continue practicing in the remaining boxes.
Remember to pay attention to stroke order.

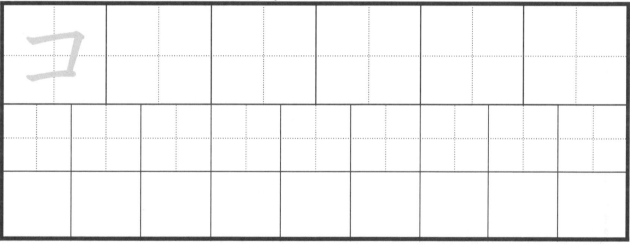

🔊 Vocabulary – Write the character in the boxes below.

1. kōhī (Coffee)　　　　　　　　　　2. komedi (Comedy)

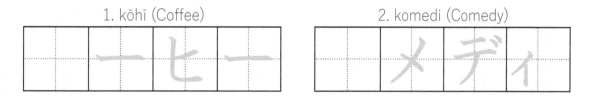

3. kōsu (Course)　　　4. kōto (Coat)　　　5. koiru (Coil)

| Pronunciation | "sa" as in <u>sa</u>ndwich | 【Write the character in the boxes】 |

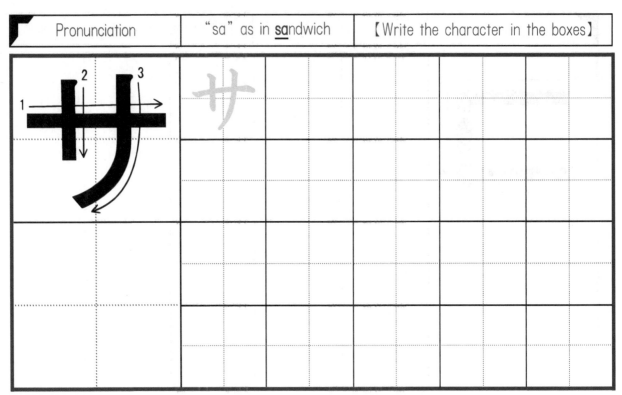

Continue practicing in the remaining boxes.

Remember to pay attention to stroke order.

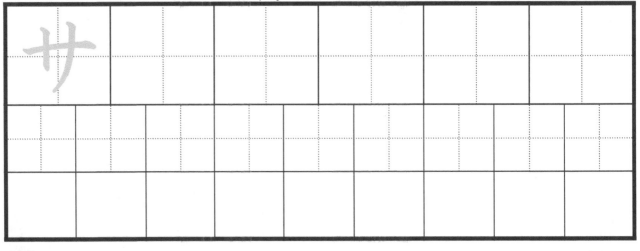

🔊 Vocabulary - Write the character in the boxes below.

1. sakkā (Soccer)

2. sandaru (Sandals)

3. saizu (Size)   4. sain (Sign)   5. sarada (Salad)

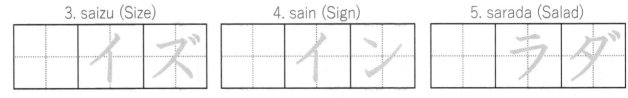

Pronunciation	"shi" as in **she**	【Write the character in the boxes】

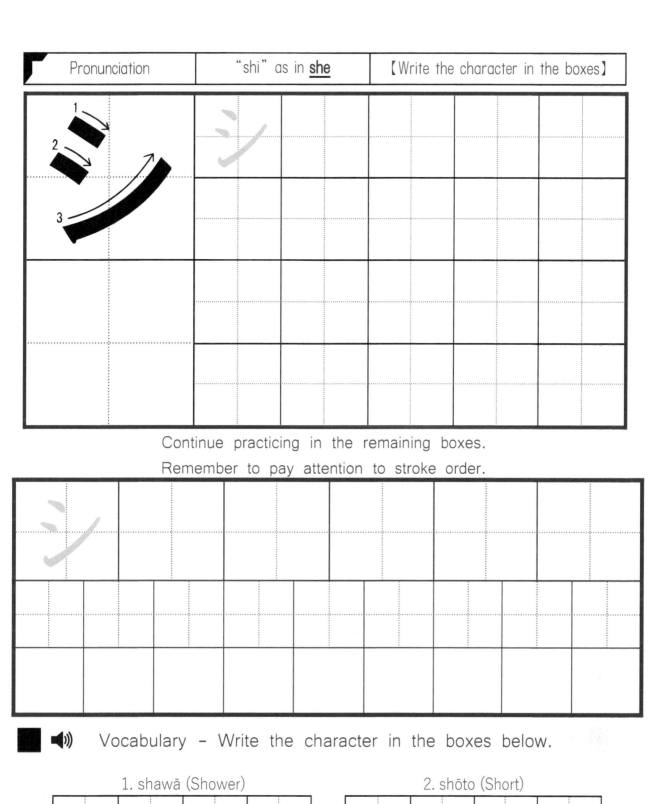

Continue practicing in the remaining boxes.

Remember to pay attention to stroke order.

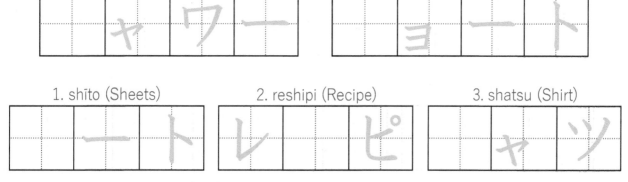

Vocabulary – Write the character in the boxes below.

1. shawā (Shower)   2. shōto (Short)

1. shīto (Sheets)   2. reshipi (Recipe)   3. shatsu (Shirt)

| Pronunciation | "su" as in <u>sue</u> | 【Write the character in the boxes】 |

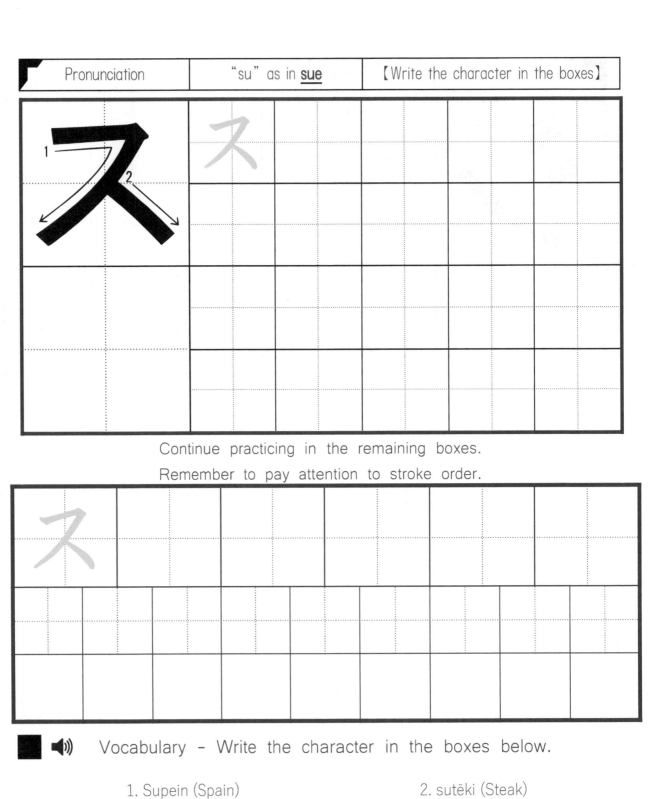

Continue practicing in the remaining boxes.

Remember to pay attention to stroke order.

🔊 Vocabulary – Write the character in the boxes below.

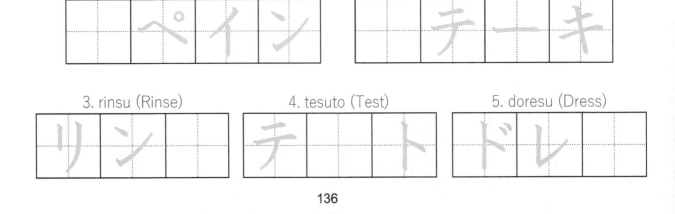

1. Supein (Spain)

2. sutēki (Steak)

3. rinsu (Rinse)

4. tesuto (Test)

5. doresu (Dress)

Pronunciation	"se" as in <u>se</u>t	【Write the character in the boxes】

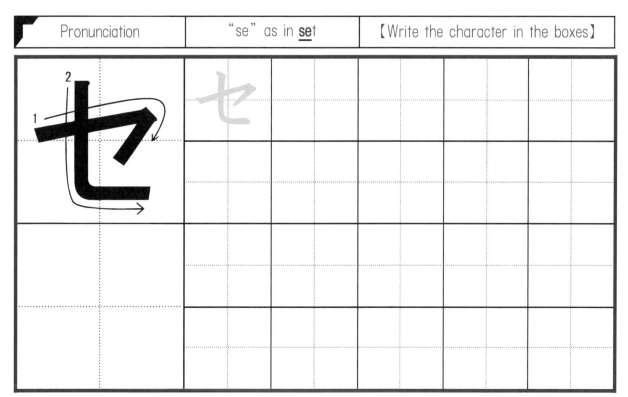

Continue practicing in the remaining boxes.

Remember to pay attention to stroke order.

🔊 Vocabulary - Write the character in the boxes below.

1. sētā (Sweater)

2. sensā (Sensor)

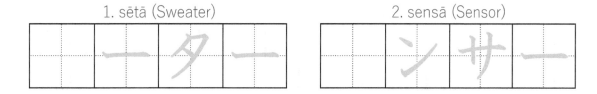

3. sēfu (Safe)

4. setto (Set)

5. sēru (Sale)

| Pronunciation | "so" as in <u>so</u>le | 【Write the character in the boxes】 |

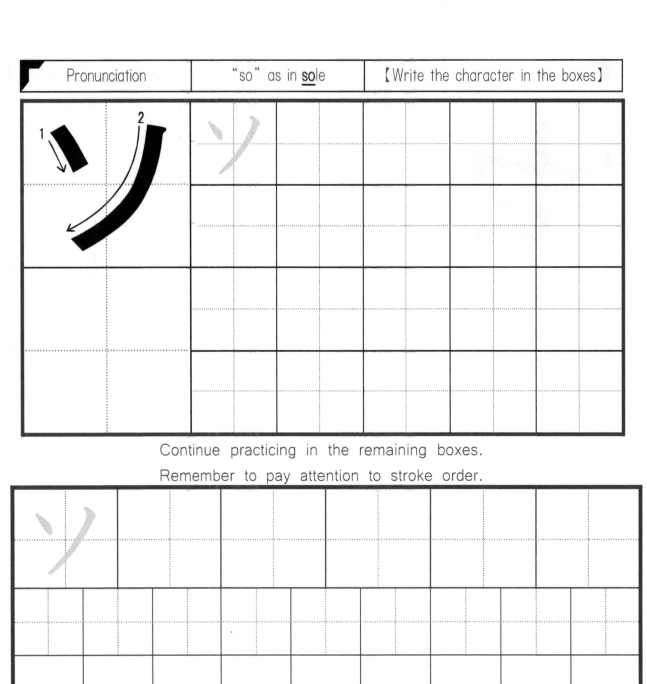

Continue practicing in the remaining boxes.

Remember to pay attention to stroke order.

Vocabulary - Write the character in the boxes below.

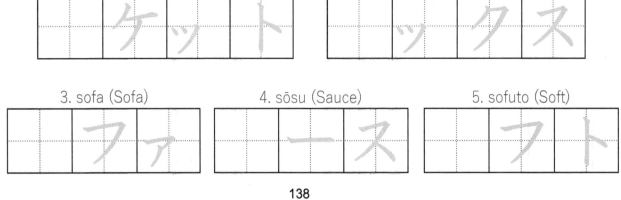

1. soketto (Socket)

2. sokkusu (Socks)

3. sofa (Sofa)

4. sōsu (Sauce)

5. sofuto (Soft)

THE BASIC 46 KATAKANA CHARACTERS

Pronunciation	"ta" as in <u>ta</u>p	【Write the character in the boxes】

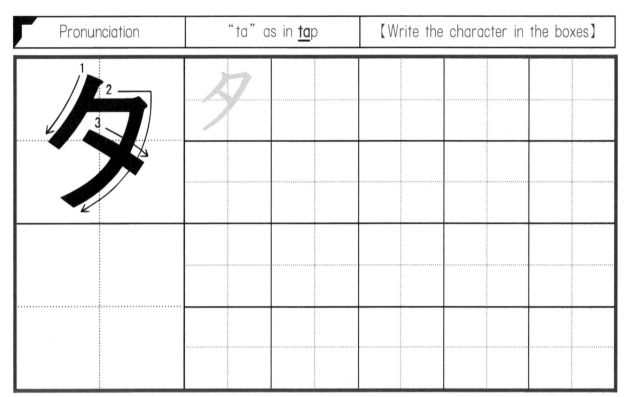

Continue practicing in the remaining boxes.
Remember to pay attention to stroke order.

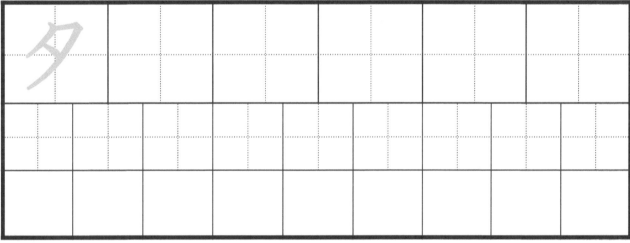

🔊 Vocabulary – Write the character in the boxes below.

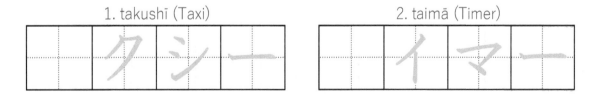

1. takushī (Taxi)　　　　　　　　2. taimā (Timer)

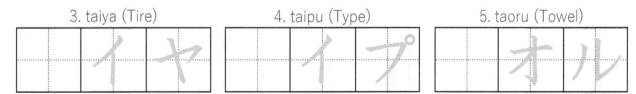

3. taiya (Tire)　　　4. taipu (Type)　　　5. taoru (Towel)

Pronunciation	"chi" as in <u>che</u>ese	【Write the character in the boxes】

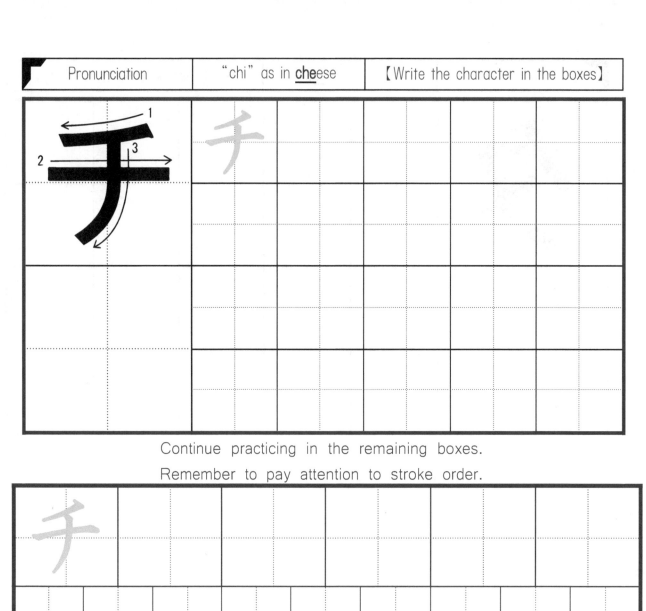

Continue practicing in the remaining boxes.
Remember to pay attention to stroke order.

 Vocabulary – Write the character in the boxes below.

1. chansu (Chance)

ャ　ン　ス

2. chenji (Change)

エ　ン　ジ

3. chesu (Chess)

ェ　ス

4. chīzu (Cheese)

ー　ズ

5. chikin (Chicken)

キ　ン

Pronunciation	"tsu" as in <u>tsu</u>nami	【Write the character in the boxes】

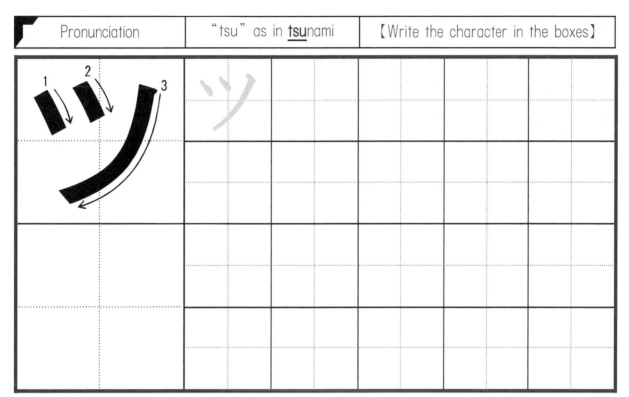

Continue practicing in the remaining boxes.

Remember to pay attention to stroke order.

🔊 Vocabulary – Write the character in the boxes below.

1. supōtsu (Sports)

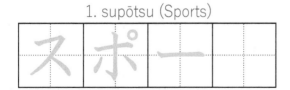

2. kyabetsu (Cabbage)

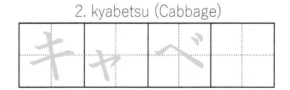

3. tsuā (Tours)

4. tsuin (Twin)

5. tsūru (Tool)

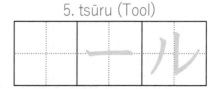

Pronunciation	"te" as in <u>te</u>mple	【Write the character in the boxes】

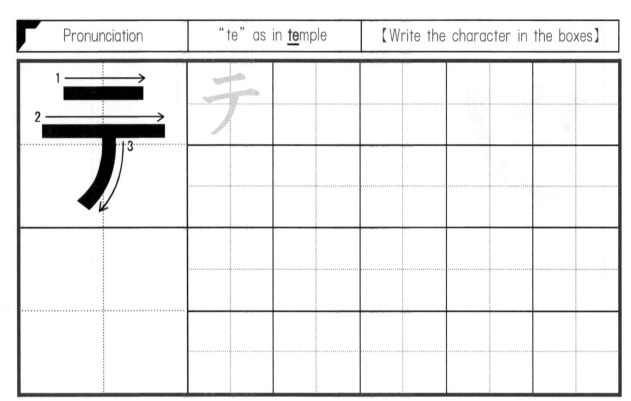

Continue practicing in the remaining boxes.
Remember to pay attention to stroke order.

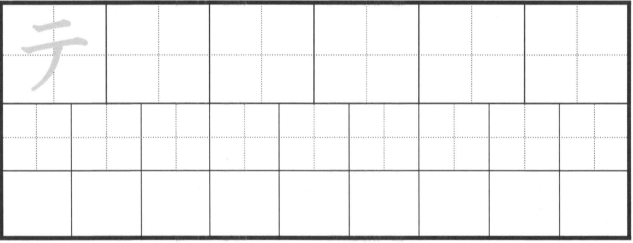

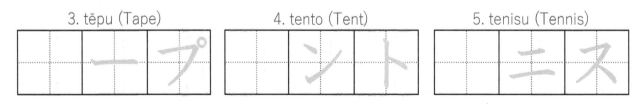 Vocabulary – Write the character in the boxes below.

1. tēburu (Table)

2. Tekisasu (Texas)

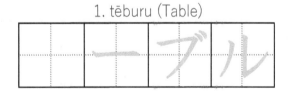

3. tēpu (Tape)

4. tento (Tent)

5. tenisu (Tennis)

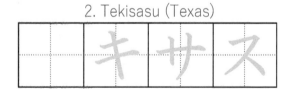

142

| Pronunciation | "to" as in <u>to</u>y | 【Write the character in the boxes】 |

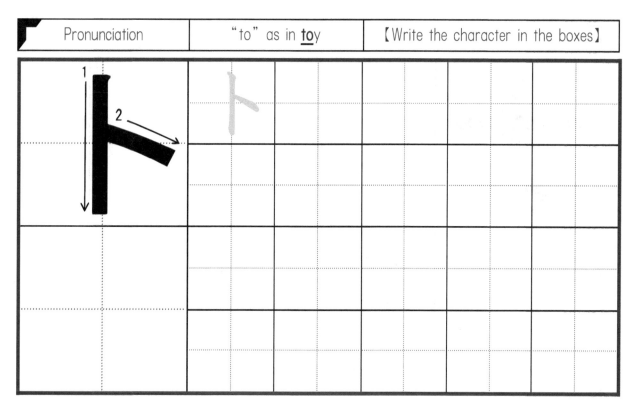

Continue practicing in the remaining boxes.

Remember to pay attention to stroke order.

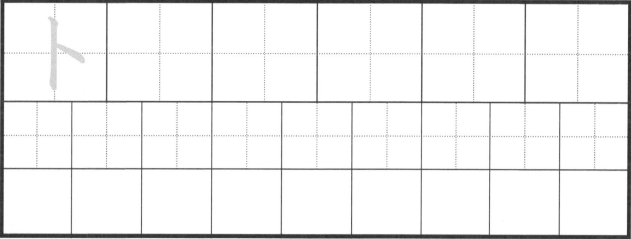

🔊 Vocabulary – Write the character in the boxes below.

1. Toronto (Toronto)

2. tōsuto (Toast)

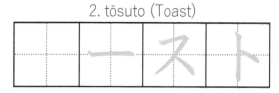

3. toire (Toilet)

4. tomato (Tomato)

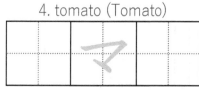

5. torē (Tray)

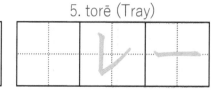

| Pronunciation | "na" as in **na**p | 【Write the character in the boxes】 |

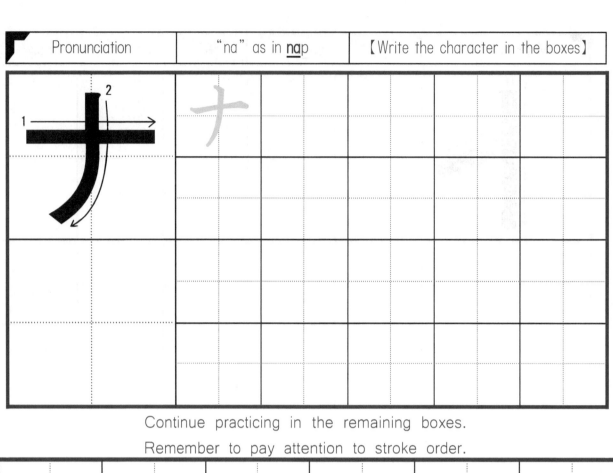

Continue practicing in the remaining boxes.

Remember to pay attention to stroke order.

🔊 Vocabulary – Write the character in the boxes below.

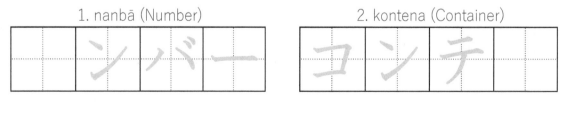

1. nanbā (Number)

2. kontena (Container)

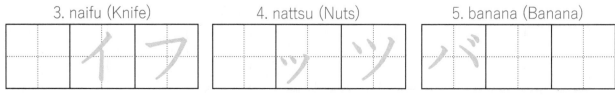

3. naifu (Knife)

4. nattsu (Nuts)

5. banana (Banana)

Pronunciation	"ni" as in **knee**	【Write the character in the boxes】

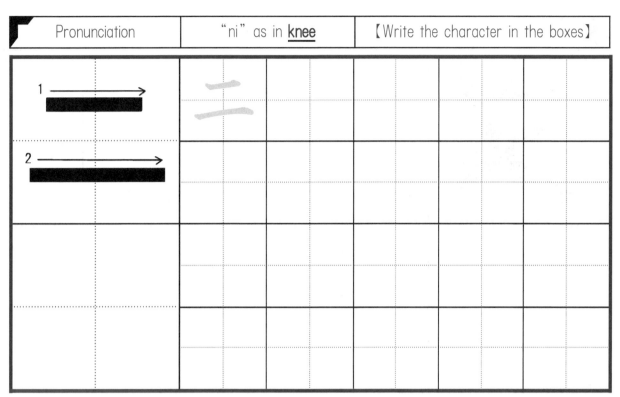

Continue practicing in the remaining boxes.

Remember to pay attention to stroke order.

Vocabulary – Write the character in the boxes below.

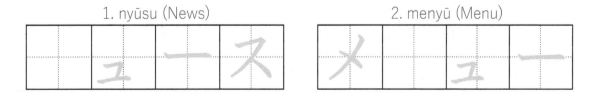

1. nyūsu (News)　　　　　　　　　　　2. menyū (Menu)

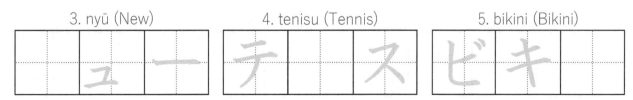

3. nyū (New)　　　　4. tenisu (Tennis)　　　　5. bikini (Bikini)

145

| Pronunciation | "nu" as in **noo**dles | 【Write the character in the boxes】 |

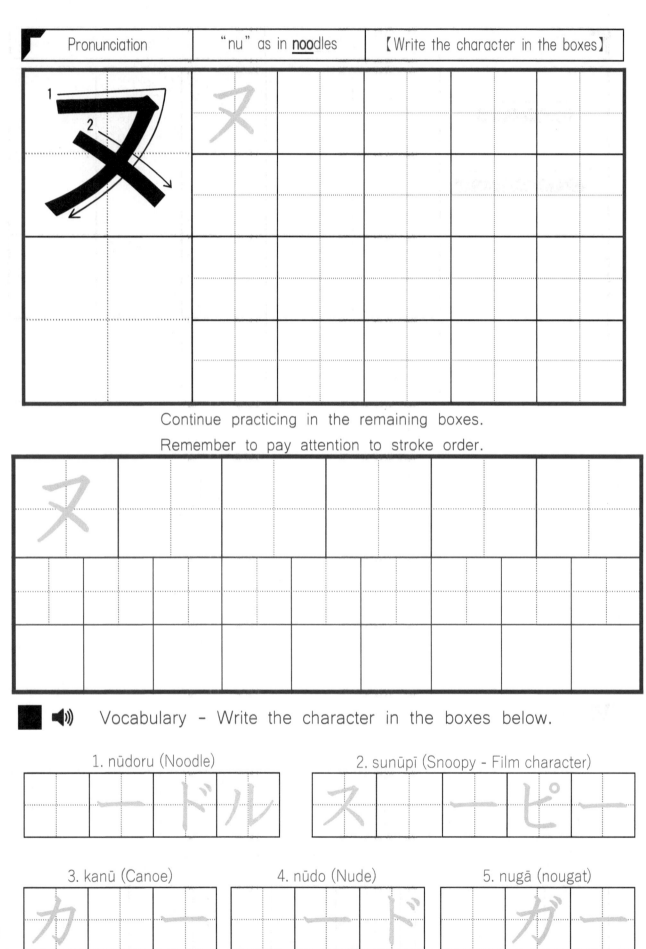

Continue practicing in the remaining boxes.

Remember to pay attention to stroke order.

🔊 Vocabulary – Write the character in the boxes below.

1. nūdoru (Noodle)

2. sunūpī (Snoopy - Film character)

3. kanū (Canoe)

4. nūdo (Nude)

5. nugā (nougat)

| Pronunciation | "ne" as in **ne**st | 【Write the character in the boxes】 |

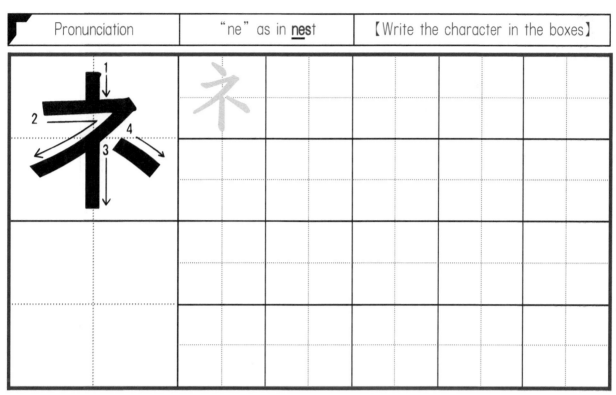

Continue practicing in the remaining boxes.
Remember to pay attention to stroke order.

🔊 Vocabulary – Write the character in the boxes below.

1. Nepāru (Nepal)

2. mayonēzu (Mayonnaise)

3. nekku (Neck)   4. nēmu (Name)   5. Nebada (Nevada)

Pronunciation	"no" as in <u>no</u>te	【Write the character in the boxes】

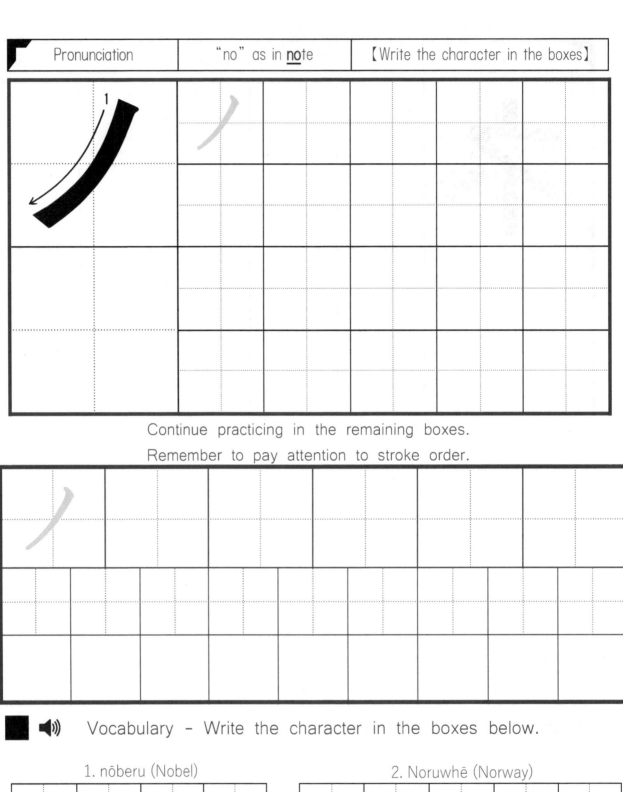

Continue practicing in the remaining boxes.

Remember to pay attention to stroke order.

Vocabulary – Write the character in the boxes below.

1. nōberu (Nobel)

ーベル

2. Noruwhē (Norway)

ルウェー

3. nōto (Note)

ート

4. piano (Piano)

ピア

5. kajino (Casino)

カジ

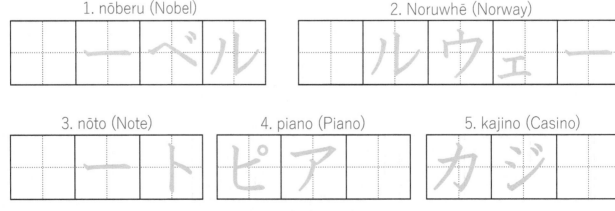

| Pronunciation | "ha" as in **ha**t | 【Write the character in the boxes】 |

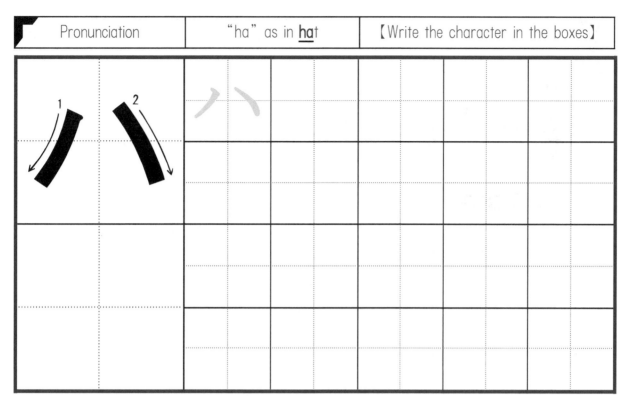

Continue practicing in the remaining boxes.
Remember to pay attention to stroke order.

Vocabulary - Write the character in the boxes below.

1. hanbāgā (Hamburger)

ンバーガー

2. hāto (Heart)

ート

3. harowhin (Halloween)

ロウィーン

4. hādo (Hard)

ード

| Pronunciation | "hi" as in yes **he** is! | 【Write the character in the boxes】 |

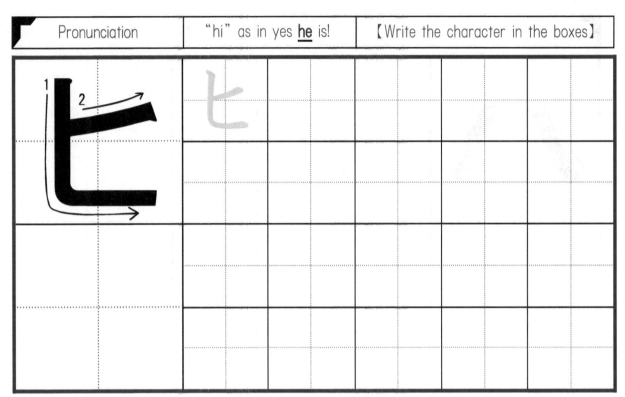

Continue practicing in the remaining boxes.

Remember to pay attention to stroke order.

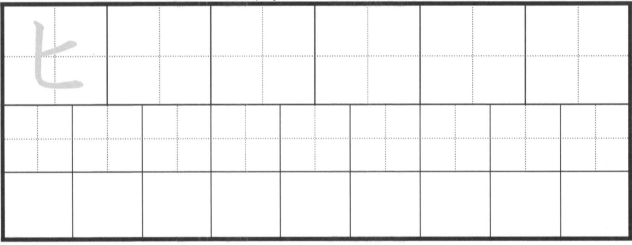

🔊 Vocabulary – Write the character in the boxes below.

1. hītā (Heater)

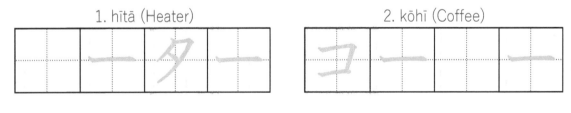

2. kōhī (Coffee)

3. hīru (Heel)   4. hitto (Hit)   5. hinto (Hint)

| Pronunciation | "fu" as in <u>fu</u>ji mount | 【Write the character in the boxes】 |

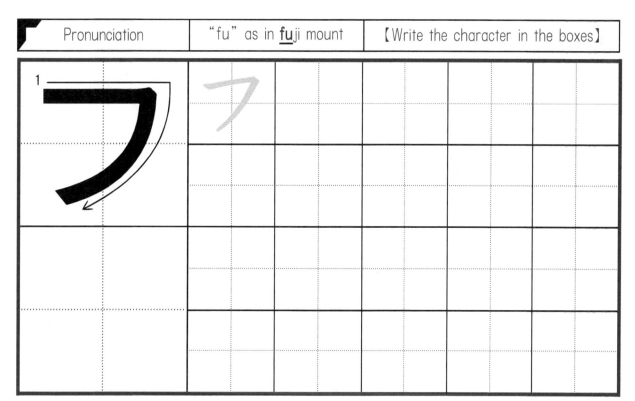

Continue practicing in the remaining boxes.
Remember to pay attention to stroke order.

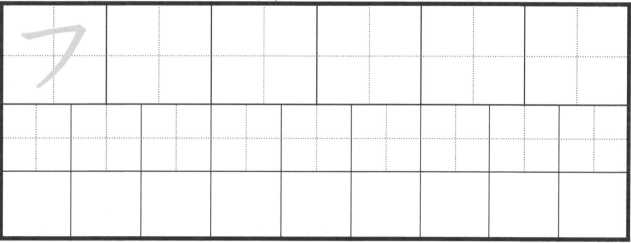

◼ 🔊 Vocabulary – Write the character in the boxes below.

1. fairu (File)

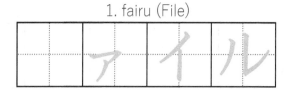

2. Furansu (France)

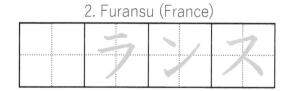

3. furūtsu (Fruits)

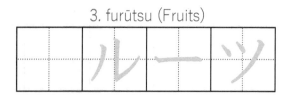

4. furonto (Front)

| Pronunciation | "he" as in **her**! | 【Write the character in the boxes】 |

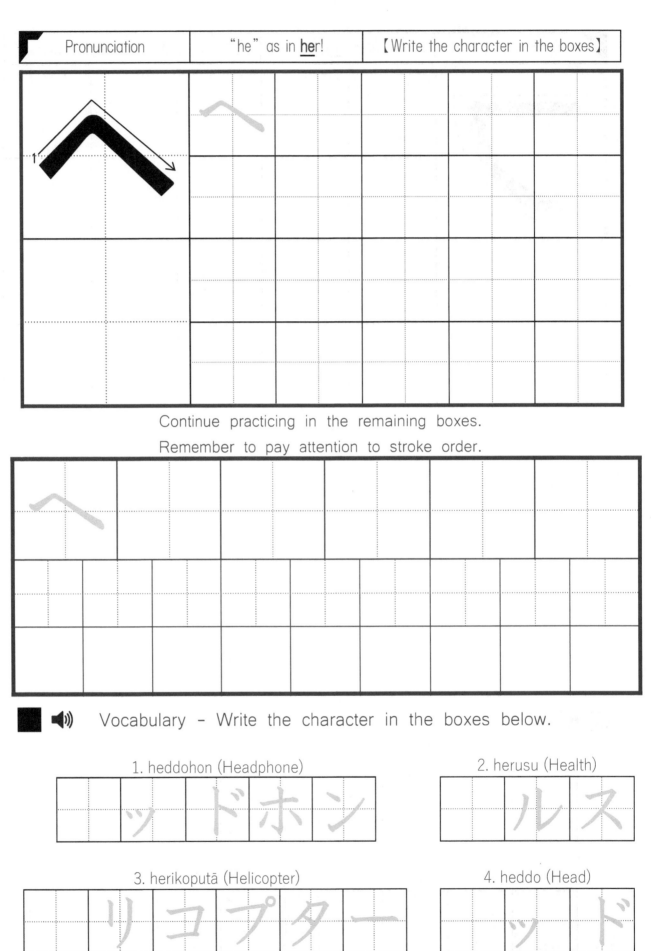

Continue practicing in the remaining boxes.
Remember to pay attention to stroke order.

🔊 Vocabulary – Write the character in the boxes below.

1. heddohon (Headphone)

ッドホン

2. herusu (Health)

ルス

3. herikoputā (Helicopter)

リコプター

4. heddo (Head)

ッド

| Pronunciation | "ho" as in **ho**pe | 【Write the character in the boxes】 |

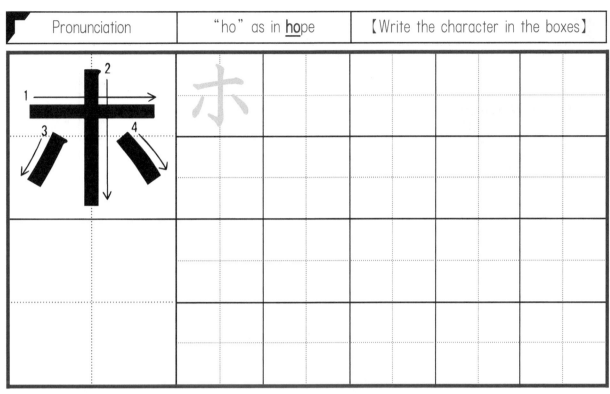

Continue practicing in the remaining boxes.
Remember to pay attention to stroke order.

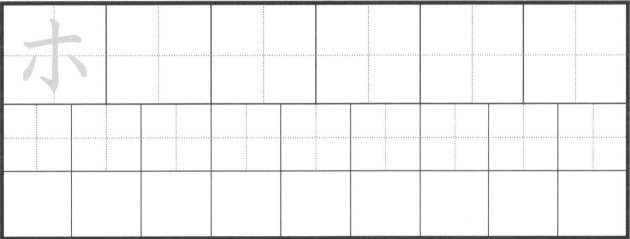

■ 🔊 Vocabulary - Write the character in the boxes below.

1. Honkon (Hong Kong)

2. hokkē (Hockey)

3. horā (Horror)

4. hotto (Hot)

5. hoteru (Hotel)

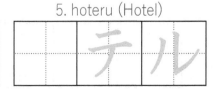

Pronunciation	"ma" as in <u>ma</u>t	【Write the character in the boxes】

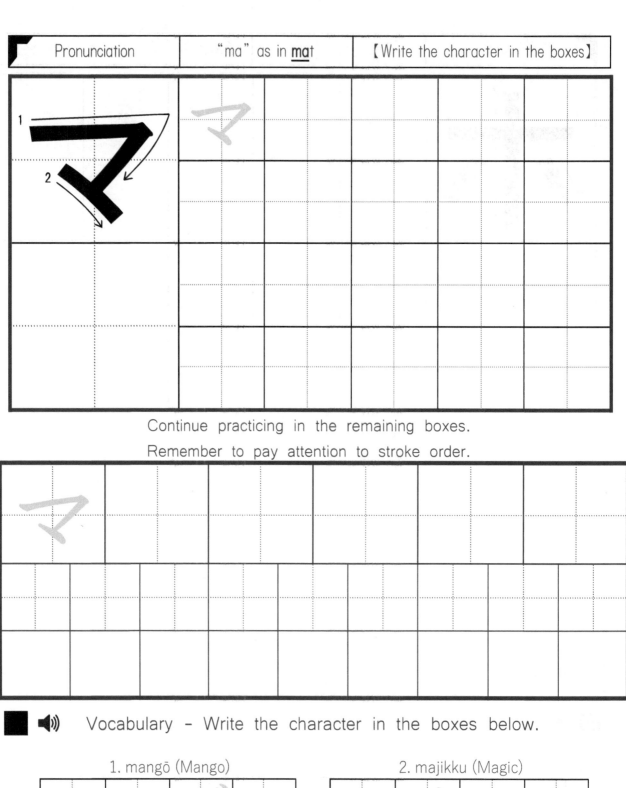

Continue practicing in the remaining boxes.

Remember to pay attention to stroke order.

 **◄))** Vocabulary - Write the character in the boxes below.

1. mangō (Mango)

2. majikku (Magic)

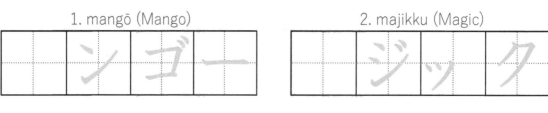

3. manga (Comics)

4. masuku (Mask)

5. māku (Mark)

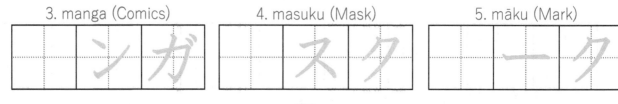

Pronunciation	"mi" as in **me**!	【Write the character in the boxes】

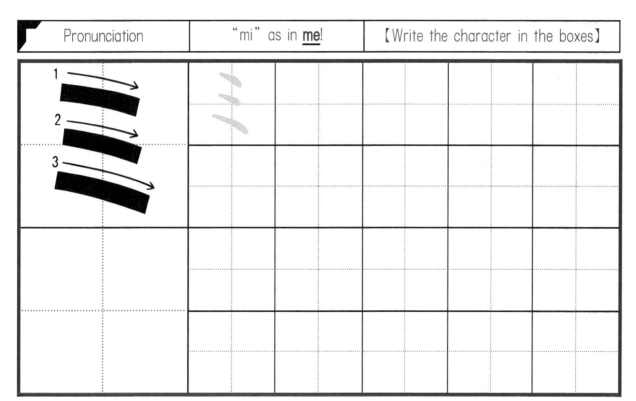

Continue practicing in the remaining boxes.

Remember to pay attention to stroke order.

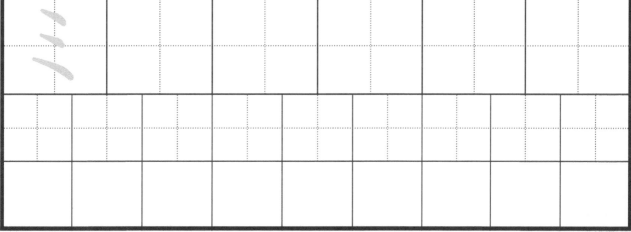

■ 🔊 Vocabulary – Write the character in the boxes below.

1. mikkusu (Mix)   2. mineraru (Mineral)

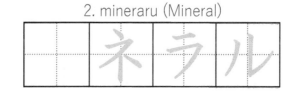

3. mīru (Meal)   4. mīto (Meat)   5. miruku (Milk)

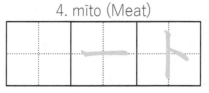

| Pronunciation | "mu" as in **moo**d | 【Write the character in the boxes】 |

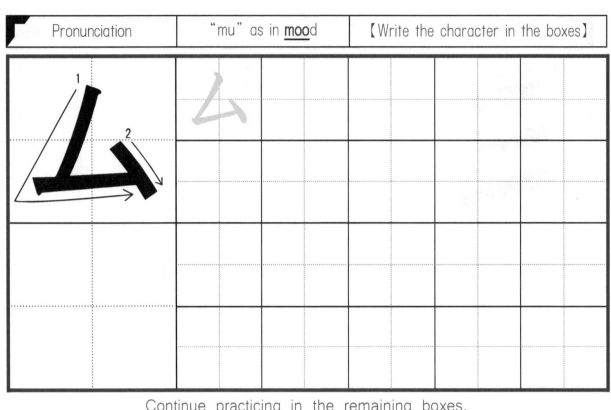

Continue practicing in the remaining boxes.
Remember to pay attention to stroke order.

Vocabulary – Write the character in the boxes below.

1. Betonamu (Vietnam)

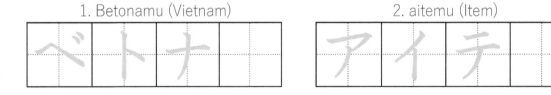

2. aitemu (Item)

3. chīmu (Team)   4. nēmu (Name)   5. Adamu (Adam)

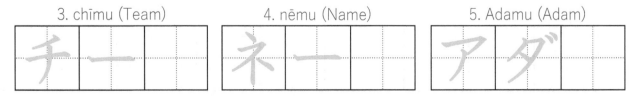

156

Pronunciation	"me" as in <u>Me</u>xico	【Write the character in the boxes】

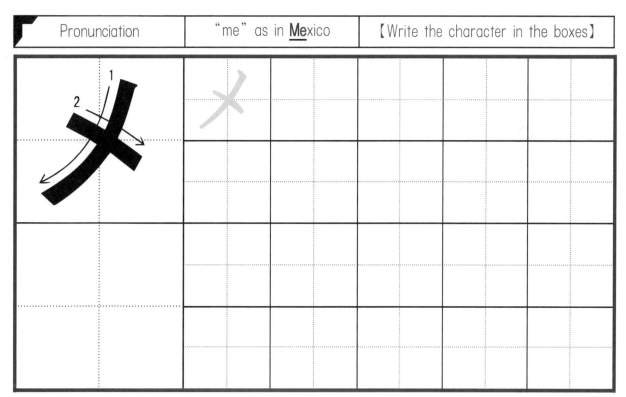

Continue practicing in the remaining boxes.

Remember to pay attention to stroke order.

🔊 Vocabulary – Write the character in the boxes below.

1. Mekishiko (Mexico)

2. menyū (Menu)

3. mēru (Email)

4. anime (Animation)

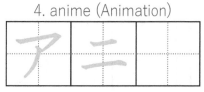

5. meron (Melon)

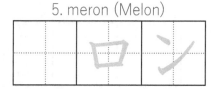

Pronunciation	"mo" as in <u>mo</u>re	【Write the character in the boxes】

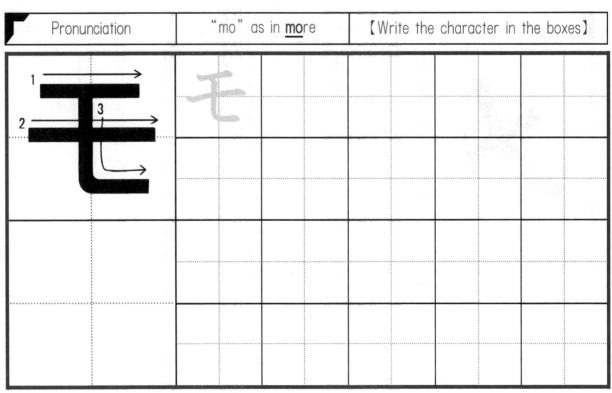

Continue practicing in the remaining boxes.

Remember to pay attention to stroke order.

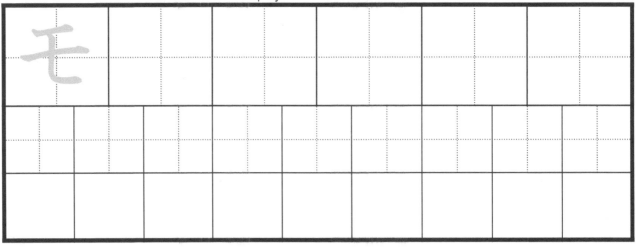

 Vocabulary – Write the character in the boxes below.

1. Morokko (Morocco)

2. mōtā (Motor)

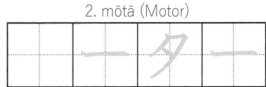

3. mōru (Mall)

4. modemu (Modem)

5. moderu (Model)

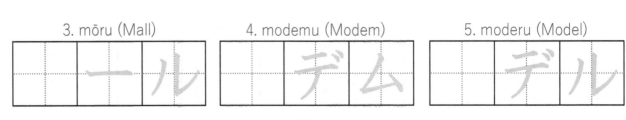

Pronunciation	"ya" as in **ya**cht	【Write the character in the boxes】

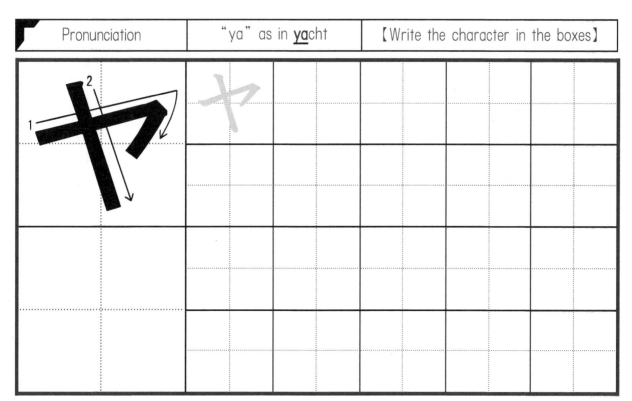

Continue practicing in the remaining boxes.
Remember to pay attention to stroke order.

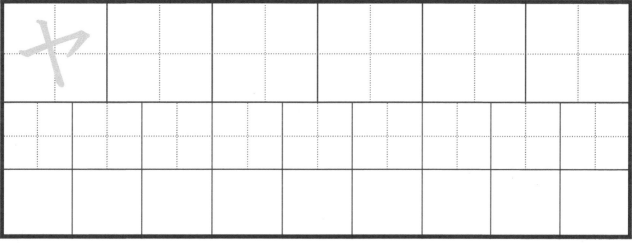

🔊 Vocabulary – Write the character in the boxes below.

1. daiyaru (Dial)　　　　　2. kanariya (Canary)

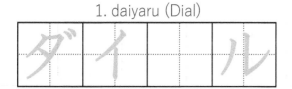

1. taiya (Tire)　　2. yādo (Yard)　　3. daiya (Diamond)

THE BASIC 46 KATAKANA CHARACTERS

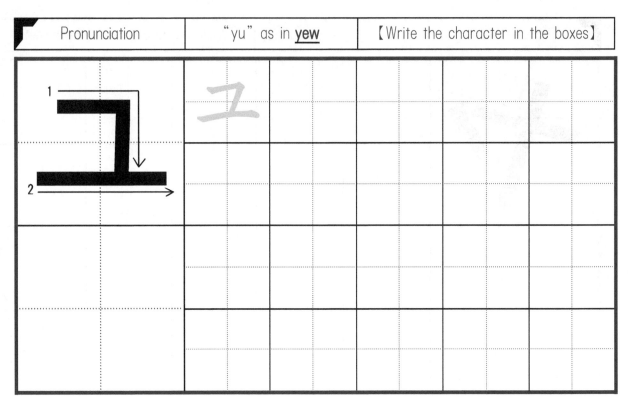

Continue practicing in the remaining boxes.

Remember to pay attention to stroke order.

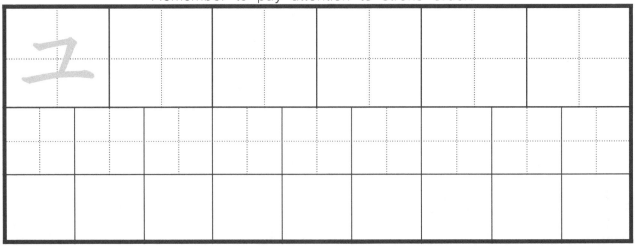

 Vocabulary – Write the character in the boxes below.

1. yūzā (User)

2. yunitto (Unit)

3. yunifōmu (Uniform)

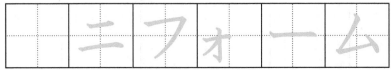

| Pronunciation | "yo" as in **yo**ga | 【Write the character in the boxes】 |

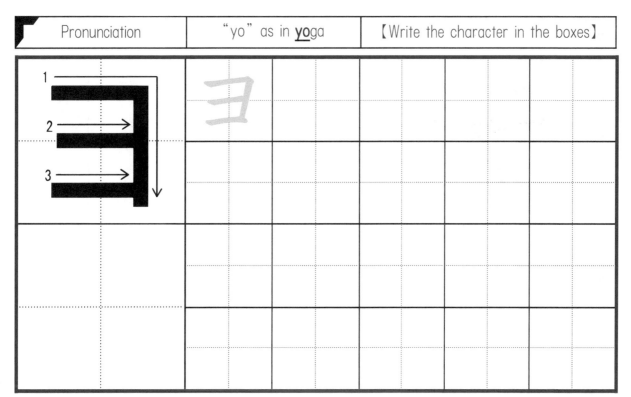

Continue practicing in the remaining boxes.
Remember to pay attention to stroke order.

Vocabulary - Write the character in the boxes below.

1. yōguruto (Yogurt)

2. mayonēzu (Mayonnaise)

3. Nyūyōku (New York)

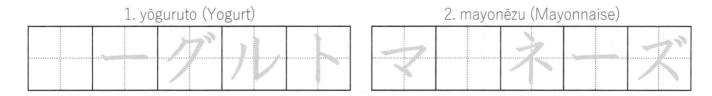

161

Pronunciation	"ra" as in <u>ra</u>men	【Write the character in the boxes】

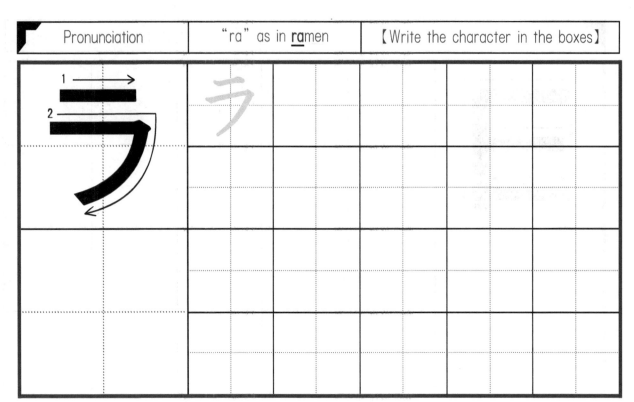

Continue practicing in the remaining boxes.

Remember to pay attention to stroke order.

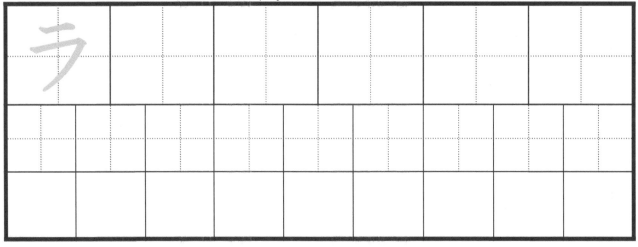

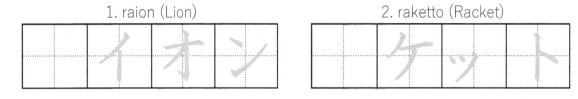 Vocabulary – Write the character in the boxes below.

1. raion (Lion)

2. raketto (Racket)

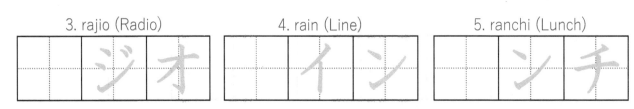

3. rajio (Radio)

4. rain (Line)

5. ranchi (Lunch)

Pronunciation	"ri" as in <u>ri</u>ng	【Write the character in the boxes】

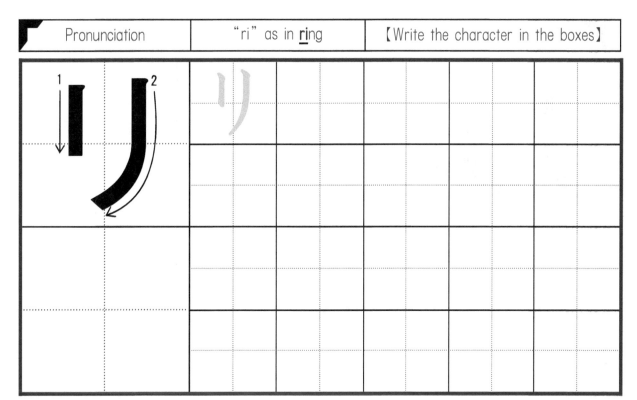

Continue practicing in the remaining boxes.

Remember to pay attention to stroke order.

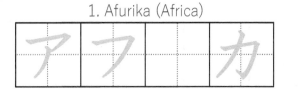

Vocabulary – Write the character in the boxes below.

1. Afurika (Africa)

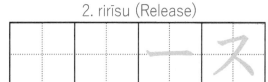

2. ririsu (Release)

3. ribon (Ribbon)

4. ringu (Ring)

5. rinku (Link)

Pronunciation	"ru" as in <u>ru</u>by	【Write the character in the boxes】

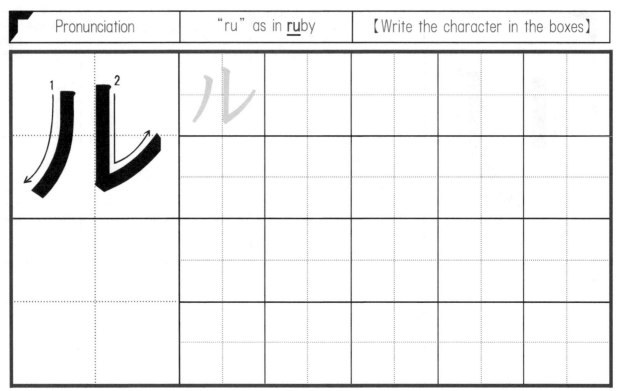

Continue practicing in the remaining boxes.
Remember to pay attention to stroke order.

Vocabulary – Write the character in the boxes below.

1. sutairu (Style)

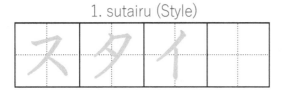

2. fairu (File)

3. rubī (Ruby)

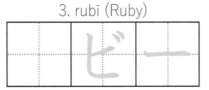

4. rūfu (Roof)

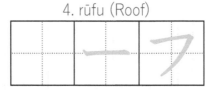

5. paneru (Panel)

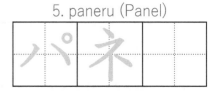

| Pronunciation | "re" as in <u>ra</u>dio | 【Write the character in the boxes】 |

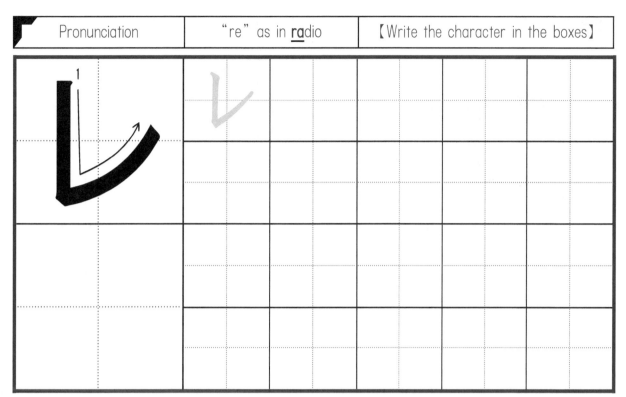

Continue practicing in the remaining boxes.
Remember to pay attention to stroke order.

🔊 Vocabulary – Write the character in the boxes below.

1. repōto (Report)

2. rekōdo (Record)

3. remon (Lemon)

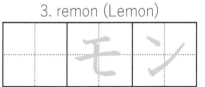

4. reberu (Level)

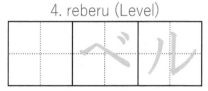

5. terebi (TV)

Pronunciation	"ro" as in **ro**pe	【Write the character in the boxes】

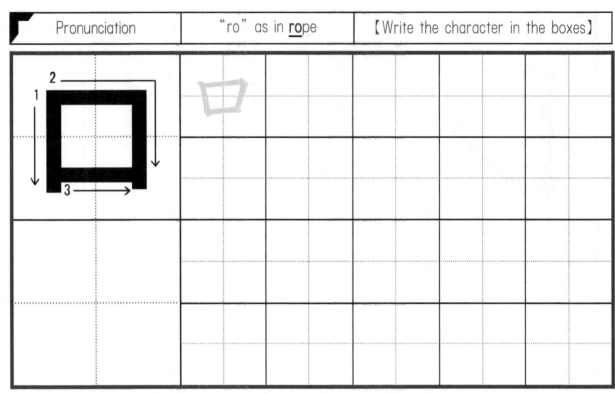

Continue practicing in the remaining boxes.

Remember to pay attention to stroke order.

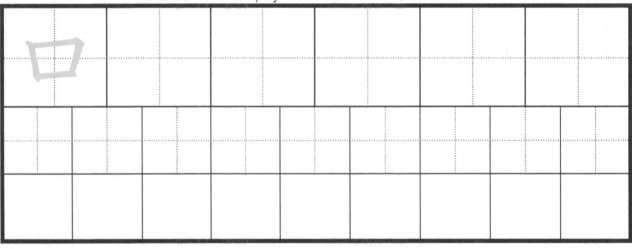

■ 🔊 Vocabulary - Write the character in the boxes below.

1. Rondon (London)

2. robotto (Robot)

3. robī (Lobby)

4. rōpu (Rope)

5. Rōma (Rome)

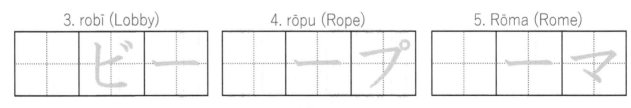

| Pronunciation | "wa" as in **wa**ter | 【Write the character in the boxes】 |

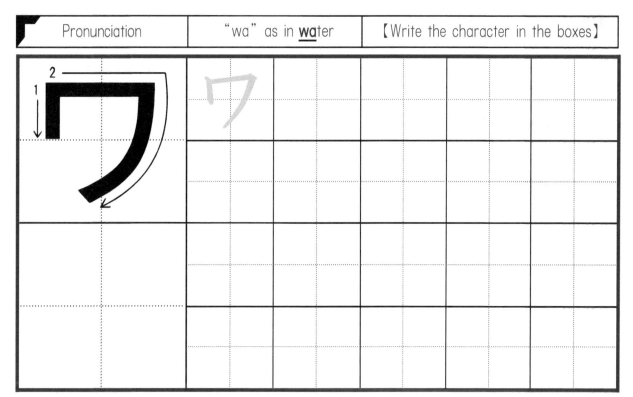

Continue practicing in the remaining boxes.
Remember to pay attention to stroke order.

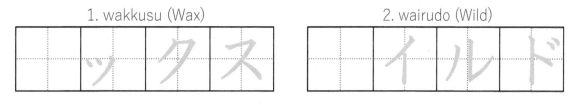

Vocabulary – Write the character in the boxes below.

1. wakkusu (Wax)

2. wairudo (Wild)

3. wain (Wine)

4. Hawai (Hawaii)

5. waipu (Wipe)

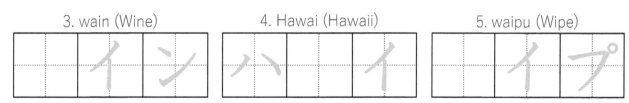

167

Pronunciation	"wo" as in **wo**rry	【Write the character in the boxes】

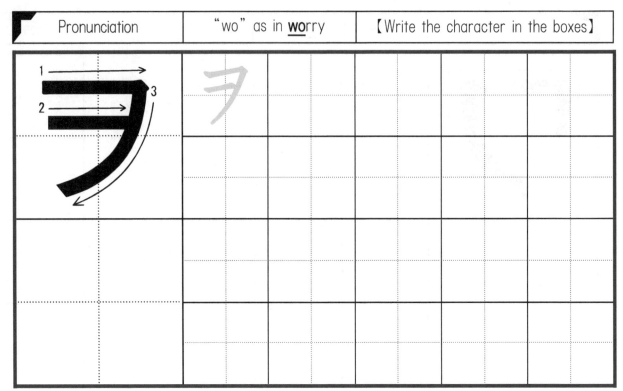

Continue practicing in the remaining boxes.

Remember to pay attention to stroke order.

Note: ヲ "wo" is rarely used to write sentences, except in some video games.

❖ This is an old katakana, so now it's rarely used in modern Japanese.

(＊Almost Same pronunciation as オ).

Pronunciation	"n" as in <u>in</u>k	【Write the character in the boxes】

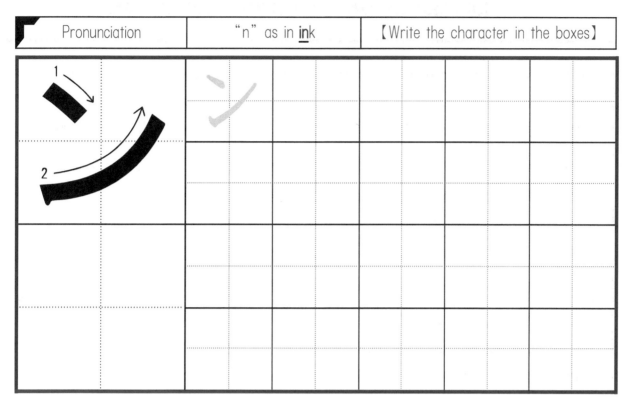

Continue practicing in the remaining boxes.
Remember to pay attention to stroke order.

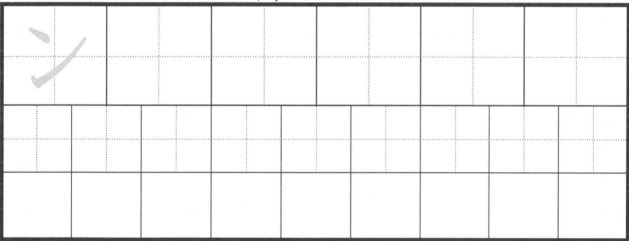

■ **Note:** ン "n" and ソ "so" look similar.

A big difference is that "n" is written more from left to right, and "so" is written more from top to bottom.

■ ◀)) Vocabulary – Write the character in the boxes below.

1. ramen (Noodles)　　　　　　　　2. meron (Melon)

KATAKANA - DAKUTEN AND HANDAKUTEN

Katakana has the same concept as Hiragana when it comes to these Dakuten and Handakuten syllables.

❖ This means ka (カ) turns to ga (ガ) and ha (ハ) turns to pa (パ) for Katakana.

__The first__ diacritical mark is called a dakuten or ten-ten and looks like this ﾞ, two diagonal strokes placed on the top right corner of a character.

Its job is to change an unvoiced sound into its voiced counterpart. 〈k〉 changes to 〈g〉, 〈sa〉 changes to 〈za〉, 〈t〉 changes to 〈d〉 and 〈h〉 changes to 〈b〉.

__The second__ diacritical mark is the handakuten or maru and looks like this ﾟ, a circle which is also placed on the top right corner of a character.
The handakuten is only used with Hiragana in the h- column and turns the consonant 〈h〉 into a 〈p〉.

The additional Katakana chart below shows those with 濁音 (dakuten) and 半濁音 (handakuten).

Normal sound		With dakuten		With handakuten	
ハ	ha	バ	ba	パ	pa
ヒ	hi	ビ	bi	ピ	pi
フ	hu	ブ	bu	プ	pu
ヘ	he	ベ	be	ペ	pe
ホ	ho	ボ	bo	ポ	po

Dakuten

ガ ga	ギ gi	グ gu	ゲ ge	ゴ go
ザ za	ジ zi(ji)	ズ zu	ゼ ze	ゾ zo
ダ da	ヂ di(ji)	ヅ du	デ de	ド do
バ ba	ビ bi	ブ bu	ベ be	ボ bo

Handakuten

パ pa	ピ pi	プ pu	ペ pe	ポ po

□ﾞ **dakuten**
□ﾟ **handakuten**

Note:

Pronunciation	"ga" as in **got**	【Write the character in the boxes】

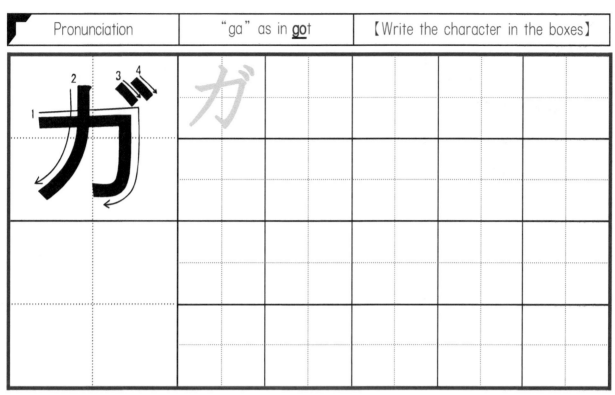

Continue practicing in the remaining boxes.
Remember to pay attention to stroke order.

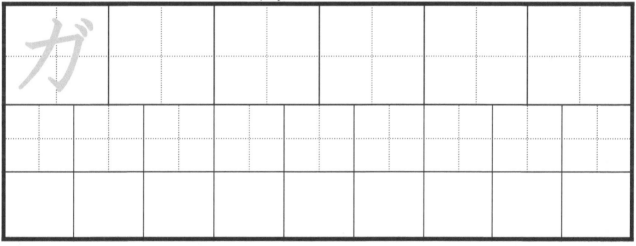

■ 🔊 Vocabulary – Write the character in the boxes below.

1. gasorin (Gasoline)   2. gāden (Garden)

3. garasu (Glass)   4. gaun (Gown)   5. gaido (Guide)

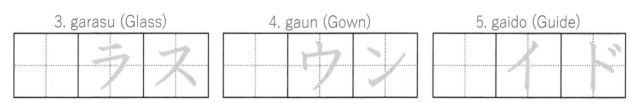

Pronunciation	"gi" as in **gi**ft	【Write the character in the boxes】

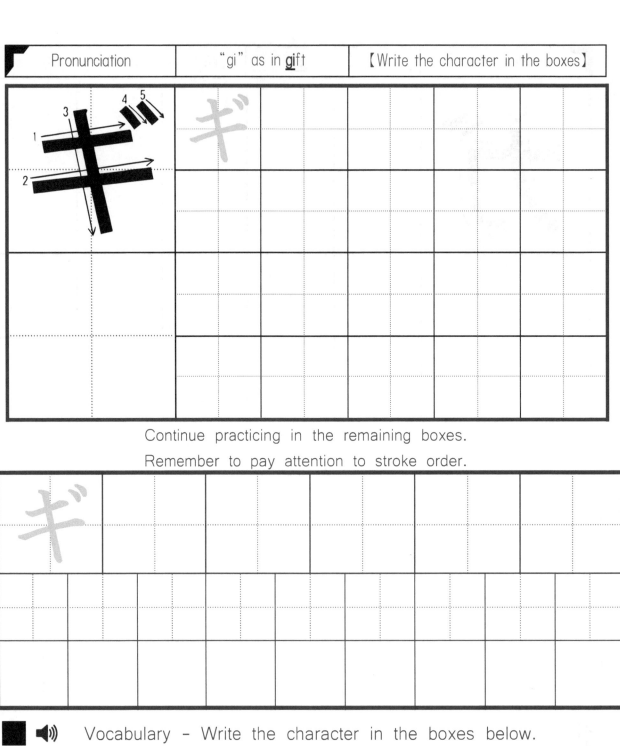

Continue practicing in the remaining boxes.

Remember to pay attention to stroke order.

🔊 Vocabulary – Write the character in the boxes below.

1. Igirisu (England)

イ　リ　ス

2. pengin (Penguin)

ペ　ン　　ン

3. gitā (Guitar)

ター

4. gifuto (Gift)

フト

5. ginesu (Guinness)

ネ　ス

172

Pronunciation	"gu" as in **goo**d	【Write the character in the boxes】

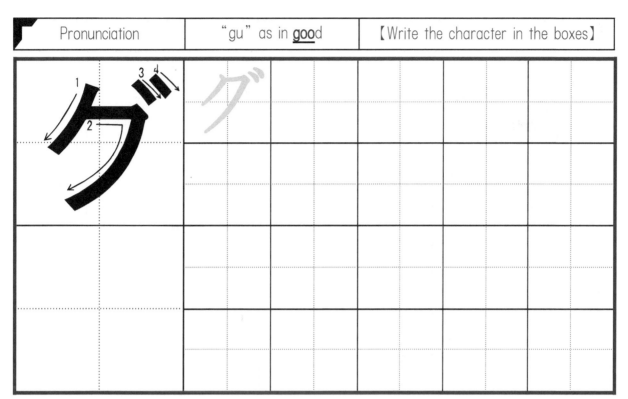

Continue practicing in the remaining boxes.
Remember to pay attention to stroke order.

Vocabulary – Write the character in the boxes below.

1. gurūpu (Group)

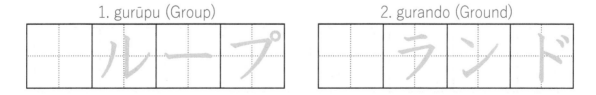

2. gurando (Ground)

3. gurē (Grey)

4. guramu (Gram)

5. kingu (King)

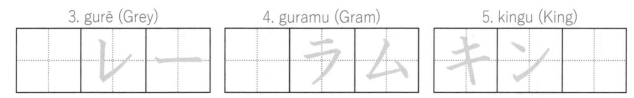

173

Pronunciation	"ge" as in **get**	【Write the character in the boxes】

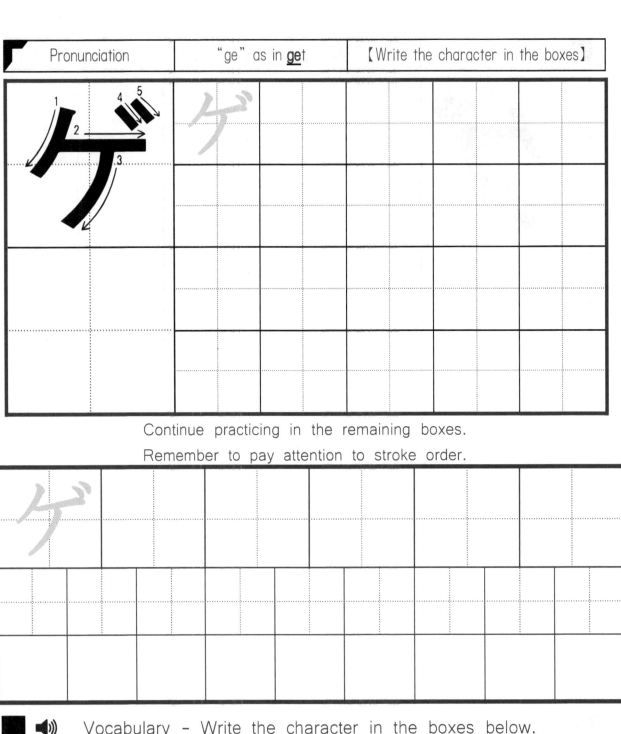

Continue practicing in the remaining boxes.

Remember to pay attention to stroke order.

🔊 Vocabulary – Write the character in the boxes below.

1. gēji (Gauge)

2. getto (Get)

3. gēto (Gate)

4. gēmu (Game)

5. gerira (Guerrilla)

6. gesuto (Guest)

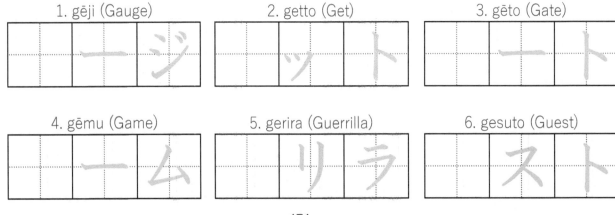

Pronunciation	"go" as in **go**!	【Write the character in the boxes】

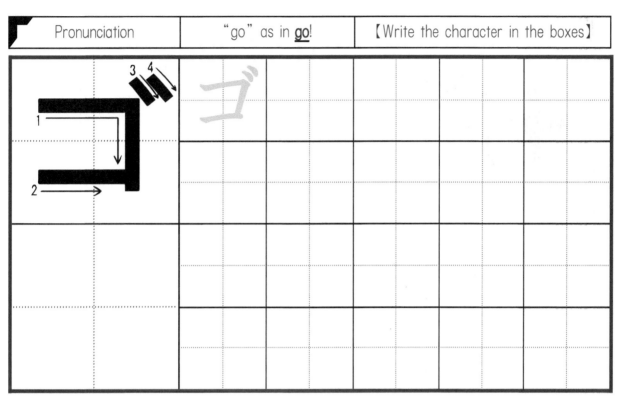

Continue practicing in the remaining boxes.
Remember to pay attention to stroke order.

🔊 Vocabulary - Write the character in the boxes below.

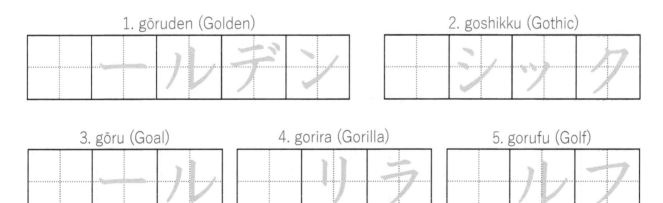

1. gōruden (Golden)

2. goshikku (Gothic)

3. gōru (Goal)

4. gorira (Gorilla)

5. gorufu (Golf)

175

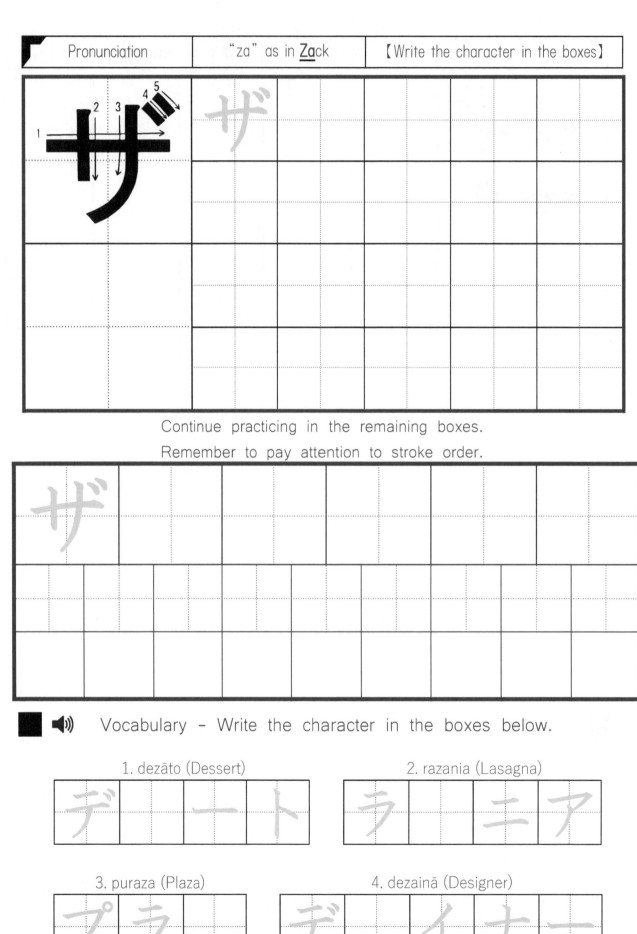

| Pronunciation | "za" as in <u>Z</u>ack | 【Write the character in the boxes】 |

Continue practicing in the remaining boxes.

Remember to pay attention to stroke order.

Vocabulary - Write the character in the boxes below.

1. dezāto (Dessert)

2. razania (Lasagna)

3. puraza (Plaza)

4. dezainā (Designer)

Pronunciation	"zi (ji)" as in Kan**ji**	【Write the character in the boxes】

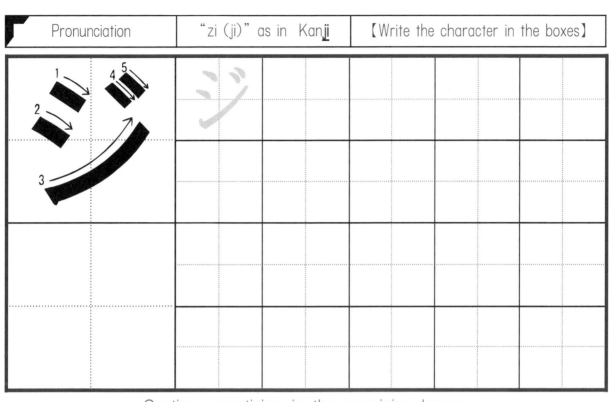

Continue practicing in the remaining boxes.
Remember to pay attention to stroke order.

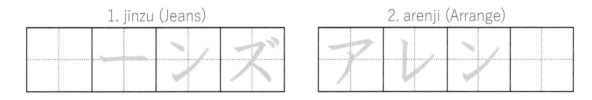

🔊 Vocabulary - Write the character in the boxes below.

1. jīnzu (Jeans)   2. arenji (Arrange)

3. Ajia (Asia)   4. ejji (Edge)   5. pēji (Page)

Pronunciation	"zu" as in <u>zo</u>o	【Write the character in the boxes】

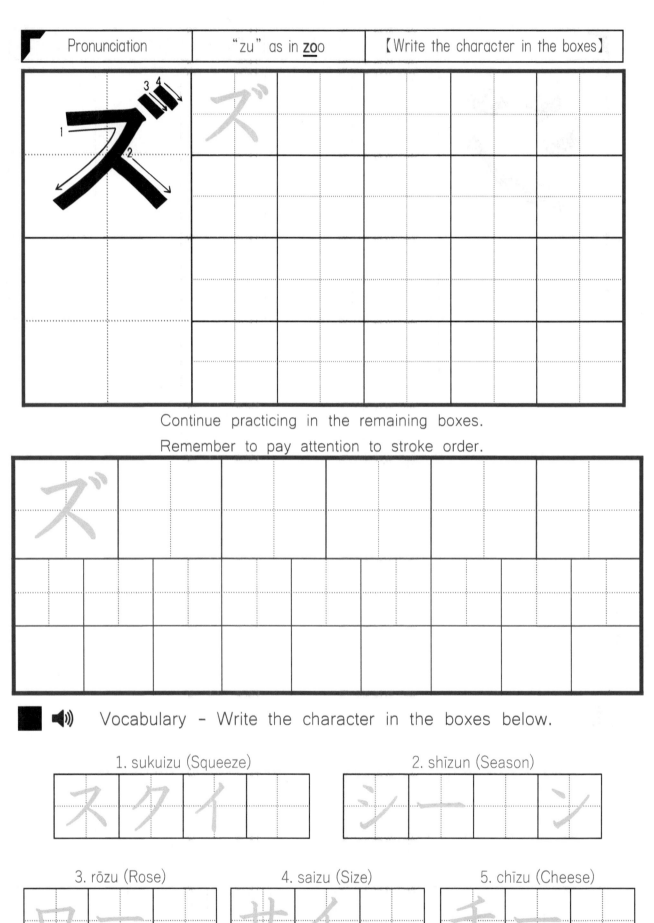

Continue practicing in the remaining boxes.
Remember to pay attention to stroke order.

 Vocabulary - Write the character in the boxes below.

1. sukuizu (Squeeze)

ス　ク　イ

2. shīzun (Season)

シ　ー　ン

3. rōzu (Rose)

ロ　ー

4. saizu (Size)

サ　イ

5. chīzu (Cheese)

チ　ー

178

Pronunciation	"ze" as in **zeh**	【Write the character in the boxes】

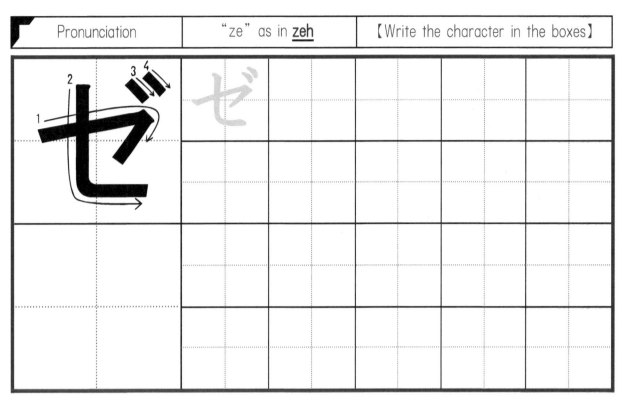

Continue practicing in the remaining boxes.
Remember to pay attention to stroke order.

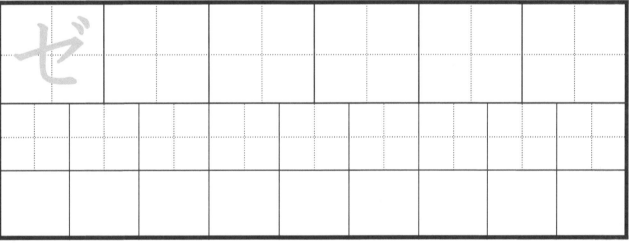

Vocabulary – Write the character in the boxes below.

1. enzeru (Angel)

2. zeneraru (General)

3. zerī (Jelly)

4. gāze (Gauze)

5. zeusu (Zeus)

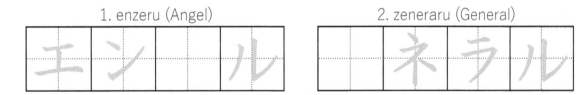

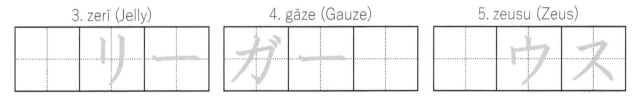

| Pronunciation | "zo" as in <u>ZO</u>ne | 【Write the character in the boxes】 |

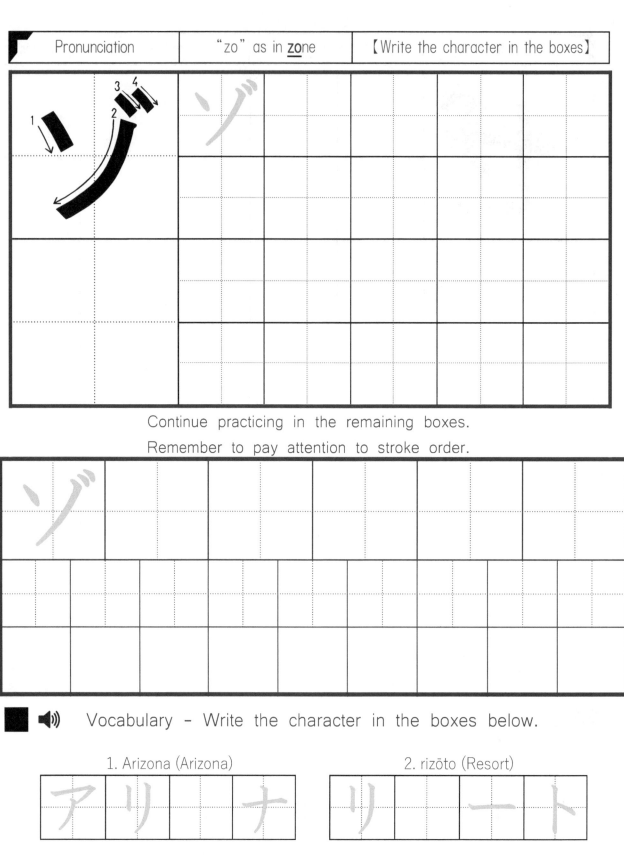

Continue practicing in the remaining boxes.

Remember to pay attention to stroke order.

Vocabulary - Write the character in the boxes below.

1. Arizona (Arizona)

アリ　ナ

2. rizōto (Resort)

リ　ート

3. zōn (Zone)

ーン

4. ozon (Ozone)

オ　ン

5. zonbi (Zombie)

ンビ

180

| Pronunciation | "da" as in **da**nce | 【Write the character in the boxes】 |

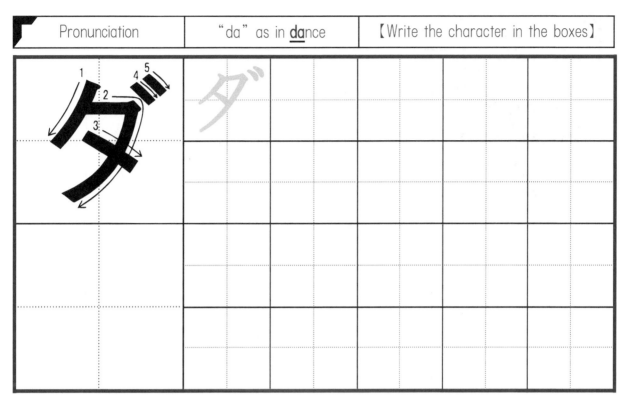

Continue practicing in the remaining boxes.

Remember to pay attention to stroke order.

🔊 Vocabulary – Write the character in the boxes below.

1. sōda (Soda)

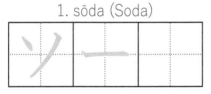

2. daun (Down)

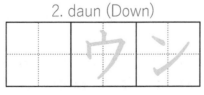

3. dātsu (Darts)

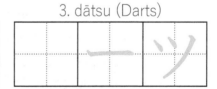

4. dansu (Dance)

5. sarada (Salad)

6. daburu (Double)

181

Pronunciation	"di"	【Write the character in the boxes】

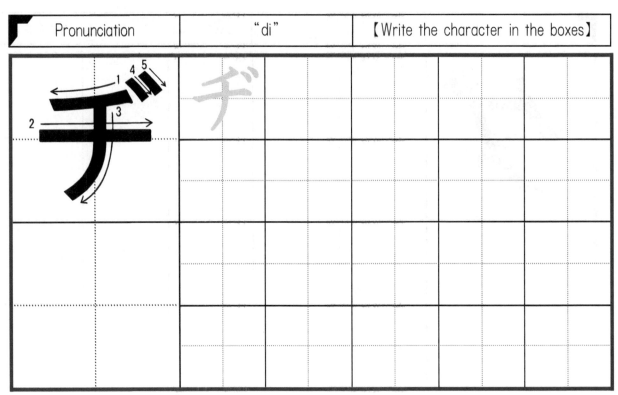

Continue practicing in the remaining boxes.

Remember to pay attention to stroke order.

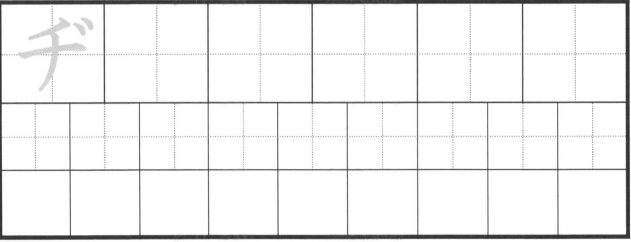

■ **Note:** About "zi" and "di", and "zu" and "du"

In the olden days, the pronunciation of "da(ダ)· di(ヂ)· du(ヅ)· de(デ) ·do(ド)"

was pronounced "da(ダ)· di(ディ)· du(デュ)· de(デ)· do(ド)".

The difference between the Japanese voices "zi" and "di", and "zu" and "du"

has completely disappeared. In both cases, the pronunciations of "di" and "du" are unified,

so the notation of "di" and "du" is not necessary.

However, you may have to always use "di" and "du" when writing.

Rules for using "di" and "du"

"di" and "du" are caused by repeated calls of the same sound.

"di" and "du" were created by the union of two words.

Keep in mind that we are focusing on how to write letters here.

Pronunciation	"du"	【Write the character in the boxes】

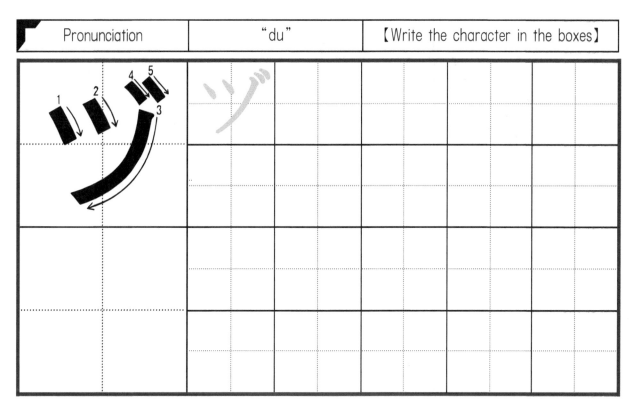

Continue practicing in the remaining boxes.

Remember to pay attention to stroke order.

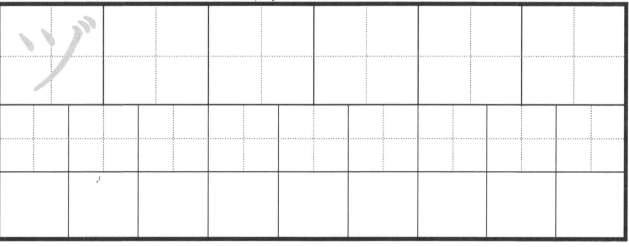

◼ **Note:** About "zi″ and "di″, and ″zu″ and "du″

In the olden days, the pronunciation of "da(ダ)・ di(ヂ)・ du(ヅ)・ de(デ) ・do(ド)"
was pronounced "da(ダ)・ di(ディ)・ du(デュ)・ de(デ)・ do(ド)".

The difference between the Japanese voices "zi" and "di", and "zu" and "du"
has completely disappeared. In both cases, the pronunciations of "di" and "du" are unified,
so the notation of "di" and "du" is not necessary.

However, you may have to always use "di″ and "du″ when writing.

Rules for using "di″ and "du″

"di″ and "du″ are caused by repeated calls of the same sound.

"di″ and "du″ were created by the union of two words.

Keep in mind that we are focusing on how to write letters here.

KATAKANA - DAKUTEN AND HANDAKUTEN

Pronunciation	"de" as in <u>de</u>sk	【Write the character in the boxes】

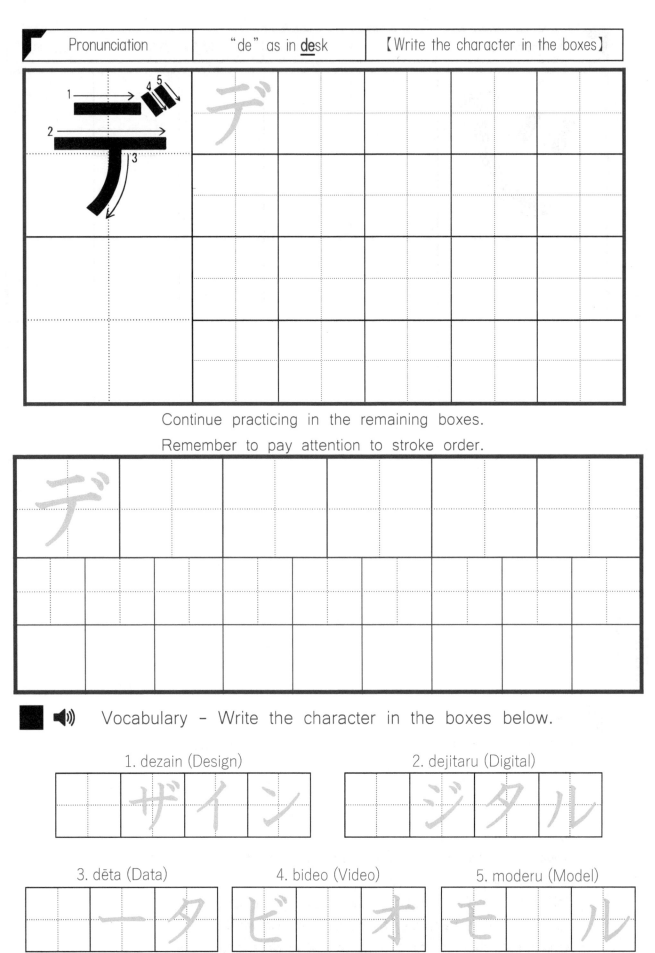

Continue practicing in the remaining boxes.
Remember to pay attention to stroke order.

Vocabulary – Write the character in the boxes below.

1. dezain (Design)

ザイン

2. dejitaru (Digital)

ジタル

3. dēta (Data)

ータ

4. bideo (Video)

タビ

オ

5. moderu (Model)

モル

Pronunciation	"do" as in <u>do</u>or	【Write the character in the boxes】

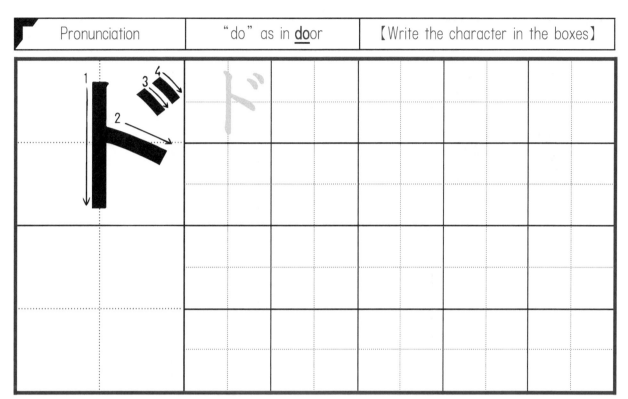

Continue practicing in the remaining boxes.

Remember to pay attention to stroke order.

Vocabulary – Write the character in the boxes below.

1. doraibu (Drive)

2. burando (Brand)

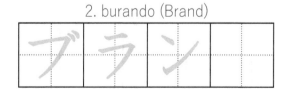

3. dorai (Dry)

4. Doitsu (Germany)

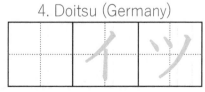

5. doresu (Dress)

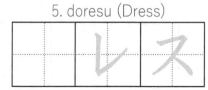

Pronunciation	"ba" as in **ba**t	【Write the character in the boxes】

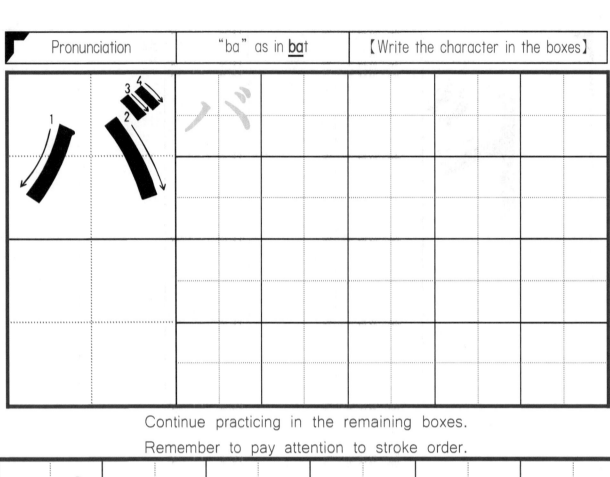

Continue practicing in the remaining boxes.
Remember to pay attention to stroke order.

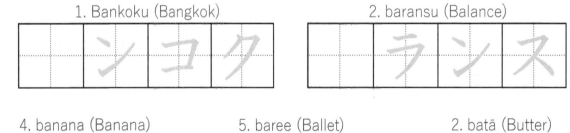

■ 🔊 Vocabulary – Write the character in the boxes below.

1. Bankoku (Bangkok)   2. baransu (Balance)

4. banana (Banana)   5. baree (Ballet)   2. batā (Butter)

186

| Pronunciation | "bi" as in **bee** | 【Write the character in the boxes】 |

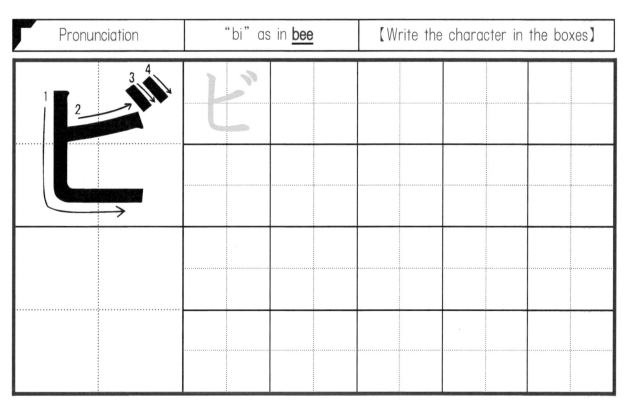

Continue practicing in the remaining boxes.
Remember to pay attention to stroke order.

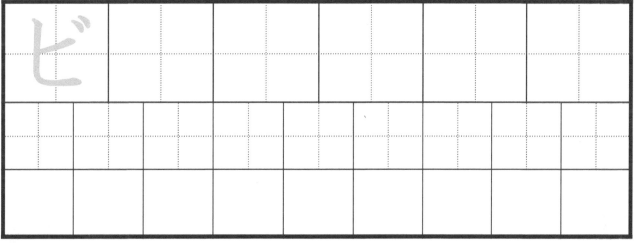

🔊 Vocabulary – Write the character in the boxes below.

1. bitamin (Vitamin)

2. bijinesu (Business)

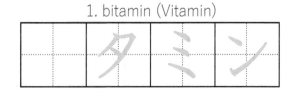

3. bīru (Beer)   4. bīfu (Beef)   5. bideo (Video)

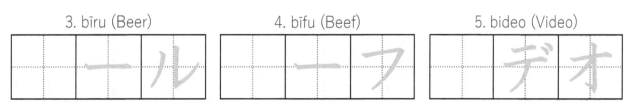

187

| Pronunciation | "bu" as in **boo**m | 【Write the character in the boxes】 |

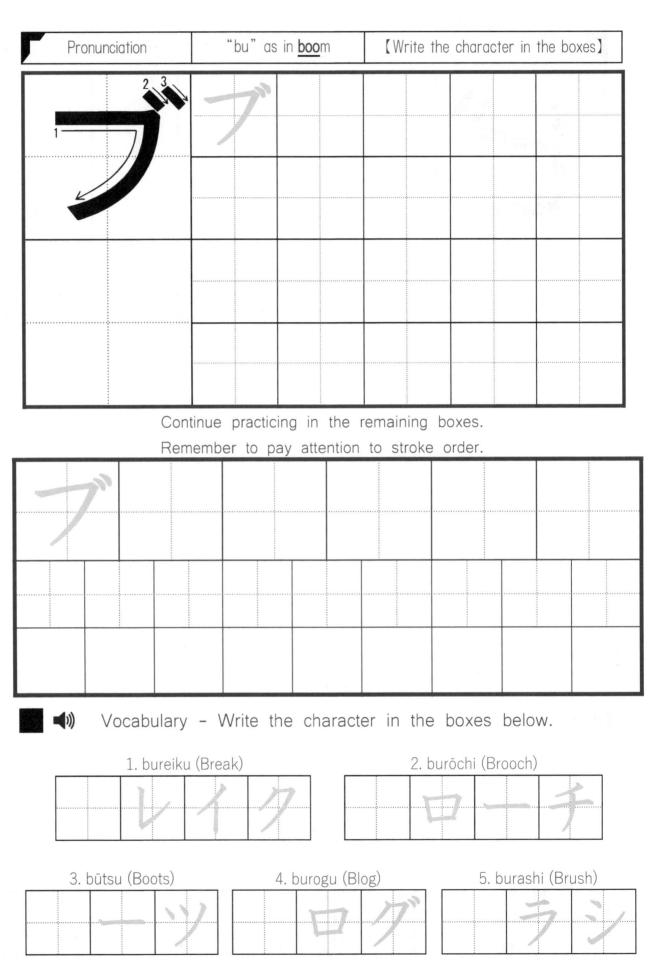

Continue practicing in the remaining boxes.
Remember to pay attention to stroke order.

Vocabulary - Write the character in the boxes below.

1. bureiku (Break)

レイク

2. burōchi (Brooch)

ローチ

3. būtsu (Boots)

ーツ

4. burogu (Blog)

ログ

5. burashi (Brush)

ラシ

188

Pronunciation	"be" as in <u>Be</u>n	【Write the character in the boxes】

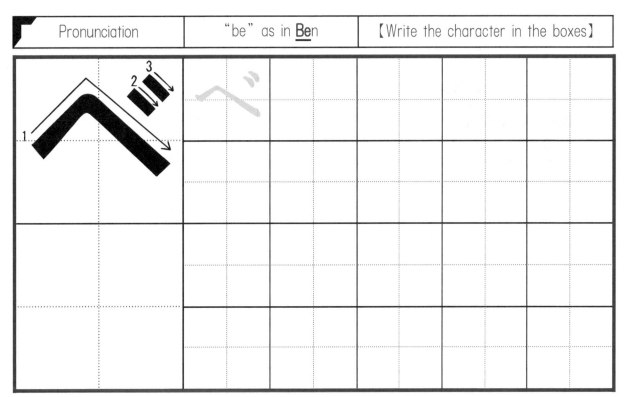

Continue practicing in the remaining boxes.

Remember to pay attention to stroke order.

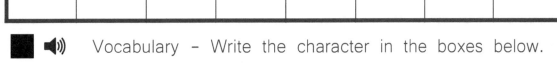

Vocabulary - Write the character in the boxes below.

1. bēkon (Bacon)

2. bēkarī (Bakery)

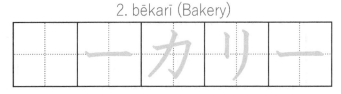

3. bēsu (Base)   4. beddo (Bed)   5. beruto (Belt)

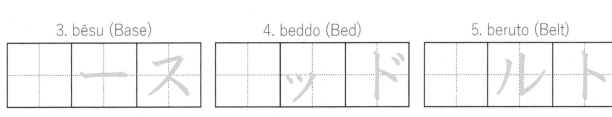

189

| Pronunciation | "bo" as in **bo**y | 【Write the character in the boxes】 |

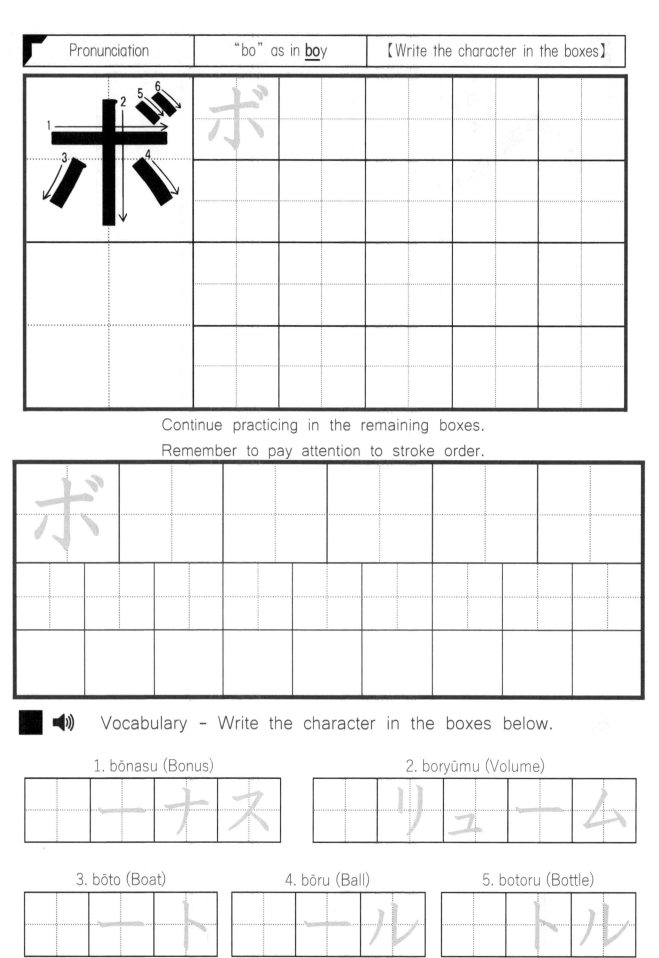

Continue practicing in the remaining boxes.
Remember to pay attention to stroke order.

Vocabulary - Write the character in the boxes below.

1. bōnasu (Bonus)

2. boryūmu (Volume)

3. bōto (Boat)

4. bōru (Ball)

5. botoru (Bottle)

190

Pronunciation	"pa" as in **pa**ckage	【Write the character in the boxes】

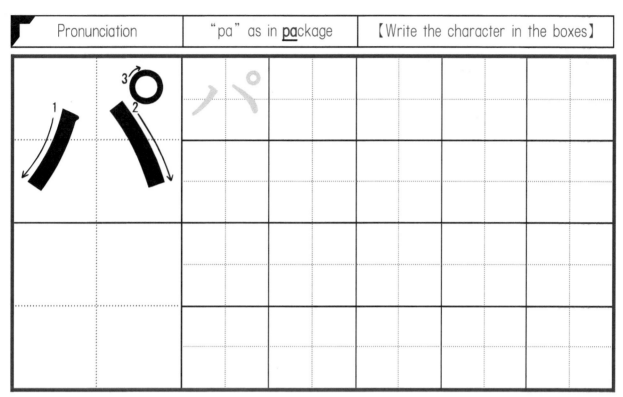

Continue practicing in the remaining boxes.
Remember to pay attention to stroke order.

Vocabulary - Write the character in the boxes below.

1. pajama (Pajamas)

2. pasupōto (Passport)

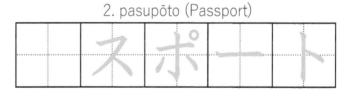

3. panda (Panda)   4. pasuta (Pasta)   5. pāku (Park)

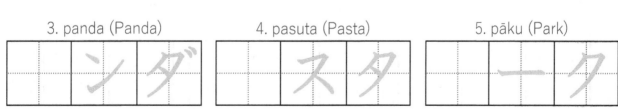

| Pronunciation | "pi" as in **pee** | 【Write the character in the boxes】 |

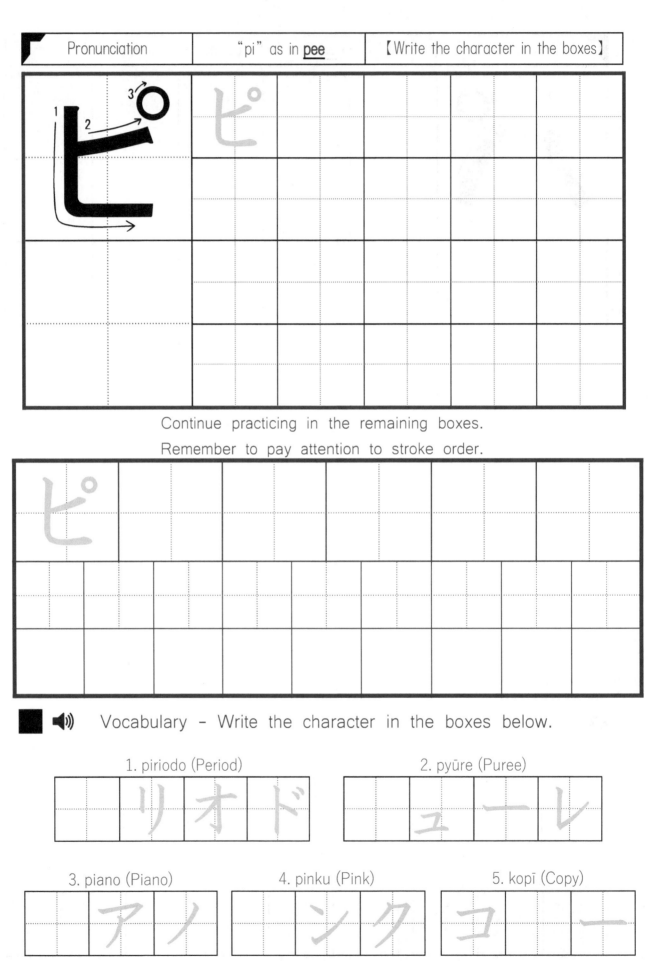

Continue practicing in the remaining boxes.
Remember to pay attention to stroke order.

Vocabulary - Write the character in the boxes below.

1. piriodo (Period)

リオド

2. pyūre (Puree)

ューレ

3. piano (Piano)

アノ

4. pinku (Pink)

ンク

5. kopī (Copy)

コー

| Pronunciation | "pu" as in **poo**r | 【Write the character in the boxes】 |

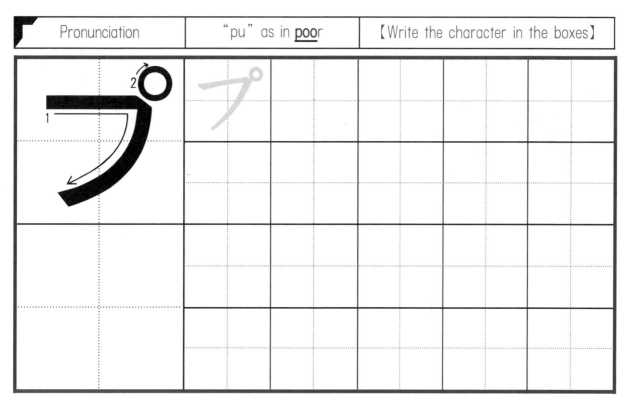

Continue practicing in the remaining boxes.
Remember to pay attention to stroke order.

Vocabulary - Write the character in the boxes below.

1. purinto (Print)

2. purachina (Platinum)

3. pūru (Pool)

4. puragu (Plug)

5. purasu (Plus)

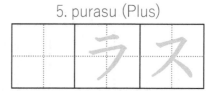

Pronunciation	"pe" as in **pay**	【Write the character in the boxes】

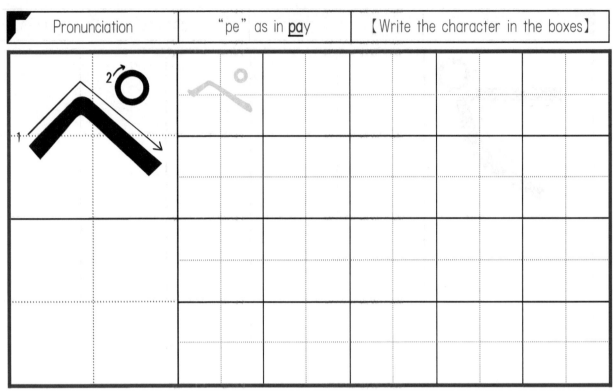

Continue practicing in the remaining boxes.

Remember to pay attention to stroke order.

🔊 Vocabulary – Write the character in the boxes below.

1. peinto (Paint)

2. pēpā (Paper)

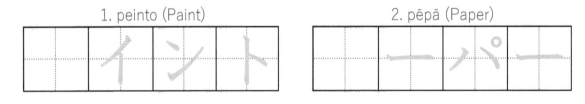

3. pēji (Page)

4. Perū (Peru)

5. petto (Pets)

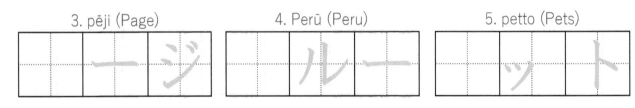

| Pronunciation | "po" as in **po**int | 【Write the character in the boxes】 |

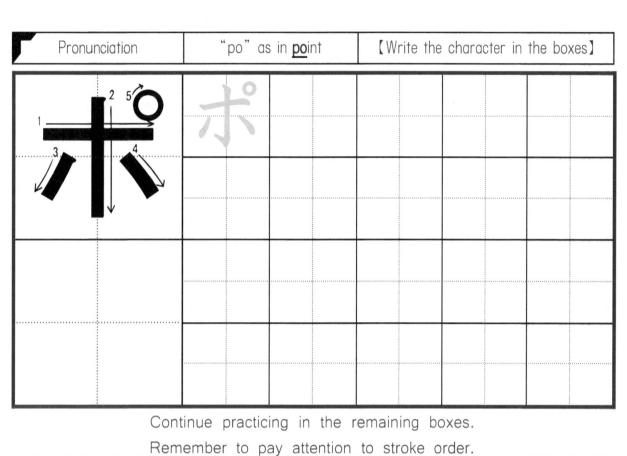

Continue practicing in the remaining boxes.
Remember to pay attention to stroke order.

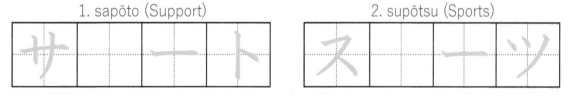

◼ 🔊 Vocabulary - Write the character in the boxes below.

1. sapōto (Support)　　　　　　　　2. supōtsu (Sports)

3. poteto (Potato)　　4. posuto (Post)　　5. pōku (Pork)

KATAKANA - ADDITIONAL SOUNDS YOUON

You have learnt basic 46 Hiragana Katakana and Dakuon Handakuten Hiragana Katakana And Youon Of Hiragana.

Now you are going to learn **Youon Katakana** which is a combination of two sounds, the pronunciation will change, When combined in this way "ya," "yu" and "yo" are written small characters, as in the examples below.

キャ kya	キュ kyu	キョ kyo
シャ sha(sya)	シュ shu(syu)	ショ sho(syo)
チャ cha(tya)	チュ chu(tyu)	チョ cho(tyo)
ニャ nya	ニュ nyu	ニョ nyo
ヒャ hya	ヒュ hyu	ヒョ hyo

ギャ gya	ギュ gyu	ギョ gyo
ジャ zya(ja)	ジュ zyu(ju)	ジョ zyo(jo)

ビャ bya	ビュ byu	ビョ byo
ピャ pya	ピュ pyu	ピョ pyo

ミャ mya	ミュ myu	ミョ myo
リャ rya	リュ ryu	リョ ryo

✓ **Review** ☐**Awesome!** ☐**Excellent!** ☐**Good!** ☐**Average!** ☐**Poor!**

Note:

Vocabulary – Complete the example words with the correct combined characters.

KATAKANA - ADDITIONAL SOUNDS YOON

kya   kyu   kyo

 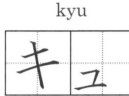 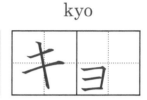

1. kyasshu (Cache)

2. manikyua (Manicure)

sha   shu   sho

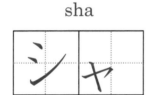  

1. shawā (Shower)

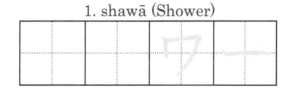

2. rōshon (Lotion)

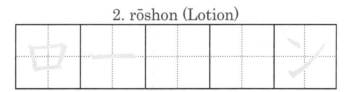

✓ **Review** ☐**Awesome！** ☐**Excellent！** ☐**Good！** ☐**Average！** ☐**Poor！**

Note: kyo and sho character combinations are only used in less common words, which are not included here.

🔊 Vocabulary – Complete the example words with the correct combined characters.

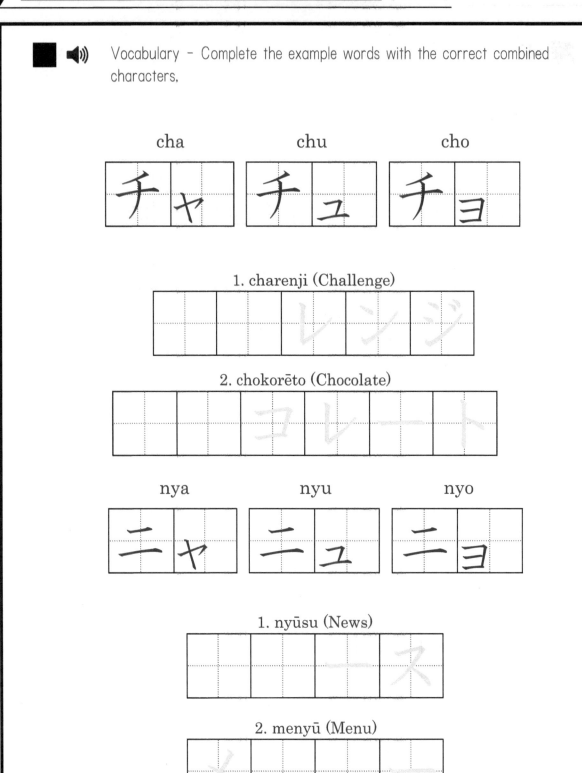

cha   chu   cho

チャ   チュ   チョ

1. charenji (Challenge)

レンジ

2. chokorēto (Chocolate)

コレート

nya   nyu   nyo

ニャ   ニュ   ニョ

1. nyūsu (News)

ース

2. menyū (Menu)

メ

✓ **Review** ☐**Awesome!** ☐**Excellent!** ☐**Good!** ☐**Average!** ☐**Poor!**

Note: chu , nya and nyo are only used in less common words, which are not included here.

Vocabulary – Complete the example words with the correct combined characters.

hya   hyu   hyo

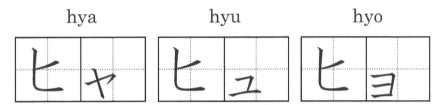

1. behhyā (Becher-German poet)

2. hyūman (Human)

mya   myu   myo

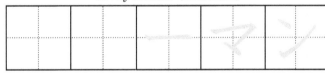

1. myūto (Mute – Volume)

2. myūjikku (Music)

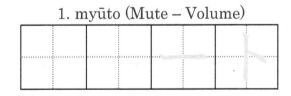

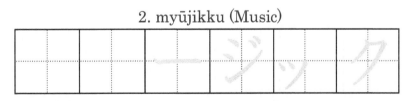

KATAKANA - ADDITIONAL SOUNDS YOON

✓ **Review** ☐**Awesome!** ☐**Excellent!** ☐**Good!** ☐**Average!** ☐**Poor!**

Note: hyo ,mya and **myo** are only used in less common words, which are not included here.

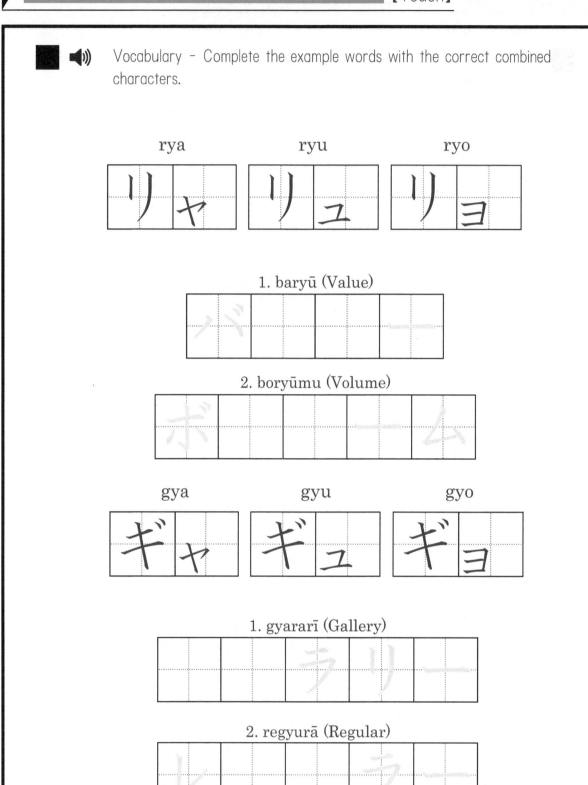

KATAKANA - ADDITIONAL SOUNDS YOON

Vocabulary – Complete the example words with the correct combined characters.

rya   ryu   ryo

リャ   リュ   リョ

1. baryū (Value)

バ   ー

2. boryūmu (Volume)

ボ   ー ム

gya   gyu   gyo

ギャ   ギュ   ギョ

1. gyararī (Gallery)

ラ リ ー

2. regyurā (Regular)

レ   ラ ー

✓ **Review** ☐**Awesome!** ☐**Excellent!** ☐**Good!** ☐**Average!** ☐**Poor!**

Note: gyo , rya and ryo are only used in less common words, which are not included here.

KATAKANA-ADDITIONAL SOUNDS YOON

Vocabulary – Complete the example words with the correct combined characters.

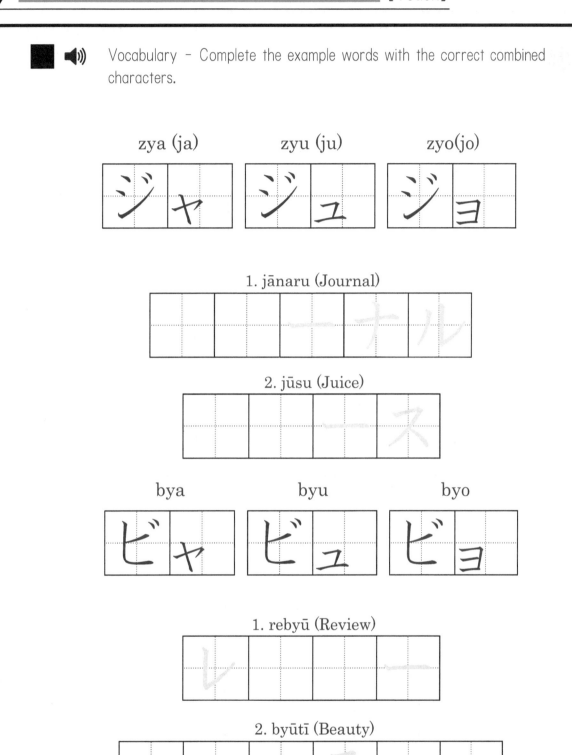

zya (ja)   zyu (ju)   zyo(jo)

ジャ   ジュ   ジョ

1. jānaru (Journal)

ーナル

2. jūsu (Juice)

ース

bya   byu   byo

ビャ   ビュ   ビョ

1. rebyū (Review)

レ ー

2. byūtī (Beauty)

ーティー

✓ **Review** ☐**Awesome!** ☐**Excellent!** ☐**Good!** ☐**Average!** ☐**Poor!**

Note: zyo(jo) , bya and byo are only used in less common words, which are not included here.

Vocabulary – Complete the example words with the correct combined characters.

pya   pyu   pyo

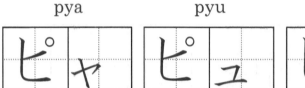 

1. pyua (Pure)

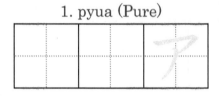

2. konpyūtā (Computer)

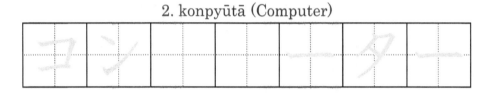

3. pyūma (Puma)

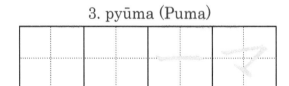

4. pyūre (Puree)

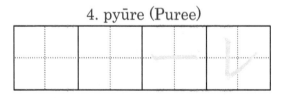

✓ **Review** ☐**Awesome!** ☐**Excellent!** ☐**Good!** ☐**Average!** ☐**Poor!**

Note: pya and pyo are only used in less common words, which are not included here.

KATAKANA - ADDITIONAL SOUNDS YOON

A LINE アイウエオ & K LINE カキクケコ

Activity 1

You should now be able to read and write the characters below.

A.   Try reading them aloud, repeat them until the sounds come fluently.

B.   Write them in romaji.

オ	イ	ア	ウ	エ	ク	コ	カ	ケ	キ

Activity 2

A.   Match the katakana character to the hiragana character with the same sound.

B.   Write the following words into katakana.

エ	お	カ	き	Italy		Taxi	
ウ	え	ク	こ	Coffee		Cake	
イ	あ	キ	か	America		Jacket	
オ	う	コ	け	Wedding		Orange	
ア	い	ケ	く	Elevator		Camera	

Activity 3

A.   Read these words, and write their romaji and meaning.

イス _____ _____   チキン _____ _____

トイレ _____ _____   ミルク _____ _____

ワイン _____ _____   タオル _____ _____

クラス _____ _____   カナダ _____ _____

ウイルス _____ _____   コメディ _____ _____

エンジン _____ _____   メキシコ _____ _____

A LINE アイウエオ & K LINE カキクケコ

Activity 3

B. Read the following words in katakana, and pick out the ones which mean "Tire" and "Tray." Then write all the words out in romaji.

ライス	アイテム	オフィス	カプセル
トレイ	エベレスト	タイヤ	スキー

Activity 4

A. Fill in each space with the appropriate katakana to make words.

1. _____ラーム   (Alarm)

2. _____タリア   (Italy)

3. _____リーブ   (Olive)

4. _____ジプト   (Egypt)

5. _____ャベツ   (Cabbage)

6. _____ッキー   (Cookie)

7. _____リーム   (Cream)

8. _____ットン   (Cotton)

9. _____ープ   (Cape)

10. _____ラス   (Class)

イ	エ	オ	ア	ウ	ク	カ	コ	ケ	キ

B. Write the following words in katakana.

1. takushī   (Taxi)   _____

2. fōku   (Fork)   _____

3. karorī   (Calorie)   _____

4. kitchin   (Kitchen)   _____

5. Kanada   (Canada)   _____

6. pinku   (Pink)   _____

7. epuron   (Apron)   _____

8. burausu   (Blouse)   _____

9. whedingu   (Wedding)   _____

10. karaoke   (Karaoke)   _____

KATAKANA EXERCISES ACTIVITY

A LINE アイウエオ ＆ K LINE カキクケコ

Activity 5

A. Complete the following table using the words from the writing practice pages.

English	Romaji	Katakana
【Asia】		
	aidea	
【Wedding】		
		エレベーター
【Contact】		

B. Circle the English and Japanese romaji words, and then circle the same words in katakana.

America	Album	Club	Adult	Ukraine
Sign	Allergic	Indonesia	Cable	Napkin
Dress	Accessories	Waiter	Australia	Christmas
Kiwi	Guide	Elegant	Cut	Tobacco

kēburu	ueitā	kurisumasu	akusesarī	doresu
arerugī	katto	Amerika	adaruto	tabako
ereganto	gaido	napukin	arubamu	kiui
sain	Ōsutoraria	kurabu	Indoneshia	Ukuraina

キウイナプキンアメリカサインアクセサリーガイドアルバムアレルギー
インドネシアウェイターエレガントクラブカットケーブルクリスマスドレス
オーストラリアアダルトウクライナタバコ

A LINE　アイウエオ　&　K LINE　カキクケコ

Activity 6

A.　Write the meaning for below romaji and circle the correct katakana words for the them.

1	furaido	(	)	a. フルイド	b. フライド	c. フライト
2	bōru	(	)	a. ボーロ	b. ボール	c. ボウル
3	orenji	(	)	a. オレンジ	b. オリンジ	c. オルンジ
4	kemikaru	(	)	a. ケミカリ	b. ケミカル	c. ケミカロ
5	masuku	(	)	a. マソク	b. ムスク	c. マスク
6	konpasu	(	)	a. コンポス	b. コンパス	c. コンピス

B.　Rewrite the following words in the correct order.

1	【kyandī】	Candy	ンデキャィー	
2	【katorikku】	Catholic	トリカック	
3	【kechappu】	Ketchup	プチャッケ	
4	【kurashikku】	Classic	シラックク	

C.　Match the katakana character to the hiragana character with the same sound.

オ　　あ　　　　　ケ　　こ

イ　　え　　　　　カ　　き

エ　　い　　　　　コ　　く

ア　　う　　　　　ク　　か

ウ　　お　　　　　キ　　け

SLINE サ シ ス セ ソ & TLINE タ チ ツ テ ト

Activity 1

A. Write the following romaji into katakana.

Romaji	Katakana	Meaning
sandoitchi		Sandwiches
sarada		Salad
sakkā		Soccer
shatsu		Shirt
shawā		Shower
Supein		Spain
kyanseru		Cancel

Romaji	Katakana	Meaning
sētā		Sweater
sentā		Center
sofa		Sofa
sōsu		Sauce
taipu		Type
chīzu		Cheese
supōtsu		Sports

Activity 2

A. Circle the katakana characters for sa, shi, tsu, te, and to.

B. Find the Katakana word that has the same meaning as the English word below.

C. Read the following words, and write their romaji and meaning.

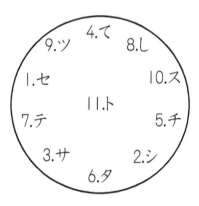

Table ( )	Tunnel ( )	Test ( )	Check ( )
Texas ( )	Shirt ( )	Song ( )	Ticket ( )

1. シャツ	2. テスト	3. テキサス	4. テーブル
5. チェック	6. ソング	7. トンネル	8. チケット

スーツ _____ _____   テニス _____ _____

スタイル _____ _____   ターン _____ _____

シリーズ _____ _____   ソース _____ _____

アクセス _____ _____   チャンス _____ _____

SLINE サ シ ス セ ソ & T LINE タ チ ツ テ ト

Activity 3

A.　Try reading them aloud, repeat them until the sounds come fluently.

B.　Write them in romaji.

セ	サ	ソ	ス	シ	テ	チ	タ	ト	ツ

C.　Test yourself — check that you have learned the S & T lines of katakana well by filling in the missing kana.

サ				ソ					ト

Activity 4

A.　With the 'S' & 'T' line you can extend your range of vocabulary quite a bit. Try reading these words and filling the missing with the appropriate katakana .

トロント	【　　　　　】	Toronto		【　　　　　】	Spain
トースト	【　　　　　】	Toast	スポーツ	【　　　　　】	
	【 teikuauto 】	Take-out		【 chokorēto 】	Chocolate
	【　　　　　】	Tent		【 shatsu 】	

B.　These are common English names, How would you write them?

Charlotte	Victoria	Lucas	Thomas
(Shārotto)	(Bikutoria)	(Rūkasu)	(Tōmasu)

_____　　_____　　_____　　_____

C.　Rewrite the following words in the correct order.

I	【toire】	Toilet	イトレ	
2	【takushī】	Taxi	クーシタ	
3	【sandaru】	Sandals	ルサダン	
4	【shinguru】	Single	ングシル	

KATAKANA EXERCISES ACTIVITY

<u>S LINE</u> サ シ ス セ ソ & <u>T LINE</u> タ チ ツ テ ト

Activity 5

A. Match the katakana character to the hiragana character with the same sound.

ス	せ	チ	た
ソ	し	ト	つ
サ	そ	タ	て
シ	さ	テ	と
セ	す	ツ	ち

B. Write the following romaji into katakana.

setto	_____	【Set】	sofuto	_____	【Soft】
rinsu	_____	【Rinse】	sōda	_____	【Soda】
nyūsu	_____	【News】	taipu	_____	【Type】
reshipi	_____	【Recipe】	chesu	_____	【Chess】
shisutemu	_____	【System】	sararī	_____	【Salary】
sābisu	_____	【Service】	sākasu	_____	【Circus】

C. Practice reading the following words aloud, then rewrite them.

ソルト	【soruto】	Salt	
シャンプー	【shanpū】	Shampoo	
テキスト	【tekisuto】	Text	
リラックス	【rirakkusu】	Relax	
ターミナル	【tāminaru】	Terminal	
ドレッシング	【doresshingu】	Dressing	

ALL KATAKANA LINES

Activity 1

A.   Write the romaji for the following katakana characters.

Katakana	Romaji	Katakana	Romaji	Katakana	Romaji	Katakana	Romaji
イ	i	ネ		ツ		ミ	
ロ		ナ		ソ		シ	
ハ		ラ		レ		ヒ	
ニ		ム		タ		ス	
ホ		ウ		フ		セ	
ヘ		ノ		コ		メ	
ト		オ		エ		キ	
チ		ク		テ		ヲ	
リ		ヤ		ア		ル	
ヌ		マ		ユ		ネ	
ヨ		ケ		モ		サ	

Katakana	Romaji	Katakana	Romaji	Katakana	Romaji	Katakana	Romaji
パ		シャ		ニュ		ザ	
ピ		シュ		ニョ		ジ	
バ		ショ		ヒャ		ゾ	
プ		チャ		ゲ		ダ	
ボ		チュ		ギャ		ゴ	
ベ		チョ		リュ		ポ	
ド		ニャ		ヒョ		ガ	

✓ **Review ☐Awesome! ☐Excellent! ☐Good! ☐Average! ☐Poor!**

Note:

Activity 1

B.   Write the correct katakana for the following romaji.

Romaji	Katakana	Romaji	Katakana	Romaji	Katakana
be		do	ド	gu	
bu		di(ji)		kya	
da		gi		nyo	
pa		chu		kyu	
go		rya		gya	
sha		pe		ga	
ba		cho		hya	
pu		ryu		ze	
de		po		kyo	
tsu		ryo		zu	
hyo		nya		ge	
bo		n		zo	
shu		nyu		du	
za		zi(ji)		pi	
sho		bi		po	

✓ **Review** ☐**Awesome !** ☐**Excellent !** ☐**Good !** ☐**Average !** ☐**Poor !**

Note:

Activity 2

A.   Write the following words in romaji and give the translations.

1.	ホテル	_____	_____
2.	レストラン	_____	_____
3.	ブック	_____	_____
4.	スケジュール	_____	_____
5.	サンドイッチ	_____	_____
6.	ファックス	_____	_____
7.	マカロニ	_____	_____

Activity 2

B.   Write the following words in Katakana.

1.   Ham   【hamu】   _____

2.   Cheese   【chīzu】   _____

3.   Shower   【shawā】   _____

4.   Massage   【massāji】   _____

5.   Shampoo   【Shanpū】   _____

6.   Schedule   【sukejūru】   _____

7.   Sandwich   【sandoitchi】   _____

8.   Ice cream   【aisukurīmu】   _____

Activity 2

C.   Guess the meaning of these Katakana words and practice writing them.

1. アニメ	3. セーター	5. ソース	7. ミルク
2. ニュース	4. ソーセージ	6. メール	8. ターミナル
1. _____	3. _____	5. _____	7. _____
2. _____	4. _____	6. _____	8. _____

✓ **Review** □**Awesome!** □**Excellent!** □**Good!** □**Average!** □**Poor!**

Note:

KATAKANA EXERCISES ACTIVITY

KATAKANA EXERCISES

Activity 3

A.   Guess the meaning of these Katakana words and practice writing them.
The first one has been done as an example.

EX: アメリカ   Amerika   America   アメリカ

　　　　　　Igirisu   _____   _____

　　　　　　Supein   _____   _____

　　　　　　Kanada   _____   _____

　　　　　　Suisu   _____   _____

　　　　　　gitā   _____   _____

　　　　　　kēki   _____   _____

　　　　　　kukkī   _____   _____

　　　　　　kōhī   _____   _____

Activity 3

B.   Complete the table by filling up the empty boxes.

Romaji	Katakana	English
Itaria		
	フランス	
		Coffee
Igirisu		
	カレーライス	
Burajiru		

✓ **Review** ☐Awesome! ☐Excellent! ☐Good! ☐Average! ☐Poor!

Note:

KATAKANA EXERCISES ACTIVITY

Activity 4

A.   Guess the meaning of these Katakana words and practice writing them.

サッカー	sakkā	_____	_____
チーズ	chīzu	_____	_____
スポーツ	supōtsu	_____	_____
テレビ	terebi	_____	_____
ドイツ	Doitsu	_____	_____
ダンス	dansu	_____	_____
ピアノ	piano	_____	_____
ビジネス	bijinesu	_____	_____
サンプル	sample	_____	_____

Activity 4

B.   Complete the table by filling up the empty boxes.

Romaji	Katakana	English
arubamu		
	ワイン	
		Lemon
antena		
	チケット	
		Mail
moderu		

✓ **Review** ☐**Awesome!** ☐**Excellent!** ☐**Good!** ☐**Average!** ☐**Poor!**

Note:

KATAKANA EXERCISES ACTIVITY

Activity 5

Food Menu - メニューをよみましょう！ Let's read the menu!

1.カレーライス	900 円
2.エビピラフ	600 円
3.バタートースト	500 円
4.ツナサラダ	300 円
5.ハンバーガー	400 円
6.サンドイッチ	450 円
7.ビーフシチュー	920 円
8.タラコスパゲティ	800 円

お飲み物(おのみもの)

1.コーヒー(アイス/ホット)	350 円
2.カフェオレ	400 円
3.アイスティ	350 円
4.レモンティ	300 円
5.オレンジジュース	400 円
6.コカ·コーラ	250 円
7.クリームソーダ	450 円
8.ビール	750 円

デザート

1.バニラアイスクリーム	350 円
2.イチゴパフェ	650 円
3.ケーキセット(ケーキ·コーヒー)	700 円

✓ **Review** □**Awesome！** □**Excellent！** □**Good！** □**Average！** □**Poor！**

Note:

Activity 6

Countries/Cities 1-2 Match the Countries and Cities to their correct katakana.

インドネシア	Italy
マレーシア	Indonesia
バンコク	Malaysia
シドニー	Vietnam
ベトナム	Bangkok
ロンドン	France
アメリカ	Germany
シンガポール	London
ブラジル	America
ドイツ	Toronto
ニューヨーク	Melbourne
フランス	Thailand
イタリア	Brazil
オーストラリア	Sydney
メルボルン	New York
タイ	Singapore
トロント	Australia

✓ **Review** ☐**Awesome!** ☐**Excellent!** ☐**Good!** ☐**Average!** ☐**Poor!**

Note:

Activity 7

Countries/Cities 2-2 Match the Countries and Cities to their correct katakana.

イギリス	England
フィンランド	New Zealand
トルコ	Canada
アデレード	Turkey
ナイジェリア	Ireland
アイルランド	Finland
スリランカ	Nigeria
ニュージーランド	Sweden
インド	Spain
スペイン	India
ハワイ	Adelaide
カナダ	Boston
エジプト	Egypt
アラスカ	Hawaii
スエーデン	Iraq
イラク	Sri Lanka
ボストン	Alaska
オランダ	Jamaica
ジャマイカ	Netherlands

✓ **Review** ☐**Awesome!** ☐**Excellent!** ☐**Good!** ☐**Average!** ☐**Poor!**

Note:

KATAKANA EXERCISES ACTIVITY

Activity 8

Match the Animals to their correct katakana.

ポッサム	Lion
タイガー	Salmon
カンガルー	Chihuahua
ラット	koala
ポメラニアン	Pomeranian
ライオン	Tiger
オーストリッチ	Husky
ドンキー	Kangaroo
チキン	Rat
コアラ	Possum
フラミンゴ	Hamster
パンダ	Flamingo
チワワ	Panda
サーモン	Bison
バイソン	Oyster
オイスター	Ostrich
ハスキー	Donkey
ゴリラ	Penguin
ハムスター	Chicken
ペンギン	Gorilla

✓ **Review** □**Awesome!** □**Excellent!** □**Good!** □**Average!** □**Poor!**

Note:

KATAKANA EXERCISES ACTIVITY

Activity 9

Sports / Write the following words in Katakana.

For an extra challenge try to write them by covering the Katakana.

Hiking		Squash	
Swimming		Sky diving	
Tennis		Cricket	
Soccer		Badminton	
Golf		Rugby	
Basketball		Volleyball	
Jogging		Wrestling	
Aerobics		Boxing	
Skiing		Yoga	
Skate		Hockey	

1	ハイキング	11	スクワシュ
2	スウィミング	12	スカイダイビング
3	テニス	13	クリケット
4	サッカー	14	バドミントン
5	ゴルフ	15	ラグビー
6	バスケットボール	16	バレーボール
7	ジョギング	17	レスリング
8	エアロビクス	18	ボクシング
9	スキー	19	ヨガ
10	スケート	20	ホッケー

KATAKANA EXERCISES ACTIVITY

Activity 10

Clothes & Accessories/ Practice reading the following aloud, and repeat them until the sounds come fluently. For an extra challenge try to write them in the blanks.

ピアス	piasu	Earrings	
Tシャツ	tīshatsu	T-shirt	
スカーフ	sukāfu	Scarf	
スカート	sukāto	Skirt	
ネクタイ	nekutai	Tie	
ジャンパー	janpā	Jumper	
スニーカー	sunīkā	Sneakers	
ハイヒール	haihīru	High heels	
ローラーブレード	rōrāburēdo	Rollerblade	
シングレット	shinguretto	Singlet	
ヘアバンド	hea bando	Hair band	
バンダナ	bandana	Bandana	
キャップ	kyappu	Cap	
リストバンド	risuto bando	Wristband	
セーター	sētā	Sweater	
シャツ	shatsu	Shirt	
ジーンズ	jīnzu	Jeans	
ブーツ	būtsu	Boots	
パンプス	panpusu	Pumps	
ソックス	sokkusu	Socks	
アイシャドウ	aishadō	Eye shadow	
ヘアピン	hea pin	Hairpin	
シャンプー	shanpū	Shampoo	
コンディショナー	kondishon	Conditioner	

✓ **Review** □**Awesome！** □**Excellent！** □**Good！** □**Average！** □**Poor！**

Note:

KATAKANA EXERCISES ACTIVITY

Activity 11 - LONG VOWELS

Katakana, long sounds are represented by a dash —

Note : When you see the — character, know that all it's doing is extending the vowel sound that comes before it. This is really common in katakana words, especially foreign words.

It's important to know that there are many words that look the same, where the only difference is that one has a long vowel and the other doesn't. Using the wrong pronunciation can change the meaning of a word entirely.

Practice reading and writing the following and give the translations.

1	コーヒー		11	ステーキ	
2	タクシー		12	キーボード	
3	カレー		13	ダウンロード	
4	セーター		14	ハンバーガー	
5	ビール		15	デパート	
6	チーズ		16	アパート	
7	コピー		17	スーパー	
8	ケーキ		18	カード	
9	メール		19	テーブル	
10	ゲーム		20	ジュース	

Hint:
chīzu, bīru, takushī, kōhī, mēru, sētā, kēki, karē, gēmu, kopī, kādo, depāto apāto, daunrōdo, sutēki, jūsu, hanbāgā, sūpā, kībōdo, tēburu

✓ **Review** □**Awesome !** □**Excellent !** □**Good !** □**Average !** □**Poor !**

Note:

Activity 12 - Katakana Double Consonants (Small Tsu ッ)

Double consonants "kka", "tte", "ppu", etc.

Note : A small "tsu" indicates the double consonants sound.

This "tsu" forms the double consonants with the following character.

ロケット	⟹	roke**tto**	Rocket
ベッド	⟹	be**ddo**	Bed

	Words	Rewrite	Meaning
1	ネット		
2	ペット		
3	ロケット		
4	トラック		
5	インターネット		
6	チケット		
7	ヨット		
8	サッカー		
9	スイッチ		
10	ポケット		
11	ネットワーク		Network

✓ **Review** ☐**Awesome!** ☐**Excellent!** ☐**Good!** ☐**Average!** ☐**Poor!**

Note:

KATAKANA EXERCISES ACTIVITY

KATAKANA EXERCISES ACTIVITY

Activity 13 - Katakana Youon

Practice reading and writing the following

Example	Practice	Example	Practice
スキャナ [sukyana] scanner	スキャナ	チャット [chatto] chat	チャット
セキリュティ [sekyuriti] security	セキュリティ	チョコレート [chokorēto] chocolate	チョコレート
ギャップ [gappu] gap	ギャップ	ニュース [nyūsu] news	ニュース
ギリシャ [girisha] Greek	ギリシャ	ニューヨーク [nyūyōku] New York	ニューヨーク
キャッシュ [Kyasshu] cache	キャッシュ	オフショア [ofushoa] offshore	オフショア
ミャンマー [myanmaa] Myanmā	ミャンマー	ソリューション [soryūshon] solution	ソリューション
ミュージック [myūjikku] music	ミュージック	ジュース [jūsu] juice	ジュース
ジャーナリスト [jānarisuto] jounalist	ジャーナリスト	コンピュータ [konpyūta] computer	コンピュータ

✓ **Review** ☐**Awesome!** ☐**Excellent!** ☐**Good!** ☐**Average!** ☐**Poor!**

Note:

Japanese Language Difficulty Points

The Japanese language is challenging for non-native speakers. Japanese is not an easy language to learn, especially if you live in the United States or Europe.

The Japanese language has several elements, including grammar, pronunciation, reading, and writing character, a foreigner who wishes to learn Japanese may wonder why even Japanese people find it difficult to understand, Japanese is a language that even Japanese people find difficult because it's difficult to use honorifics and grammar, and there are multiple readings for each kanji.

- A particularly difficult aspect of communication is the fact that words that are similar in meaning can convey different meanings.

Kanji

There are multiple ways to read kanji, and even Japanese people find it difficult to read all of them correctly. For example: 店 which means shop or store has two readings (てん)ten and (みせ) mise.

Honorifics

Honorifics(謙譲語-kenjougo) are used to show respect, using honorific language can be polite, respectful, or humble, the honorific is a form of expressing respect for other people, this form of speech may have the purpose of showing respect and humbling yourself down when talking to someone of a higher status than yourself.

When you talk to a "superior" or someone older than you, or higher ranking in your company like your boss, or manager you need to show respect to like customers, clients, etc.) you have to use polite Japanese.

- You have to change the politeness level depending on who you are talking to, using the wrong honorifics is rude, so you need to learn how to use them correctly.

Grammar

Grammar is the rule for creating sentences. Grammar has different types such as particles and parts of speech, in particular, if you make a mistake in using particles such as "〜は", "〜が", "〜を", the sentence will be completely different from the intended content.

- The meaning of a sentence changes depending on how the particles are used.

	MEANING	One
① 一	ONYOMI	イチ、イツ Ichi, Itsu
	KUNYOMI	ひと(つ) Hito(tsu)

EXAMPLE				EXAMPLE SENTENCE
いっかい 一回	Ikkai	–	One time	ひとり がっこう い 一人で学校へ行きます。
ひとくち 一口	Hitokuchi	–	One bite	Hitori de gakkou he ikimasu.
いちえん 一円	Ichien	–	One yen	I go to school alone.

	MEANING	Two
① ② 二	ONYOMI	ニ Ni
	KUNYOMI	ふた, ふた(つ) Futa, Futa(tsu)

EXAMPLE				EXAMPLE SENTENCE
ふたり 二人	Futari	–	Two persons	にがつ さむ 二月はとても寒いです。
にがつ 二月	Nigatsu	–	February	Nigatu wa totemo samui desu.
ふつか 二日	Futsuka	–	2nd Day	February is very cold.

✓ Review ☐Awesome! ☐Excellent! ☐Good! ☐Average! ☐Poor!

	MEANING	Three
① ② ③ 三	ONYOMI	サン　San
	KUNYOMI	みっ(つ)，み，Mit(tsu)，Mi

EXAMPLE	EXAMPLE SENTENCE
さんかい 三回　Sankai　－　Three times みっか 三日　Mikka　－　The 3rd さんがつ 三月　Sangatsu　－　March	みっ　　たまご ここには、三つの卵があります。 Koko niwa, mittsu no tamago ga arimasu. There are three eggs here.

	MEANING	Four
② ① ③ ④ 四 ⑤	ONYOMI	シ　Shi
	KUNYOMI	よ、よ(つ)、よっ(つ)、よん　Yo, Yo(tsu), Yot(tsu), Yon

EXAMPLE	EXAMPLE SENTENCE
よじ 四時　Yoji　－　4 o'clock しき 四季　Shiki　－　The 4 seasons よんかい 四回　Yonkai　－　Four times	よじ　き 四時に来てください。 Yoji ni kite kudasai. Please come by four o'clock.

✓ **Review** ☐**Awesome！** ☐**Excellent！** ☐**Good！** ☐**Average！** ☐**Poor！**

	MEANING	Five	
① 五 ② ③ ④	ONYOMI	ゴ Go	
	KUNYOMI	いつ(つ)、いつ　Itsu(tsu), Itsu	
	EXAMPLE		**EXAMPLE SENTENCE**

	ごかい 五回　Gokai　－　Five times	ごじ　あ 五時に会いましょう。
	いつか 五日　Itsuka　－　5th day	Goji ni aimashou.
	ごまい 五枚　Gomai　－　Five sheets	See you at five o'clock.

	MEANING	Six	
① ② 六 ③ ④	ONYOMI	ロク、リク Roku, Riku	
	KUNYOMI	む、むつ、むっ(つ)、むい　Mu, Mutsu, Mut(tsu), Mui	
	EXAMPLE		**EXAMPLE SENTENCE**

	むいか 六日　Muika　－　6th day	ろくじ　はじ 六時に始めます。
	ろくがつ 六月　Roku gatsu　－　June	Rokuji ni hajimemasu.
	ろっかい 六回　Rokkai　－　Six times	Start at 6 o'clock.

✓ **Review** ☐Awesome！ ☐Excellent！ ☐Good！ ☐Average！ ☐Poor！

	MEANING	Seven
	ONYOMI	シチ Shichi
	KUNYOMI	なな、なな(つ)、なの Nana, Nana(tsu), Nano

EXAMPLE	EXAMPLE SENTENCE
しちがつ 七月 Shichigatsu – July	しちじ むか い 七時に迎えに行きます。
なな 七つ Nanatsu – Seven	Shichiji ni mukae ni ikimasu.
なのか 七日 Nanoka – 7th day	I will pick you up at 7 o'clock.

	MEANING	Eight
	ONYOMI	ハチ Hachi
	KUNYOMI	や(つ)、やっ(つ)、よう Ya(tsu), Yat(tsu), You

EXAMPLE	EXAMPLE SENTENCE
はちかい 八回 Hachikai – Eight times	ぜんぶ やっ 全部でそれは八つありました。
ようか 八日 Youka – The 8th	Zenbu de sore wa yattsu arimashita.
はちがつ 八月 Hachigatsu – August	In all, it was eight.

✓ Review □Awesome！ □Excellent！ □Good！ □Average！ □Poor！

		MEANING	Nine
① ② 九		ONYOMI	キュウ、ク Kyuu, ku
		KUNYOMI	ここの、ここの(つ) Kokono, Kokono(tsu)
		EXAMPLE	**EXAMPLE SENTENCE**

	くがつ 九月 Kugatsu – September		ここの 九つしか、それはありません。			
	ここのか 九日 Kokonoka – The 9th		Kokonotsu shika sore wa arimasen.			
	くじ 九時 Kuji – Nine o'clock		There are only nine.			

		MEANING	Ten
② ① 十		ONYOMI	ジュウ、ジッ Jyuu, Ji
		KUNYOMI	とお、と To o, To
		EXAMPLE	**EXAMPLE SENTENCE**

	とおか 十日 To o ka – The 10th		とおか ともだち あ 十日に友達と会います。			
	じゅっかい 十回 Jyukkai – Ten times		Tooka ni tomodachi to aimasu.			
	じゅうじ 十時 Jyuuji – Ten o'clock		I will meet my friends on the 10th.			

✓ **Review** ☐Awesome！ ☐Excellent！ ☐Good！ ☐Average！ ☐Poor！

	MEANING	Hundred
① ② ④ ③ ⑤ ⑥ 百	ONYOMI	ヒャク Hyaku
	KUNYOMI	もも Momo

EXAMPLE	EXAMPLE SENTENCE
ひゃっかい 百回　Hyakkai － Hundred times やおや 八百屋 Yaoya － Greengrocer ひゃくにん 百人　Hyakunin － 100 peoples	ひゃくにん　き 百人くらい来ました。 Hyakunin kurai kimashita. About 100 peoples came.

	MEANING	Thousand
① ② ③ 千	ONYOMI	セン Sen
	KUNYOMI	ち Chi

EXAMPLE	EXAMPLE SENTENCE
さんぜん 三千　Sanzen － Three thousand せんかい 千回　Senkai － Thousand times ちばけん 千葉県 Chiba ken － Chiba prefecture	いま せんえん　も 今は千円しか持っていない。 Ima wa sen en shika motteinai. I only have 1,000 yen now.

✓ Review □Awesome! □Excellent! □Good! □Average! □Poor!

	MEANING	Ten thousand
① ③ ② 万	ONYOMI	マン、バン Man, Ban
	KUNYOMI	よろず Yorozu

EXAMPLE	EXAMPLE SENTENCE
いちまんえん 一万円 Ichiman en — 10thousand Yen ひゃくまん 百万 Hyaku man — A million ばんにん 万人 Ban'nin — All people	いちまんえん それは一万円ぐらいするだろう。 Sore wa ichiman en gurai surudarou. It'll cost around ten thousand yen.

	MEANING	Water
① ③ ② 水 ④	ONYOMI	スイ Sui
	KUNYOMI	みず Mizu

EXAMPLE	EXAMPLE SENTENCE
すいどう 水道 Suidou — Water pipe すいようび 水曜日 Suiyoubi — Wednesday おおみず 大水 Oomizu — Flood	みず か 水を買ってきます。 Mizu wo katte kimasu. I will buy water.

✓ **Review** ☐**Awesome!** ☐**Excellent!** ☐**Good!** ☐**Average!** ☐**Poor!**

	MEANING	Fire
① 火 ② ④	ONYOMI	カ　Ka
	KUNYOMI	ひ、び、ほ　Hi, Bi, Ho

EXAMPLE	EXAMPLE SENTENCE
かざん 火山　　Kazan　　–　　Volcano かようび 火曜日　Kayoubi　–　　Tuesday はなび 花火　　Hanabi　–　　Fireworks	かじ　ちゅうい 火事に注意してください。 Kaji ni chuui shite kudasai. Be careful of fire.

	MEANING	Tree, Wood
① 木 ② ③ ④	ONYOMI	ボク、モク　Boku, Moku
	KUNYOMI	き、こ　Ki, Ko

EXAMPLE	EXAMPLE SENTENCE
もくようび 木曜日　Mokuyoubi –　Thursday ぼくとう 木刀　　Bokutou　–　Wooden sword こだち 木立　　Kodachi　–　Grove of trees	こうえん　まつ　き 公園に松の木があります。 Kouen ni matsu no ki ga arimasu. There is a pine tree at the park.

✓ **Review** □**Awesome !** □**Excellent !** □**Good !** □**Average !** □**Poor !**

	MEANING	Hevens, Sky, Imperial
① 天 ③ ② ④	ONYOMI	テン Ten
	KUNYOMI	あま、あめ、そら、ぞら　Ama, Ame, Sora, Zora

EXAMPLE	EXAMPLE SENTENCE
てんき 天気　Tenki　－　Weather てんごく 天国　Tengoku　－　The 9th あま　がわ 天の川　Amanogawa　－　Milky Way	てんき　よほう 天気予報はどうですか。 Tenkeyohou wa, doudesuka. How about the weather forecast?

	MEANING	Soil, Earth, Ground
① 土 ② ③	ONYOMI	ト、ド　To, Do
	KUNYOMI	つち Tsuchi

EXAMPLE	EXAMPLE SENTENCE
つち 土　Tsuchi　－　Soil ねんど 粘土　Nendo　－　Clay どようび 土曜日　Doyoubi　－　Saturday	どようび　で 土曜日に出かけます。 Doyoubi ni dekakemasu. I'm going out on Saturday.

✓ **Review** □**Awesome!** □**Excellent!** □**Good!** □**Average!** □**Poor!**

	MEANING	North
北	ONYOMI	ホク Hoku
	KUNYOMI	きた Kita
	EXAMPLE	EXAMPLE SENTENCE

	EXAMPLE	EXAMPLE SENTENCE
	ほっかいどう 北海道 Hokkaidou [Region of Japan] きたあめりか 北アメリカ Kita Amerika [North America]	ほっかいどう い 北海道へ行ったことがありまか。 Hokkaidou he itta koto ga arimasu ka? Have you ever been to Hokkaido?

	MEANING	East
東	ONYOMI	トウ Tou
	KUNYOMI	ひがし、あずま Higashi, Azuma
	EXAMPLE	EXAMPLE SENTENCE

	EXAMPLE	EXAMPLE SENTENCE
	とうきょう 東京 Toukyou − Tokyo. ちゅうとう 中東 Chuutou − The Middle East とうざい 東西 Touzai − East and west	とうきょう す 東京に住んでいます。 Toukyou ni sunde imasu. I live in Tokyo.

✓ **Review** ☐**Awesome!** ☐**Excellent!** ☐**Good!** ☐**Average!** ☐**Poor!**

	MEANING	West
①④⑤③②⑥ 西	ONYOMI	サイ、セイ　Sai, Sei
	KUNYOMI	にし　Nishi
	EXAMPLE	EXAMPLE SENTENCE

EXAMPLE	EXAMPLE SENTENCE
ほくせい 北西　Hokusei　− Northwest たいせいよう 大西洋 Taiseiyou − The Atlantic せいおう 西欧　Seiou　　− Western Europe	かぜ にし か 風が西に変わった。 Kaze ga nishi ni kawatta. The wind changed direction towards the west.

	MEANING	South
②①④⑤⑥③⑦⑨⑧ 南	ONYOMI	ナン　Nan
	KUNYOMI	みなみ　Minami
	EXAMPLE	EXAMPLE SENTENCE

EXAMPLE	EXAMPLE SENTENCE
なんべい 南米　Nanbei　− South America なんぼく 南北　Nanboku − North and South なんきょく 南極　Nankyoku− Antarctic	みなみ うみ 南に、海があります。 Minami ni, umi ga arimasu. There is a sea in the south.

✓ **Review** ☐Awesome！ ☐Excellent！ ☐Good！ ☐Average！ ☐Poor！

		MEANING	Left	
② ① 左 ③ ④ ⑤		ONYOMI	サ　Sa	
		KUNYOMI	ひだり　Hidari	
		EXAMPLE		EXAMPLE SENTENCE

		EXAMPLE		EXAMPLE SENTENCE
		ひだりて 左手　Hidarite　– Left hand さゆう 左右　Sayuu　– Left and Right ひだりあし 左足　Hidariashi – Left foot		わたし ひだりて　　か 私は左手で書きます。 Watashi wa hidarite de kakimasu. I write with my left hand.

		MEANING	Right	
① ② 右 ④ ③ ⑤		ONYOMI	ウ、ユウ　U, Yuu	
		KUNYOMI	みぎ　Migi	
		EXAMPLE		EXAMPLE SENTENCE

		EXAMPLE		EXAMPLE SENTENCE
		みぎて 右手　Migite　– Right hand みぎめ 右目　Migime　– Right eye さゆう 左右　Sayuu　– Left and right		みぎ　ま 右に曲がります。 Migi ni magarimasu. I'm turning to the right. (In a car for example)

✓ **Review** □**Awesome!** □**Excellent!** □**Good!** □**Average!** □**Poor!**

日	MEANING	Day, Sun
	ONYOMI	ジツ、ニチ　Jitsu, Nichi
	KUNYOMI	か、ひ　Ka, Hi

EXAMPLE	EXAMPLE SENTENCE
まいにち 毎日　Mainichi　–　Everyday きょう 今日　Kyou　　–　Today しゅうじつ 終日　Shuujitsu　–　All day	まいにち　にほんご　べんきょう 毎日、日本語を勉強します。 Mainichi, nihongo wo benkyou shimasu. Everyday I study Japanese.

月	MEANING	Month, Moon
	ONYOMI	ガツ、ゲツ　Gatsu, Getsu
	KUNYOMI	つき　Tsuki

EXAMPLE	EXAMPLE SENTENCE
いちがつ 一月　　Ichigatsu　– January こんげつ 今月　　Kongetsu　– This Month げつようび 月曜日　Getsuyoubi – Monday	きょう　　げつようび 今日は、月曜日です。 Kyou wa Getsuyoubi desu. Today is Monday.

✓ **Review** ☐**Awesome!** ☐**Excellent!** ☐**Good!** ☐**Average!** ☐**Poor!**

	MEANING	Flower, Blossom
① ② ③ ④ ⑦ ⑥ ⑤ 花	ONYOMI	カ　Ka
	KUNYOMI	はな　Hana

EXAMPLE			EXAMPLE SENTENCE
はなび 花火	Hanabi	– Firework	うつく　はな これはとても美しい花です。
ひばな 火花	Hibana	– Spark	Kore wa totemo utsukushii hana desu.
はな 花	Hana	– Flower	This is a very beautiful flower.

	MEANING	Fish
① ② ④ ③ ⑥ ⑤ ⑦ ⑧ ⑨ ⑩ ⑪ 魚	ONYOMI	ギョ　Gyo
	KUNYOMI	さかな、うお　Sakana, Uo

EXAMPLE			EXAMPLE SENTENCE
さかなつ 魚釣り	Sakanatsuri	– Fishing	しんせん さかな た 新鮮な魚を食べたいです。
うおいちば 魚市場	Uoichiba	– Fish Market	Shinsenna sakana wo tabetai desu.
きんぎょ 金魚	Kingyo	– Goldfish	I want to eat fresh fish.

✓ **Review** ☐**Awesome!** ☐**Excellent!** ☐**Good!** ☐**Average!** ☐**Poor!**

空	MEANING	Sky The air
	ONYOMI	クウ Kuu
	KUNYOMI	そら、あ（く）、から Sora, A(ku), Kara
	EXAMPLE	EXAMPLE SENTENCE

EXAMPLE				EXAMPLE SENTENCE
あおぞら 青空	Aozora	–	Blue Sky	とり そら と 鳥が空を飛んでいる。
くうき 空気	Kuuki	–	Air	Tori ga sora wo tonde iru.
くうこう 空港	Kuukou	–	Airport	Birds are flying in the sky.

山	MEANING	Mountain
	ONYOMI	サン San
	KUNYOMI	やま Yama
	EXAMPLE	EXAMPLE SENTENCE

EXAMPLE				EXAMPLE SENTENCE
やぎ 山羊	Yagi	–	A goat	はじ やま のぼ 初めて山に登った。
ふじさん 富士山	Fuji-san	–	Mt.fuji	Hajimete yama ni nobotta.
とざん 登山	Tozan	–	Climbing	I climbed the mountain for the first time.

✓ Review ☐Awesome! ☐Excellent! ☐Good! ☐Average! ☐Poor!

①川② ③		

MEANING	River, Stream
ONYOMI	セン Sen
KUNYOMI	かわ Kawa

EXAMPLE	EXAMPLE SENTENCE
かわさき 川崎　Kawasaki　– City in Japan あま がわ 天の川 Amanogawa – Milky Way かわも 川面　Kawamo　– River surface	いえ うし　かせん 家の後ろに河川があります。 Ie no ushiro ni kasen ga arimasu. There is a river behind the house.

①雨③④②⑤⑦⑥⑧		

MEANING	Rain
ONYOMI	ウ U
KUNYOMI	あめ Ame

EXAMPLE	EXAMPLE SENTENCE
おおあめ 大雨　　Ooame　– Heavy rain うてん 雨天　　Uten　– Rainy day あまぐ 雨具　　Amagu　– Rain gear	あめ　ふ 雨が、降っています。 Ame ga futte imasu. It's raining.

✓ Review ☐Awesome！☐Excellent！☐Good！☐Average！☐Poor！

①②③④⑤ 本	**MEANING**	Book, Volume, Script, Origin, True, Real, Source, Genuine.
	ONYOMI	ホン Hon
	KUNYOMI	もと Moto

EXAMPLE				EXAMPLE SENTENCE
にほん 日本	Nihon	–	Japan	ほん よ この本を読みたい。
ほんもの 本物	Honmono	–	Genuine	Kono hon wo yomitai.
ほんじつ 本日	Honjitsu	–	Today	I want to read this book.

①②③④⑤ 目	**MEANING**	Eye, Eyeball, Eyesight, Sight, Vision
	ONYOMI	モク Moku
	KUNYOMI	め Me

EXAMPLE				EXAMPLE SENTENCE
もくてき 目的	Mokuteki	–	Purpose	め あなたの目はとてもきれいです。
めぐすり 目薬	Megusuri	–	Eye drops	Anata no me wa totemo kirei desu.
めやす 目安	Meyasu	–	Criterion	Your eyes are so beautiful.

✓ **Review** ☐**Awesome!** ☐**Excellent!** ☐**Good!** ☐**Average!** ☐**Poor!**

	MEANING	Mouth, Opening
口 ②①③	ONYOMI	コウ、ク Kou, Ku
	KUNYOMI	くち Kuchi

EXAMPLE				EXAMPLE SENTENCE
りこう 利口	Rikou	–	Clever	くち あ 口を開けてください。
くちべに 口紅	Kuchibeni	–	Lipstick	Kuchi wo akete kudasai.
でぐち 出口	Deguchi	–	Exit	Please open your mouth.

	MEANING	Ear, Hearing
耳 ①②③④⑥⑤	ONYOMI	ジ Ji
	KUNYOMI	みみ Mimi

EXAMPLE				EXAMPLE SENTENCE
じびか 耳鼻科	Jibika	–	Otolaryngology	わたし みみ なが いぬ ほ 私は耳の長い犬が欲しいです。
みぎみみ 右耳	Migimimi	–	Right ear	Watashi wa mimi no nagai inu ga hoshii desu.
みみせん 耳栓	Mimisen	–	Earplug	I want a dog with long ears.

✓ **Review** ☐**Awesome!** ☐**Excellent!** ☐**Good!** ☐**Average!** ☐**Poor!**

	MEANING	Hand
	ONYOMI	シュ Shu
	KUNYOMI	て Te

EXAMPLE				EXAMPLE SENTENCE
からて 空手	Karate	–	Karate	みぎて いた 右手が痛い。
てがみ 手紙	Tegami	–	Letter	Migite ga itai.
かしゅ 歌手	Kashu	–	Singer	My right hand hurts.

	MEANING	Foot, Leg, To be Sufficient
	ONYOMI	ソク Soku
	KUNYOMI	あし、た(りる) Ashi, Ta(riru)

EXAMPLE				EXAMPLE SENTENCE
まんぞく 満足	Manzoku	–	Satisfaction	はな すいぶん ふそく その花は水分が不足しています。
あしくび 足首	Ashikubi	–	Ankle	Sono hana wa suibun ga fusoku shite imasu.
ふそく 不足	Fusoku	–	Lack	Its flowers lack water.

✓ **Review** ☐Awesome! ☐Excellent! ☐Good! ☐Average! ☐Poor!

人	MEANING	Person, Human being, People
①②	ONYOMI	ジン、ニン　Jin, Nin
	KUNYOMI	ひと　Hito

EXAMPLE	EXAMPLE SENTENCE
じんこう 人口　　Jinkou　　－　Population がいこくじん 外国人　Gaikokujin　－　Foreigner さんにん 三人　　Sannin　－　Three peoples	びじん あなたは美人です。 Anata wa bijin desu. You are a beautiful woman.

母	MEANING	Mother
②①③⑤④	ONYOMI	ボ　Bo
	KUNYOMI	はは、かあ　Haha, Kaa

EXAMPLE	EXAMPLE SENTENCE
かあ お母さん　Okaasan　－　A mother そぼ 祖母　　Sobo　　－　Grandmother ぼせい 母性　　Bosei　　－　Maternal	あした　はは　ひ 明日は母の日です。 Ashita wa haha no hi desu. Tomorrow is mother's day.

✓ **Review** □Awesome！□Excellent！□Good！□Average！□Poor！

父

①② ④③

MEANING	Father
ONYOMI	フ、ブ、プ　Fu, Bu, Pu
KUNYOMI	ちち、とう　Chichi, Tou

EXAMPLE	EXAMPLE SENTENCE

とう
お父さん　Otousan　-　A father

そふ
祖父　　Sofu　　-　Grandfather

しんぷ
神父　　Shinpu　-　Catholic priest

ちち げんき
父は元気です。

Chichi wa genki desu.

My father is fine.

女

①③②

MEANING	Woman, Female
ONYOMI	ジョ　Jo
KUNYOMI	おんな、め　Onna, Me

EXAMPLE	EXAMPLE SENTENCE

じょせい
女性　　Josei　-　Female

めがみ
女神　　Megami　-　Goddess

じょゆう
女優　　Joyuu　-　An actress

かのじょ おんな こ う
彼女は女の子を産みました。

Kanojo wa on'nanoko wo umimashita.

She gave birth to a girl.

✓ **Review** ☐**Awesome!** ☐**Excellent!** ☐**Good!** ☐**Average!** ☐**Poor!**

男		MEANING	Man, Male
		ONYOMI	ダン、ナン　Dan, Nan
		KUNYOMI	おとこ、お　Otoko, O
		EXAMPLE	EXAMPLE SENTENCE

		EXAMPLE				EXAMPLE SENTENCE
		だんじょ 男女	Danjo	–	Men & women	あか　　　　おとこ　こ 赤ちゃんは男の子です。
		だんせい 男性	Dansei	–	Male	Akachan wa otokonoko desu.
		ちょうなん 長男	Chounan	–	Eldest son	The baby is a boy.

子		MEANING	Child
		ONYOMI	シ、ス、ツ　Shi, Su, Tsu
		KUNYOMI	こ、ね　Ko, Ne
		EXAMPLE	EXAMPLE SENTENCE

		EXAMPLE				EXAMPLE SENTENCE
		こども 子供	Kodomo	–	A child	しごせん 子午線はどこにありますか。
		かし お菓子	Okashi	–	Sweets	Shigosen wa doko ni arimasu ka.
		いす 椅子	Isu	–	Chair, stool	Where is the meridian?

✓ **Review** ☐**Awesome!** ☐**Excellent!** ☐**Good!** ☐**Average!** ☐**Poor!**

		MEANING	Little, Small
① 小 ③ ②		ONYOMI	ショウ Shou
		KUNYOMI	ちい(さい)、こ-、お-、さ- Chii(sai), Ko-, O-, Sa-

	EXAMPLE			EXAMPLE SENTENCE
こむぎ 小麦	Komugi	–	Flour	おも ちい それは思っていたより小さい。
しゅくしょう 縮小	Shukushou	–	Shrink	Sore wa omotteita yori chiisai.
おがわ 小川	Ogawa	–	Stream	That's smaller than I thought it was.

		MEANING	Center, in, Inside, Middle, Mean, Inner
④ ② 中 ① ③		ONYOMI	チュウ、ジュウ Chuu , Jyuu
		KUNYOMI	なか、うち、あた(る) Naka, Uchi, Ata(ru)

	EXAMPLE			EXAMPLE SENTENCE
ちゅうこしゃ 中古車	Chuukosha	–	Used car	いま いえ なか 今は家の中にいますよ。
まんなか 真中	Man'naka	–	Middle	Ima wa ie no naka ni imasu yo.
まよなか 真夜中	Mayonaka	–	Midnight	I'm inside the house right now.

✓ **Review** ☐**Awesome!** ☐**Excellent!** ☐**Good!** ☐**Average!** ☐**Poor!**

大	MEANING	Big, Large	
②①③	ONYOMI	ダイ、タイ　Dai, Tai	
	KUNYOMI	おお(きい)　Oo(kii)	
	EXAMPLE		**EXAMPLE SENTENCE**

	EXAMPLE			EXAMPLE SENTENCE
	だいがく 大学	Daigaku	– University	らいしゅう　　　たいしかん　い 来週アメリカの大使館に行きます。
	おとな 大人	Otona	– Adult	Raishuu amerika no taishikan ni ikimasu.
	たいしかん 大使館	Taishikan	– Embassy	I'm going to the American embassy next week.

上	MEANING	Above, Up	
①② ③	ONYOMI	ジョウ、ショウ、シャン　Jou, Shou, Shan	
	KUNYOMI	うえ、うわ-、かみ、あ(げる)、のぼ(る)、たてまつ(る) Ue,　Uwa, Kami,　A(geru),　Nobo(ru), Tatematsu(ru)	
	EXAMPLE		**EXAMPLE SENTENCE**

	EXAMPLE			EXAMPLE SENTENCE
	うわぎ 上着	Uwagi	– Outerwear	おし　　　じょうず あなたは教えるのが上手です。
	じょうひん 上品	Jouhin	– Elegant	Anata wa oshieru noga jouzu desu.
	じょうげ 上下	Jouge	– Up and down	You're good at teaching.

✓ **Review** ☐Awesome! ☐Excellent! ☐Good! ☐Average! ☐Poor!

下	MEANING	Below, Down, Desend, Give, Low, Inferior
①②③	ONYOMI	カ、ゲ　Ka, Ge
	KUNYOMI	した、しも、もと、さ(げる)、くだ(る)、お(ろす) Shita, Shimo, Moto, Sa(geru), Kuda(ru), O(rosu)

EXAMPLE	EXAMPLE SENTENCE
ちかてつ 地下鉄　Chikatetsu – Subway くつした 靴下　　Kutsushita – Socks ねさ 値下げ　Nesage　– Cut in price	くだ それを下さい。 Sore wo kudasai. May I have that.

何	MEANING	What, Which
①③⑤⑦②④⑥	ONYOMI	カ　Ka
	KUNYOMI	なに　Nani

EXAMPLE	EXAMPLE SENTENCE
なんにん 何人　Nannin – How many people なに 何か　Nanika – Something なに 何？　Nani? – What?	いまなんじ 今何時ですか。 Ima nanji desu ka. What time is it now?

✓ **Review** ☐**Awesome!** ☐**Excellent!** ☐**Good!** ☐**Average!** ☐**Poor!**

行	MEANING	Going, Journey, Carry out, Line, Row, To go
	ONYOMI	コウ、ギョウ、アン　Kou, Gyou, An
	KUNYOMI	い(く)、ゆ(く)、おこな(う)　I(ku), Yu(ku), Okona(u)
	EXAMPLE	EXAMPLE SENTENCE

ぎんこう 銀行　Ginkou　－　Bank りょこう 旅行　Ryokou　－　Trip, Travel い 行く　Iku　－　To go, to move	まいとし　りょこう 毎年、旅行がしたいです。 Maitoshi ryokou ga shitai desu. I want to travel every year.	

見	MEANING	See, Hopes, Chances, Idea, Opinion, Look at, Visible
	ONYOMI	ケン　Ken
	KUNYOMI	み(る)、み(せる)　Mi(ru), Mi(seru)
	EXAMPLE	EXAMPLE SENTENCE

けんぶつ 見物　Kenbutsu　－　Sight seeing み 見る　Miru　－　To see, to look み 見せる　Miseru　－　I show you	えいが　み この映画を見たことありますか。 Kono eiga wo mita koto arimasu ka. Have you seen this movie?	

✓ **Review** ☐**Awesome!** ☐**Excellent!** ☐**Good!** ☐**Average!** ☐**Poor!**

	MEANING	Say, Word, Speech
②言 ③ ④ ⑥ ⑤⑦	ONYOMI	ゲン、ゴン　Gen, Gon
	KUNYOMI	い(う)、こと　I(u), Koto

EXAMPLE	EXAMPLE SENTENCE
い 言う　　Iu　　　－ To say, To utter ことば 言葉　　Kotoba － Dialect, Word げんご 言語　　Gengo － Language	ひと　　い　　　　わたし　い あの人が、言ったことを私は言う。 Ano hito ga, itta koto wo watashi wa iu. I say what that person said.

	MEANING	Word, Speech, Language
①　⑧ ②語⑨ ③⑩ ④⑪ ⑥　⑬ ⑤⑦⑫⑭	ONYOMI	ゴ　Go
	KUNYOMI	かた(る)　Kata(ru)

EXAMPLE	EXAMPLE SENTENCE
にほんご 日本語 Nihongo – Japanese Language ごがく 語学　　Gogaku – Study of Language かた 語らう　Katarau– To talk, To tell	にほんご　まな 日本語を学びたいです。 Nihongo wo manabi tai desu. I want to learn Japanese.

✓ **Review** ☐Awesome！ ☐Excellent！ ☐Good！ ☐Average！ ☐Poor！

食

MEANING	Eat, Food
ONYOMI	ショク、ジキ Shoku, Jiki
KUNYOMI	く(う)、た(べる)、は(む) K(u), Ta(beru), Ha(mu)

EXAMPLE				EXAMPLE SENTENCE
た もの 食べ物	Tabemono	–	Food	た もう食べましたか。
しょくじ 食事	Shokuji	–	A meal	Mou tabemashita ka.
しょっき 食器	Shokki	–	Tableware	Have you eaten yet?

飲

MEANING	Drink
ONYOMI	イン In
KUNYOMI	の(む) No(mu)

EXAMPLE				EXAMPLE SENTENCE
の 飲む	Nomu	–	To Drink	みず の 水を飲みました。
いんりょう 飲料	Inryou	–	Beverage	Mizu wo nomimashita.
いんしょくてん 飲食店	Inshokuten	–	Restaurant	I drank water.

✓ Review ☐Awesome! ☐Excellent! ☐Good! ☐Average! ☐Poor!

会	MEANING	Meeting , Meet
①②③④⑤⑥	ONYOMI	カイ Kai
	KUNYOMI	あ(う) A(u)

	EXAMPLE	EXAMPLE SENTENCE
	かいしゃ 会社　Kaisha　—　Company	にちようび　あさ　あ 日曜日の朝に会いましょう。
	しゃかい 社会　Shakai　—　Society	Nichiyoubi no asa ni aimashou.
	かいわ 会話　Kaiwa　—　Conversation	See you on Sunday morning.

学	MEANING	School, Study, Learning, Science
①②③④⑤⑥⑦⑧	ONYOMI	ガク Gaku
	KUNYOMI	まな(ぶ) Mana(bu)

	EXAMPLE	EXAMPLE SENTENCE
	だいがく 大学　Daigaku　—　University	にほんご　いっしょ　まな 日本語を一緒に学びましょう。
	がっこう 学校　Gakkou　—　School	Nihongo wo issho ni manabi mashou.
	かがく 科学　Kagaku　—　Science	Learn Japanese together.

✓ **Review** ☐Awesome! ☐Excellent! ☐Good! ☐Average! ☐Poor!

休	MEANING	Rest, Day off, Retire, Sleep
	ONYOMI	キュウ Kyuu
	KUNYOMI	やす(む) Yasu(mu)

	EXAMPLE	EXAMPLE SENTENCE
	ひるやす 昼休み Hiruyasumi – Lunch break きゅうじつ 休日　Kyuujitsu　– Day off しゅうきゅう 週休　Shuukyuu – Weekly holidays	やす　　　　　よ　ゆめ み お休みなさい。良い夢を見てください！ Oyasuminasai. Yoi yume wo mitekudasai! Good night. Have good dreams!

買	MEANING	Buy
	ONYOMI	バイ Bai
	KUNYOMI	か(う) Ka(u)

	EXAMPLE	EXAMPLE SENTENCE
	かいもの 買物　　Kaimono　–　Shopping ばいばい 売買　Baibai　–　Trade かいとり 買取　Kaitori　–　Purchase	おおがたはんばいてん　ふく か 大型販売店で服を買いました。 Oogata hanbaiten de fuku wo kaimashita. I bought clothes from a large retailer.

✓ **Review** ☐**Awesome！** ☐**Excellent！** ☐**Good！** ☐**Average！** ☐**Poor！**

聞	MEANING	To hear, to listen, to ask
	ONYOMI	ブン、モン　Bun, Mon
	KUNYOMI	き(く) き(こえる)　Ki(ku) Ki(koeru)

	EXAMPLE	EXAMPLE SENTENCE
	しんぶん 新聞　　Shinbun　－ Newspaper き じょうず 聞き上手 Kikijouzu － Good listener き ちが 聞き違い Kikichigai － Mishearing	きょう　じゅぎょう　な　き 今日は授業が無いと聞きました。 Kyou wa jugyou ga nai to kikimashita. I heard that there is no class today.

来	MEANING	Come, Due, Next, Cause, Become
	ONYOMI	ライ、タイ　Rai, Tai
	KUNYOMI	く(る)、き(たる)、き、こ　Ku(ru), Ki(taru), Ki, Ko

	EXAMPLE	EXAMPLE SENTENCE
	らいげつ 来月　　Raigetsu － Next month でき 出来る　Dekiru　－ To be able to do みらい 未来　　Mirai　　－ The future	みっかご　こ あなたも三日後ここに来れますか。 Anata mo mikkago koko ni koremasu ka. Can you come here in three days too?

✓ Review □Awesome！ □Excellent！ □Good！ □Average！ □Poor！

立	MEANING	Stand up, Rise, Establish
	ONYOMI	リツ Ritsu
	KUNYOMI	た(つ)、た(てる)、たち Ta(tsu), Ta(teru), Tachi

EXAMPLE	EXAMPLE SENTENCE
こくりつ 国立 Kokuritsu – National	た 立てますか。
りっぱ 立派 Rippa – Splendid	Tatemasu ka.
た 立つ Tatsu – To stand, to rise	Can you stand?

生	MEANING	Life, Genuine, Birth, To grow
	ONYOMI	セイ、ショウ Sei, Shou
	KUNYOMI	い(きる)、う(む)、お(う)、は(える)、なま I(kiru), U(mu), O(u), Ha(eru), Nama

EXAMPLE	EXAMPLE SENTENCE
がくせい 学生 Gakusei – Student	がくせい あなたも学生ですか。
せいぶつ 生物 Seibutsu – Living things	Anata mo gakusei desu ka.
せんせい 先生 Sensei – Teacher, Doctor	Are you also a student?

✓ **Review** ☐**Awesome!** ☐**Excellent!** ☐**Good!** ☐**Average!** ☐**Poor!**

	MEANING	Tale, Talk, Conversation
① ② ③ ④ ⑥ ⑤ ⑦ 話 ⑧ ⑨ ⑩ ⑫ ⑪ ⑬	ONYOMI	わ Wa
	KUNYOMI	はな(す)、はなし Hana(su), Hanashi

EXAMPLE	EXAMPLE SENTENCE
かいわ 会話 Kaiwa – Conversation でんわ 電話 Denwa – Phone はな 話す Hanasu – To talk, Speak	はなし ほんとう その話は本当ですか。 Sono hanashi wa hontou desu ka. Is that story true?

	MEANING	Exit, Leave, Go out
① ② ③ ④ 出 ⑤	ONYOMI	シュツ、スイ Shutsu, Sui
	KUNYOMI	で(る)、だ(す)、い(でる) De(ru), Da(su), I(deru)

EXAMPLE	EXAMPLE SENTENCE
でぐち 出口 Deguchi – Exit, Gateway ひ で 日の出 Hinode – Sunrise しゅっけつ 出血 Shukketsu – Bleeding	ひだり でぐち で 左の出口を出てください。 Hidari no deguchi wo dete kudasai. Take the exit on the left.

✓ **Review** ☐**Awesome!** ☐**Excellent!** ☐**Good!** ☐**Average!** ☐**Poor!**

		MEANING	To read
		ONYOMI	ドク、トク、トウ　Doku, Toku, Tou
		KUNYOMI	よ(む)　Yo(mu)

EXAMPLE	EXAMPLE SENTENCE
どくしょ 読書　　Dokusho　－　Reading くとうてん 句読点　Kutouten　－　Punctuation よ 読む　　Yomu　　－　To read	ほん　よ 本を読みましょう。 Hon wo yomimashou. Let's read a book.

		MEANING	Enter, Insert
		ONYOMI	ニュウ　Nyuu
		KUNYOMI	い(る)、はい(る)　I(ru), Hai(ru)

EXAMPLE	EXAMPLE SENTENCE
いりぐち 入口　　Iriguchi　－　Entrance きにゅう 記入　　Kinyuu　　－　Fill in はい 入る　　Hairu　　－　To get in	あした　だいがく　にゅうがくしき 明日は大学の入学式です。 Ashita wa daigaku no nyuugakushiki desu. Tomorrow is my university's entrance ceremony.

✓ **Review** □**Awesome!** □**Excellent!** □**Good!** □**Average!** □**Poor!**

	MEANING	Write
書	ONYOMI	ショ　Sho
	KUNYOMI	か(く)　Ka(ku)

	EXAMPLE				EXAMPLE SENTENCE

EXAMPLE			EXAMPLE SENTENCE
か 書く	Kaku	– To write	なまえ か ここに名前を書いてください。
じしょ 辞書	Jisho	– Dictionary	Koko ni namae wo kaite kudasai.
としょかん 図書館	Toshokan –	Library	Please write your name here.

	MEANING	Behind, Back, Later, After
後	ONYOMI	ゴ、コウ　Go, Kou
	KUNYOMI	のち、うし(ろ)、あと　Nochi, Ushi(ro), Ato

EXAMPLE			EXAMPLE SENTENCE
ごご 午後	Gogo	– Afternoon	あと でんわ 後で電話します。
こんご 今後	Kongo	– From now on	Ato de denwa shimasu.
あと 後	Ato	– After, Later	I'll give you a call later.

✓ Review　□Awesome！□Excellent！□Good！□Average！□Poor！

	MEANING	Old, Used
①②③④⑤ 古	ONYOMI	コ　Ko
	KUNYOMI	ふる(い)　Furu(i)

EXAMPLE	EXAMPLE SENTENCE
ここん 古今　Kokon　－　Past and present	ふる　とけい　す 古い時計が好きです。
けいこ 稽古　Keiko　－　Training	Furui tokei ga sukidesu.
ふるす 古巣　Furusu　－　Former home	I like old clocks.

	MEANING	High, Expensive, Increase, Tall
高	ONYOMI	コウ　Kou
	KUNYOMI	たか(い)　Taka(i)

EXAMPLE	EXAMPLE SENTENCE
こうこう 高校　Koukou　－　Past and present	やさい　たか 野菜が高いです。
こうそく 高速　Kousoku　－　High speed	Yasai ga takai desu.
たか 高い　Takai　－　High, Tall, Expensive	The vegetables are expensive.

✓ **Review** □**Awesome！** □**Excellent！** □**Good！** □**Average！** □**Poor！**

	MEANING	Cheap, Peace, Safety
安	ONYOMI	アン An
	KUNYOMI	やす(い) Yasu(i)

EXAMPLE	EXAMPLE SENTENCE
あんぜん 安全　Anzen　－　Safety あんしん 安心　Anshin　－　Peace of mind やす 安い　Yasui　－　Cheap	ぶっか　やす ここは物価が安いです。 Koko wa bukka ga yasui desu. Prices here are cheap.

	MEANING	Many, Frequent, Much
多	ONYOMI	タ Ta
	KUNYOMI	おお(い) Oo(i)

EXAMPLE	EXAMPLE SENTENCE
たぶん 多分　Tabun　－　Probably, Maybe おお 多い　Ooi　－　Many, Numerous たしょう 多少　Tashou　－　Somewhat	たぶん　あした　あめ 多分明日は、雨でしょう。 Tabun ashita wa, ame deshou. It might rain tomorrow.

✓ **Review** □**Awesome!** □**Excellent!** □**Good!** □**Average!** □**Poor!**

新

	MEANING	New
	ONYOMI	シン　Shin
	KUNYOMI	あたら(しい)、あら(た)　Atara(shii), Ara(ta)

EXAMPLE	EXAMPLE SENTENCE
しんしゃ 新車　　Shinsha　　－ New Car さいしん 最新　　Saishin　　－ Newest, latest しんちゃく 新着　　Shinchaku － New arrival	あたら　くるま か 新しい車を買いました。 Atarashii kuruma wo kaimashita. I bought a new car.

少

	MEANING	A little, Few
	ONYOMI	ショウ　Shou
	KUNYOMI	すく(ない)、すこ(し)　Suku(nai), Suko(shi)

EXAMPLE	EXAMPLE SENTENCE
しょうじょ 少女　　Shoujo　　－ Young girl すく 少ない　Sukunai　　－ Few, little しょうすう 少数　　Shousuu　　－ Minority	ほ　　　　すこたか これが欲しいですが少し高い。 Kore ga hoshii desuga sukoshi takai. I want this, but it's a bit expensive.

✓ **Review** □**Awesome！** □**Excellent！** □**Good！** □**Average！** □**Poor！**

	MEANING	Long, Leader, Superior, Senior
長	ONYOMI	チョウ Chou
	KUNYOMI	なが(い) Naga(i)

EXAMPLE				EXAMPLE SENTENCE
しゃちょう 社長	Shachou	−	CEO	わたし　なが　じかんはな 私たちは長い時間話しました。
せいちょう 成長	Seichou	−	Growth	Watashitachi wa nagai jikan hanashi mashita.
きなが 気長	Kinaga	−	Leisurely	We talked for a long time.

	MEANING	White
白	ONYOMI	ハク、ビャク Haku, Byaku
	KUNYOMI	しろ(い) Shiro(i)

EXAMPLE				EXAMPLE SENTENCE
よはく 余白	Yohaku	−	Margin	しろ　ねこ　か 白い猫を飼っています。
びゃくや 白夜	Byakuya	−	Midnight sun	Shiroi neko wo katteimasu.
はくちょう 白鳥	Hakuchou	−	Swan	I have a white cat.

✓ Review □Awesome! □Excellent! □Good! □Average! □Poor!

	MEANING	Minute, Part, Understand, Divide
①②③④ 分	ONYOMI	ブン、フン、ブ　Bun, Fun, Bu
	KUNYOMI	わ(ける) わ(かれる)　Wa(keru), Wa(kareru)

EXAMPLE	EXAMPLE SENTENCE
じぶん 自分　Jibun　　－Myself はんぶん 半分　Hanbun －Half なんぷん 何分　Nanpun －How many minutes	わ　　　　　わ これを分けましょう。分かりました。 Kore wo wakemashou. Wakarimashita. Let's divide this. I understand.

	MEANING	Time, Hour
②①③④ 時 ⑤⑥⑦⑧⑨⑩	ONYOMI	ジ　Ji
	KUNYOMI	とき、どき Toki, Doki

EXAMPLE	EXAMPLE SENTENCE
じかん 時間　Jikan　　－　Time ときどき 時々　Tokidoki　－　Sometimes とけい 時計　Tokei　　－　Watch, Clock	いまなんじ 今何時ですか。 Ima nanji desu ka. What time is it now?

✓ **Review** ☐**Awesome!** ☐**Excellent!** ☐**Good!** ☐**Average!** ☐**Poor!**

	MEANING	Interval, Space, During
間	ONYOMI	カン、ケン Kan, Ken
	KUNYOMI	あいだ、ま、あい Aida, Ma, Ai

EXAMPLE				EXAMPLE SENTENCE
なかま 仲間	Nakama	–	Companion	じかん 時間がありますか。
しゅうかん 週間	Shuukan	–	Week	Jikan ga arimasu ka.
きかん 期間	Kikan	–	Period	Do you have time.

	MEANING	Week
週	ONYOMI	シュウ Shuu
	KUNYOMI	めぐ(る) Megu(ru)

EXAMPLE				EXAMPLE SENTENCE
こんしゅう 今週	Konshuu	–	This week	らいしゅうとうきょう い 来週東京に行きます。
しゅうまつ 週末	Shuumatsu	–	Weekend	Raishuu toukyou ni ikimasu.
まいしゅう 毎週	Maishuu	–	Weekly	I'm going to Tokyo next week.

✓ Review □Awesome! □Excellent! □Good! □Average! □Poor!

	MEANING	Year
	ONYOMI	ネン Nen
	KUNYOMI	とし、どし Toshi, Doshi

EXAMPLE			EXAMPLE SENTENCE
いちねん 一年	Ichinen	— One year	らいねん あき にほん い 来年の秋にやっと日本に行きます。
ことし 今年	Kotoshi	— This year	Rainen no aki ni yatto Nihon ni ikimasu.
しんねん 新年	Shinnen	— New Year	I will finally go to Japan next autumn.

	MEANING	Now, The present
	ONYOMI	コン、キン Kon, Kin
	KUNYOMI	いま Ima

EXAMPLE			EXAMPLE SENTENCE
こんや 今夜	Konya	— Tonight	いまいえ つ 今家に着いたところです。
きょう 今日	Kyou	— Today	Ima ie ni tsuita tokoro desu.
けさ 今朝	Kesa	— This Morning	I just arrived home now.

✓ Review ☐Awesome! ☐Excellent! ☐Good! ☐Average! ☐Poor!

先	MEANING	Before, Ahead, Previous, Future, Precedence
	ONYOMI	セン Sen
	KUNYOMI	さき、ま(ず) Saki, Ma(zu)

		EXAMPLE			EXAMPLE SENTENCE

ま
先ず　　Mazu　　－　First of all

せんせい
先生　　Sensei　－　Teacher

さきごろ
先頃　　Sakigoro　－　Recently

さき
どうぞ、お先に。

Douzo, osaki ni.

After you, please.

前	MEANING	In front, Before
	ONYOMI	ゼン Zen
	KUNYOMI	まえ Mae

		EXAMPLE			EXAMPLE SENTENCE

なまえ
名前　　Namae　－　Name

ごぜん
午前　　Gozen　－　A.m

ぜんじつ
前日　　Zenjitsu　－　The day before

なまえ　　まえ　か
名前を、その前に書いてください。

Namae wo, sono mae ni kaite kudasai.

Please write your name before that.

✓ Review □Awesome！□Excellent！□Good！□Average！□Poor！

午	MEANING	Noon
①②④③	ONYOMI	ゴ Go
	KUNYOMI	うま Uma

EXAMPLE			EXAMPLE SENTENCE
ごご 午後	Gogo	– P.m	ぜん ごご 午前と午後のどちらにしますか。
しょうご 正午	Shougo	– Noon; midday	Gozen to gogo no dochira ni shimasu ka.
しごせん 子午線	Shigosen	– Meridian	Would you like to go in the morning or afternoon?

半	MEANING	Half, Middle, Semi
①⑤②③④	ONYOMI	ハン Han
	KUNYOMI	なか(ば) Naka(ba)

EXAMPLE			EXAMPLE SENTENCE
はんぶん 半分	Hanbun	– Half	ほん はんぶんよ この本はほとんど半分読んだ。
はんとし 半年	Hantoshi	– Half year	Kono hon wa hotondo hanbun yonda.
なか 半ば	Nakaba	– Middle	I've read about half of this book.

✓ **Review** ☐**Awesome!** ☐**Excellent!** ☐**Good!** ☐**Average!** ☐**Poor!**

	MEANING	Store, Shop
店	ONYOMI	テン　Ten
	KUNYOMI	みせ　Mise

EXAMPLE	EXAMPLE SENTENCE
ばいてん 売店　Baiten　－　Bookshop しょてん 書店　Shoten　－　Shop, Store してん 支店　Shiten　－　Branch	みせ へいてん その店は閉店する。 Sono mise wa heiten suru. The shop will be closed.

	MEANING	Outside, Other, Foreign
外	ONYOMI	ガイ、ゲ　Gai, Ge
	KUNYOMI	そと、ほか、はず(す)、と　Soto, Hoka, Hazu,(su), To

EXAMPLE	EXAMPLE SENTENCE
いがい 以外　Igai　　－　Excepting がいこく 外国　Gaikoku　－　Foreign country がいしゅつ 外出　Gaishutsu　－　Going out	そと あそ 外で遊ぼう。 Soto de asobou. Let's play outside

✓ Review □Awesome! □Excellent! □Good! □Average! □Poor!

電

	MEANING	Electricity, Electric Powered
	ONYOMI	デン Den
	KUNYOMI	いなずま Inazuma

EXAMPLE				EXAMPLE SENTENCE

でんわ
電話　Denwa　–　Telephone

でんち
電池　Denchi　–　Battery

しゅうでん
終電　Shuuden　–　Last train

がっこう でんしゃ い
学校に電車で行きます。

Gakkou ni densha de ikimasu.

I go to school by train.

道

	MEANING	Road, Way, Street, District, Journey, Course, Path
	ONYOMI	ドウ Dou
	KUNYOMI	みち Michi

EXAMPLE				EXAMPLE SENTENCE

どうぐ
道具　Dougu　–　Tool

どうとく
道徳　Doutoku　–　Morals

かたみち
片道　Katamichi　–　One way

どうろ わた とき き
道路を渡る時は気をつけなさい。

Douro wo wataru toki wa ki wo tsuke nasai.

Be careful when crossing the street.

✓ Review ☐Awesome! ☐Excellent! ☐Good! ☐Average! ☐Poor!

	MEANING	Every, Each
①②④③⑤⑥ 毎	ONYOMI	マイ Mai
	KUNYOMI	ごと(に) Goto(ni)

	EXAMPLE			EXAMPLE SENTENCE

まいあさ
毎朝　　Maiasa　－　Every morning

まいにち
毎日　　Mainichi　－　Everyday

ひごと
日毎　　Higoto　－　Daily

まいかい せんせい　はげ
毎回、先生から励まされます。

Maikai, sensei kara hagemasaremasu.

Every time, the teacher encourages me.

	MEANING	Friend
①②③④ 友	ONYOMI	ユウ Yuu
	KUNYOMI	とも Tomo

	EXAMPLE			EXAMPLE SENTENCE

ともだち
友達　　Tomodachi　－　Friend

ゆうじょう
友情　　Yuujou　－　Friendship

しんゆう
親友　　Shinyuu　－　Close friend

こうゆう かんけい きず　　じゅうよう
交友関係を築くことが重要です。

Kouyuukankei wo kizuku koto ga jyuuyou desu.

It is important to build friendships.

✓ **Review** ☐Awesome! ☐Excellent! ☐Good! ☐Average! ☐Poor!

名	MEANING	Name, Noted, Distinguished, Reputation
	ONYOMI	メイ、ミョウ　Mei, Myou
	KUNYOMI	な　Na

EXAMPLE				EXAMPLE SENTENCE
なまえ 名前	Namae	–	Name	しょめい ここに署名してください。
ゆうめい 有名	Yuumei	–	Famous	Koko ni shomei shite kudasai.
めいし 名詞	Meishi	–	Noun	Please sign here.

金	MEANING	Gold
	ONYOMI	キン、コン、ゴン　Kin, Kon, Gon
	KUNYOMI	かね、かな、がね　Kane, Kana, Gane

EXAMPLE				EXAMPLE SENTENCE
きんようび 金曜日	Kinyoubi	–	Friday	かね か　　とも うしな 金を貸せば友を失います。
かなぐ 金具	Kanagu	–	Metal fittings	Kane wo kaseba tomo wo ushinaimasu.
ぜいきん 税金	Zeikin	–	Tax, Duty	If you lend money, you will lose your friends.

✓ **Review** □**Awesome!** □**Excellent!** □**Good!** □**Average!** □**Poor!**

円	MEANING	Yen, Circle, Round
	ONYOMI	エン En
	KUNYOMI	まる(い) Maru(i)

EXAMPLE				EXAMPLE SENTENCE

いちえん
一円　　Ichien　－　One Yen

まる
円い　　Marui　－　Round, Circle

はんえん
半円　　Hanen　－　Semicircle

かれ えんけい いえ たて
彼は円形の家を建てました。

Kare wa enkei no ie wo tatemashita.

He built a circular house.

車	MEANING	Car, Wheel
	ONYOMI	シャ Sha
	KUNYOMI	くるま Kuruma

EXAMPLE				EXAMPLE SENTENCE

でんしゃ
電車　　Densha　－　Train

じてんしゃ
自転車　Jitensha　－　Bicycle

ちゅうしゃじょう
駐車場　Chuushajou　－　Parking

くるま も
車を持っていますか。

Kuruma wo motte imasu ka.

Do you have a car?

✓ **Review** ☐Awesome! ☐Excellent! ☐Good! ☐Average! ☐Poor!

駅

	MEANING	Station
	ONYOMI	エキ Eki
	KUNYOMI	うまや Umaya

EXAMPLE	EXAMPLE SENTENCE
えきちょう 駅長　Ekichou　– Station Master おおさかえき 大阪駅 Oosakaeki – Osaka Station えきいん 駅員　Ekiin　– Station staff	えき 駅は、どちらですか。 Eki wa, dochira desu ka. Where is the station?

気

	MEANING	Spirit, Mind, Air, Atmosphere, Mood, Stream
	ONYOMI	キ、ケ Ki, Ke
	KUNYOMI	いき Iki

EXAMPLE	EXAMPLE SENTENCE
てんき 天気　Tenki　–　Weather きぶん 気分　Kibun　–　Feeling にんき 人気　Ninki　–　Popular	げんき お元気ですか。 Ogenki desu ka. How are you?

✓ **Review** ☐**Awesome!** ☐**Excellent!** ☐**Good!** ☐**Average!** ☐**Poor!**

国	MEANING	Country
	ONYOMI	コク　Koku
	KUNYOMI	くに　Kuni

	EXAMPLE	EXAMPLE SENTENCE
	こくない 国内　　Kokunai　–　Domestic	くに　　き あなたはどちらの国から来ましたか。
	こくみん 国民　　Kokumin　–　Nationa	Anata wa dochira no kuni kara kimashita ka.
	ぼこく 母国　　Bokoku　–　Home country	What country did you come from?

社	MEANING	Shrine, Company, Firm, Office, Association, Society, Shinto
	ONYOMI	シャ　Sha
	KUNYOMI	やしろ　Yashiro

	EXAMPLE	EXAMPLE SENTENCE
	しゃかい 社会　　Shakai　–　Society, Public	きょうと　じんじゃ　　てら　ゆうめい 京都は神社やお寺で有名だ。
	ほんしゃ 本社　　Honsha　–　Head office	Kyouto wa jinja ya otera de yuumei da.
	やしろ 社　　　Yashiro　–　Shrine	Kyoto is famous for its shrines and temples.

✓ **Review** ☐Awesome！ ☐Excellent！ ☐Good！ ☐Average！ ☐Poor！

	MEANING	School, Exam
校	ONYOMI	コウ Kou
	KUNYOMI	（かんが（える）、くら（べる） Kanga(eru), Kura(beru)）

EXAMPLE	EXAMPLE SENTENCE
がっこう 学校　　Gakkou　　– School こうこうせい 高校生　Koukousei　– High School Std. ぜんこう 全校　　Zenkou　　– All schools	こうちょう なが はなし はじ 校長が長い話を始めました。 Kouchou ga nagai hanashi wo hajimemashita. The headmaster began a long talk.

	MEANING	
	ONYOMI	
	KUNYOMI	

EXAMPLE	EXAMPLE SENTENCE

✓ **Review** ☐**Awesome！** ☐**Excellent！** ☐**Good！** ☐**Average！** ☐**Poor！**

かず　かぞ　かた
数の数え方
How to Count numbers

にち　げつ　ねん　しゅう　かん
日、月、年、週間
Days, Months, Years

- Numbers up to one Hundred
- Bigger numbers
- Days of the week
- Counting weeks
- Useful words related to the week
- Days of the month
- Months
- Counting months
- Useful words related to the month
- Dates in Japanese
- Years
- Counting years/Vocabulary
- Years of age
- Words to talk about age in Japanese
- Japanese greetings

Counting up to 100 in Japanese becomes surprisingly easy once you understand the first ten numbers. The exciting thing is that there's a consistent pattern to follow! After you reach 10, you can just add the next number to continue counting.

Here's how that looks:

じゅういち
11 is 十一 (juuichi): 10 + 1
and so on up to 19.

じゅうに
12 is 十二 (juuni): 10 + 2

Once you get to twenty, the approach remains similar, but you start by counting the tens:

にじゅう
20 is 二十 (nijuu): 2 10's
and so on, up to 99.

にじゅういち
21 is 二十一 (nijuuichi): 2 10's + 1

When you reach 100, it's a new word: 百 (hyaku).

No.	Hiragana	Kanji	Rōmaji
1	いち	一	ichi
2	に	二	ni
3	さん	三	san
4	よん/し	四	yon/shi
5	ご	五	go
6	ろく/む	六	roku
7	なな/しち	七	nana/shichi
8	はち	八	hachi
9	きゅう/く	九	kyuu/ku
10	じゅう	十	juu

In Japanese, we express 20 as '2 of 10,' 30 as '3 of 10,' and so on. For instance, 20 is said as 'ni juu' (two ten). This pattern continues for numbers from 30 to 90. However, there's a little twist with 40, 70, and 90 because there are two ways to say the numbers 4, 7, and 9 in Japanese, 40 can be pronounced as 'yonjuu' or 'shijuu,' while 70 can be 'nanajuu' or 'shichijuu.'

No.	Hiragana	Kanji	Rōmaji
11	じゅういち	十一	juuichi
12	じゅうに	十二	juuni
13	じゅうさん	十三	juusan
14	じゅうよん/じゅうし	十四	juuyon/juushi
15	じゅうご	十五	juugo
16	じゅうろく	十六	juuroku
17	じゅうなな/じゅうしち	十七	juunana/jyuushichi
18	じゅうはち	十八	juuhachi
19	じゅうく/じゅうきゅう	十九	juukyu/juukyuu
20	にni　じゅうjuu　にじゅうnijuu 2　X　10　=　20	二十	nijuu

No.	Hiragana	Kanji	Rōmaji
30	さんじゅう	三十	sanjuu
40	よんじゅう	四十	yonjuu
50	ごじゅう	五十	gojuu
60	ろくじゅう	六十	rokujuu
70	ななじゅう/しちじゅう	七十	nanajuu/shitijyuu
80	はちじゅう	八十	hachijuu
90	きゅうじゅう	九十	kyuujuu
100	ひゃく	百	hyaku

The primary unit in the English number system is one thousand (1,000), and one million is one thousand thousand.

However, in the Japanese number system, the primary unit is ten thousand (10,000), and ten thousand (万 – man) forms the next unit, "hundred million" (億 – oku). Translating large numbers between English and Japanese can be challenging for language learners.

Numbers	Kanji	Kana + Romaji
1	一	いち (ichi)
2	二	に (ni)
3	三	さん (san)
4	四	よん (yon)
5	五	ご (go)
6	六	ろく (roku)
7	七	なな (nana)
8	八	はち (hachi)
9	九	きゅう (kyuu)
10	十	じゅう (juu)
100	百	ひゃく (hyaku)
1,000	千	せん (sen)
10,000	万	まん (man)
100,000	十万	じゅうまん (juuman)
1,000,000	百万	ひゃくまん (hyakuman)
10,000,000	千万	せんまん (senman)
100,000,000	一億	いちおく (ichioku)
1,000,000,000	十億	じゅうおく (juuoku)
1,000,000,000,000	一兆	いっちょう (icchou)

The Week 週 (しゅう-shuu)

In Japanese, the days of the week are represented by specific kanji characters, each connected to one of the five elements (wood, fire, earth, metal, and water) and the sun and moon.

Remember that each day ends with the kanji "曜日-よう び" (youbi), and they are associated with different elements of nature. "Youbi" means "day of the week" and is pronounced like "yoh" in yo-yo and "bee," with emphasis on "yoh." The varying part in the names of the days is what comes first.

The good news is that the first part of each day's name has a straightforward meaning and corresponding kanji, making them easy to remember.

◀))

Hiragana	Kanji	Rōmaji	English	Radical
げつようび	月曜日	getsu you bi	Monday	Moon
かようび	火曜日	ka you bi	Tuesday	Fire
すいようび	水曜日	sui you bi	Wednesday	Water
もくようび	木曜日	moku you bi	Thursday	Tree
きんようび	金曜日	kin you bi	Friday	Gold
どようび	土曜日	do you bi	Saturday	Earth
にちようび	日曜日	nichi you bi	Sunday	Sun

週間 (shuukan)

After learning about the days of the week, let's move on to counting weeks in Japanese.

Below is a table showing how to count the weeks:

◀))

Hiragana	Kanji	Rōmaji	English
いっしゅうかん	1週間	i sshuu kan	One week
にしゅうかん	2週間	ni shuu kan	Two weeks
さんしゅうかん	3週間	san shuu kan	Three weeks
よんしゅうかん	4週間	yon shuu kan	Four weeks
ごしゅうかん	5週間	go shuu kan	Five weeks

■ You can use the same pattern as other counters to count more than five weeks in Japanese. Here are the numbers for counting weeks:

6週間	roku shuu kan	6 weeks
7週間	nana shuu kan	7 weeks
8週間	ha sshuu kan	8 weeks
9週間	kyuu shuu kan	9 weeks
10週間	ju sshuu kan	10 weeks
11週間	juu i sshuu ka	11 weeks
12週間	juu ni shuu kan	12 weeks

Useful Words Related to the Week in Japanese 1-2

1. konshuu (こんしゅう)

"This week" is pronounced, "konshuu"(今週). The first kanji is ″今″ just like with ″今日″ and the second kanji is ″週″(shuu), meaning "week."

Example 1:　こんしゅうとうきょう　い
今週は東京に行きます。
(**konshuu** wa toukyou ni ikimasu.)
I'm going to Tokyo this week.

Example 2:　こんしゅうてんき
今週は天気がいい。
(**konshuu** wa tenki ga ii.)
The weather is nice this week.

Example 3:　こんしゅう　にほんご
今週は日本語のテストがあります。
(**konshuu** wa nihongo no tesuto ga arimasu.)
I have a Japanese test this week.

2. senshuu (せんしゅう)

"Last week" is pronounced, "senshuu"(先週). The first kanji is ″先″(sen) and means "previous".

Example 1:　せんしゅう　　　　い
先週、東京に行きました。
(**senshuu**, toukyou ni ikimashita.)
I went to Tokyo last week.

Example 2:　せんしゅう　しごと　やす
先週は仕事を休みました。
(**senshuu** wa shigoto wo yasumimashita.)
I was off work last week.

Useful Words Related to the Week in Japanese 2-2

🔊

1. raishuu (らいしゅう)

"Next week" is pronounced, "raishuu"(来週). The first kanji is ″来″(rai), and it means "next."

Example 1:　来週はアメリカに行きます。
　　　　　　（raishuu wa amerika ni ikimasu.）
　　　　　　　I'm going to America next week.

Example 2:　来週、連絡いたします。
　　　　　　（raishuu, renraku itashimasu.）
　　　　　　　I will contact you next week.

Example 3:　ぼくのたんじょうびは来週です。
　　　　　　（boku no tanjoubi wa raishuu desu.）
　　　　　　　My birthday's next week.

2. saraishuu (さらいしゅう)

"The week after next" is pronounced, "saraishuu"(再来週). The first kanji is 再(sai), and it means again; twice.

Example 1:　再来週の木曜日はどう。
　　　　　　（saraishuu no mokuyoubi wa dou ?）
　　　　　　　How about Thursday 2 weeks from now?

Example 2:　また、再来週。
　　　　　　（mata,saraishuu.）
　　　　　　　See you the week after next week.

1st	ついたち tsuitachi 一日	11th	じゅういちにち juuichi-nichi 十一日	21st	にじゅういちにち nijuuichi-nichi 二十一日
2nd	ふつか futsuka 二日	12th	じゅうににち juuni-nichi 十二日	22nd	にじゅうににち nijuuni-nichi 二十二日
3rd	みっか mikka 三日	13th	じゅうさんにち juusan-nichi 十三日	23rd	にじゅうさんにち nijuusan-nichi 二十三日
4th	よっか yokka 四日	14th	じゅうよっか juuyokka 十四日	24th	にじゅうよっか nijuuyokka 二十四日
5th	いつか itsuka 五日	15th	じゅうごにち juugo-nichi 十五日	25th	にじゅうごにち nijuugo-nichi 二十五日
6th	むいか muika 六日	16th	じゅうろくにち juuroku-nichi 十六日	26th	にじゅうろくにち nijuuroku-nichi 二十六日
7th	なのか nanoka 七日	17th	じゅうしちにち juushiti-nichi 十七日	27th	にじゅうしちにち nijuushichi-nichi 二十七日
8th	ようか youka 八日	18th	じゅうはちにち juuhati-nichi 十八日	28th	にじゅうはちにち nijuuhachi-nichi 二十八日
9th	ここのか kokonoka 九日	19th	じゅうくにち juuku-nichi 十九日	29th	にじゅうくにち nijuuku-nichi 二十九日
10th	とおか tooka 十日	20th	はつか hatsuka 二十日	30th	さんじゅうにち sanjuu-nichi 三十日
				31st	さんじゅういちにち sanjuu-ichinichi 三十一日`

As opposed to English where every month has its name, the months in Japanese are named with numbers "いち"(ichi), "に"(ni), "さん"(san), "し"(shi).

- When it comes to months in Japanese, things can get a bit confusing. There are three ways to talk about months: "がつ" (gatsu), "つき" (tsuki), and "かげつ" (ka-getsu).

Let's break down the differences:

1. "がつ"(月 in Kanji) "gatsu" → for the name of each month (January, February, etc.).

2. "つき"(月 in Kanji) "tsuki" → for counting months with traditional Japanese numbers.

3. "かげつ"(か月 or ケ月 using Kanji) "ka-getsu" → for counting months with Kanji numbers.

Hiragana	Kanji	Rōmaji	English
いち がつ	一月	ichi-gatsu	January
に がつ	二月	ni-gatsu	February
さん がつ	三月	san-gatsu	March
し がつ	四月	shi-gatsu	April
ご がつ	五月	go-gatsu	May
ろく がつ	六月	roku-gatsu	June
しち/なな がつ	七月	shichi/nana-gatsu	July
はち がつ	八月	hachi-gatsu	August
く がつ	九月	ku-gatsu	September
じゅう がつ	十月	juu-gatsu	October
じゅういち がつ	十一月	juuichi-gatsu	November
じゅうに がつ	十二月	juuni-gatsu	December

❖ Pay attention when mentioning April, July, and September in Japanese because there are two ways to say the numbers four, seven, and nine.

❖ (Not "yon" gatsu) , (Not "nana" gatsu) , (Not "kyuu" gatsu).

LESSON 9 — Counting Months

The Japanese counter for months very simple, all you have to do is add "ヶ月"(kagetsu).

Hiragana	Kanji	Rōmaji	English
いっかげつ	一ヶ月	i kka getsu	One month
にかげつ	二ヶ月	ni ka getsu	Two months
さんかげつ	三ヶ月	san ka getsu	Three months
よんかげつ	四ヶ月	yon ka getsu	Four months
ごかげつ	五ヶ月	go ka getsu	Five months
ろっかげつ	六ヶ月	ro kka getsu	Six months
ななかげつ	七ヶ月	nana ka getsu	Seven months
はちかげつ	八ヶ月	hachi ka getsu	Eight months
きゅうかげつ	九ヶ月	kyuu ka gatsu	Nine months
じゅっかげつ	十ヶ月	ju kka getsu	Ten months
じゅういっかげつ	十一ヶ月	juu i kka getsu	Eleven months
じゅうにかげつ	十二ヶ月	juu ni ka getsu	Twelve months

❖ Take note that the "月" kanji is pronounced as "gatsu" (がつ) when referring to "January" as a calendar month. However, it is pronounced as "getsu" (げつ) when expressing "one month" or counting lengths of time. These are two distinct readings of the same kanji, depending on the usage context.

❖ Some numbers in Japanese have multiple readings:
   ▪ The number four (四) can be pronounced as "shi" (し) or "yon" (よん).
   ▪ The number seven (七) can be pronounced as "shichi" (しち) or "nana" (なな).
   ▪ The number nine (九) can be pronounced as "ku" (く) or "kyuu" (きゅう).

❖ There are multiple ways to write "か月" (kagetsu) in Japanese"か月"(kagetsu) months: "ヵ月", "ヶ月", "箇月" etc.

Useful Words Related to the Month in Japanese

1. kongetsu (こんげつ) 🔊

"This Month" kongetsu — 今月(こんげつ)：a noun meaning 'this month' in Japanese.

Example 1:
今月は、とても暑い。
(kongetsu wa, totemo atsui.)
It is very hot this month.

Example 2:
今月、毎日勉強します。
(kongetsu wa, mainichi benkyou shimasu.)
I will study every day this month.

Example 3:
今月は、とても忙しい。
(kongetsu wa, totemo isogashii.)
I'm very busy this month.

2. sengetsu (せんげつ) 🔊

"Last month" is pronounced "sengetsu."

Example 1:
私達は、先月から忙しい。
(watashitachi wa **sengetsu** kara isogashii.)
We have been busy since last month.

Example 2:
母は、先月から病気だ。
(haha wa, **sengetsu** kara byouki da.)
My mother has been ill since last month.

Example 3:
私は、先月風邪を引いた。
(watashi wa **sengetsu** kaze wo hiita.)
I caught a cold last month.

Useful Words Related to the Month in Japanese.

1. raigetsu（らいげつ）🔊

"Next month" is pronounced, "raigetsu"（来月）.

Example 1: 私は、来月あたらしい車を買います。
　　　　　　（watashi wa, **raigetsu** atarashii kuruma wo kaimasu.）
　　　　　　I will buy a new car next month.

Example 2: 彼女は来月、東京を離れます。
　　　　　　（kanojo wa **raigetsu**, Toukyou wo hanare masu.）
　　　　　　She will leave Tokyo next month.

Example 3: 来月、友達の家に行きます。
　　　　　　（**raigetsu**, tomodachi no ie ni ikimasu.）
　　　　　　I will go to my friend's house next month.

2. saraigetsu（さらいげつ）🔊

"The month after next" is pronounced, "saraigetsu"（再来月）.

Example 1: 再来月は、十二月です。
　　　　　　（**saraigetsu** wa, juu-ni-gatsu desu.）
　　　　　　The month after next is December.

Example 2: 再来月、私はあたらしい仕事を始めます。
　　　　　　（**saraigetsu**, watashi wa atarashii shigoto wo hajime masu.）
　　　　　　I will start a new job, the month after next.

再　さい sai
6 strokes (JLPT 2)
(It's not required for beginners level.)

Meaning:
again, twice, second time, repeated

On'yomi: サイ、サ (sai, sa)

Kun'yomi: ふたた.び (futata. bi)

In Japanese, saying dates is straightforward. Dates are written with the year first, then the month, and finally the day.

Dates in Japanese are Written as Follows:

- 年 (nen) : Year
- 月 (gatsu) : Month
- 日 (nichi) : Day

❑ Japanese date includes days of the week is written as follows:

2022年4月30日（火曜）or（火）

Reading : ni-sen ni-juu-ni nen/ shi-gatsu/ san-juu-nichi/ ka-you.

Tuesday, April 30th, 2022

- In Japanese, the days of the week are often written in a round bracket "( )" after the day's name. The day's name is usually expressed in a short form. For example, Tuesday is 火曜日 (ka-youbi), but in written form, it's commonly simplified to 火曜 (ka-you) or just 火 (ka).

🔊
Example 1: 　　きょう　　にせんにじゅうにねんにがつじゅうごにち
今日は、二千二十二年二月十五日です。
(kyou wa, ni-sen ni-juu-ni-nen ni-gatsu juu-go-nichi desu.)
Today is February 15th, 2022.

🔊
Example 2: テストは、2022年8月30日です。
(tesuto wa, ni-sen ni-juu-ni-nen hachi-gatsu san-juu-nichi desu.)
The examination is on August 30th, 2022.

To express the year in Japanese, simply state the year and then add "nen 年" (ねん), which is a year counter.

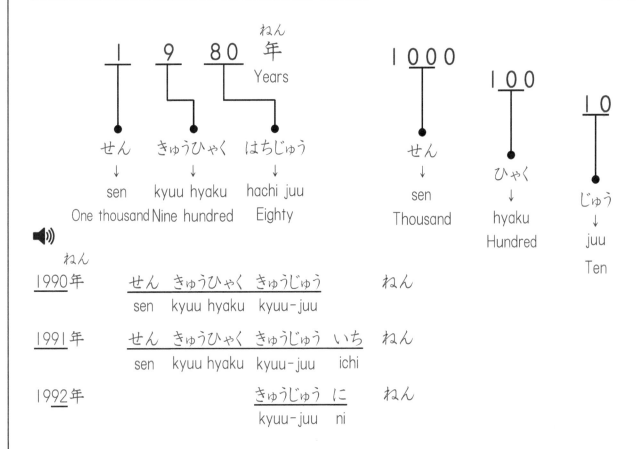

1990年 せん きゅうひゃく きゅうじゅう ねん
sen kyuu hyaku kyuu-juu

1991年 せん きゅうひゃく きゅうじゅう いち ねん
sen kyuu hyaku kyuu-juu ichi

1992年 きゅうじゅう に ねん
kyuu-juu ni

1993年	きゅうじゅうさん ねん	kyuu-juu-san nen
1994年	きゅうじゅうよ ねん	kyuu-juu-yo nen
1995年	きゅうじゅうご ねん	kyuu-juu-go nen
1996年	きゅうじゅうろく ねん	kyuu-juu-roku nen
1997年	きゅうじゅうなな/しち ねん	kyuu-juu-nana/shichi nen
1998年	きゅうじゅうはち ねん	kyuu-juu-hachi nen
1999年	きゅうじゅうく/きゅう ねん	kyuu-juu-ku/kyuu nen
2000年	にせん ねん	ni sen nen
2001年	いち ねん	ni sen ichi nen
2010年	じゅう ねん	ni sen juu nen

Japanese Era Calendar

The Japanese-era calendar, known as 和暦 (wareki) This calendar system is established according to the rule of Japanese emperors.

The current era is called 令和 (reiwa), beginning on May 1, 2019.

This traditional Japanese era calendar is commonly used for official occasions and in written records, like those used in government services at city offices.

In Japanese, "年" (ねん or nen) is the character used for counting years.
It represents the concept of "year" and is commonly used in various time-related expressions.

🔊

Hiragana	Kanji	Rōmaji	English
いちねん	一年	ichi nen	One year
にねん	二年	ni-nen	Two years
さんねん	三年	san-nen	Three years
じゅうねん	十年	juu nen	Ten years
ひゃくねん	百年	hyaku nen	100 years

❏   Now that you've familiarized yourself with the time units for days, months, and years, you can confidently talk about and understand specific dates.

Useful Words for Describing Relative Years 🔊

- 今年 ことし (kotoshi) : This year
- 去年 きょねん (kyonen) : Last year
- 一昨年 おととし (ototoshi) : The year before last
- 来年 らいねん (rainen) : Next year
- 再来年 さらいねん (sarainen) : The year after next
- 閏年 うるうどし (uruudoshi) : Leap year
- 毎年 まいとし (maitoshi) : Every year

Examples: 🔊

ことし　　　ねん
1. 今年は2022年です。
   kotoshi wa ni-sen ni juu-nen desu.
   This year is 2022.

わたしらいねん だいがくせい
2. 私は来年に大学生になる。
   watashi wa rainen ni daigakusei ni naru.
   I will become a university student next year.

In Japanese, the term for "years old" is expressed as "歳" (さい or sai). Similar to how we say "years old" in English, you need to add (才sai) after each number when indicating someone's age.

🔊

Hiragana	Kanji	Rōmaji	English
いっさい	一歳/才	i ssai	1 year old
にさい	二歳/才	ni sai	2 years old
さんさい	三歳/才	san sai	3 years old
よんさい	四歳/才	yon sai	4 years old
ごさい	五歳/才	go sai	5 years old
ろくさい	六歳/才	roku sai	6 years old
ななさい	七歳/才	nana sai	7 years old
はち/はっさい	八歳/才	hachi sai/ha ssai	8 years old
きゅうさい	九歳/才	kyuu sai	9 years old
じゅっさい	十歳/才	jussai	10 years old

❑ However, there are some pronunciation adjustments for specific numbers. For instance, when referring to 1-year-old, 8 years old, and 10 years old, adjustments occur as below:

1 year old → "i ssai" → ×いちさい'Not ichi sai'
4 years old → "yon sai" → ×しさい'Not shi sai'
7 years old → "nana sai" → ×しちさい'No shichi sai'
8 years old → "ha ssai" → ×はちさい'Not hachi sai'
9 years old → "kyuu sai" → ×くさい'Not ku sai'
10 years old 10才/歳:じゅっさい → "ju ssai" → ×じゅうさい'Not juu sai'
20 years old 20才/歳:はたち/にじゅっさい → "hatachi/ni ju ssai" → ×にじゅうさい'Not ni juu sai'

❖ Note that writing the kanji character "歳" (sai) can be challenging. As a result, there are instances where it is substituted with another kanji, "才" (sai), which is more straightforward and more commonly used.

In Japanese, you use the counter "才" (sai) when indicating your age. To express your age, you start by saying "私は" (watashi wa), which means "I am." Then, add your age and the counter "才" (sai). This structure allows you to tell others how old you are in Japanese.

Telling your age in Japanese is straightforward. If someone asks how old you are, you can simply state the number followed by "才-さい" (sai) and then "です" (desu). Here are some examples:

watashi wa [number] sai desu.)

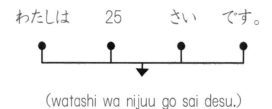

(watashi wa nijuu go sai desu.)

Example: 🔊

20 years old – はたち (hatachi) です。

33 years old – さんじゅうさんさい (san juu san sai) です。

40 years old –よんじゅっさい (yon juu sai) です。

60 years old – ろくじゅっさい (roku juu sai) です。

Question:

なんさい
何歳ですか。　(nan sai desu ka.)（Casual）.
おいくつですか。(o ikutsu desu ka.)（Polite）.

Note: There are more polite ways to ask someone's age, like:

❑ toshi wa ikutsu desu ka? としはいくつですか。

❑ otoshi wa ikutsu desu ka? おとしはいくつですか。

Nenrei – 年齢（ねんれい） is the Japanese word for 'age'

In Japanese, "年齢" （ねんれい or nenrei) is the word for 'age.' It's a noun used to refer to someone's age or how old they are. Native speakers commonly use "nenrei" when discussing age in Japanese society.

It's essential to note that "nenrei" refers to the age in general and does not specify a particular age, such as "30 years of age," for example. It is a more general term used to discuss age without being specific about the exact number of years.

🔊

Examples:

かのじょ　ぼく　ねんれい　し
彼女は僕の年齢を知らない。
(kanojo wa boku no nenrei wo shira nai .)
　She doesn't know my age.

かのじょ　ねんれい　　　　わか
彼女は年齢よりずっと若いです。
(kanojo wa nenrei yori zutto wakai desu.)
　She looks younger than her age.

The Japanese word "nenrei" is composed of two kanji characters:

1. 年 （ねん or nen): This kanji is commonly used for 'age' or 'year' in Japanese.

2. 齢 （れい or rei): This kanji specifically means 'age.'

Note that the word "toshi" （年) can refer to "year" in a general sense, like any year.
For example, "今年" (kotoshi) means "this (current) year." However, when combined with the character 齢, it forms "年齢" (nenrei), which specifically denotes a person's 'age.'

Aging and Getting Old

When talking about age and aging, the word "年" (toshi) is used in various other terms. For instance, to express someone being older or younger than another person, the word "toshi" is combined with directional words in Japanese to create "年上" (toshiue) and "年下" (toshishita). These phrases literally mean "year above" (elder) and "year below" (junior), respectively.

| 1. | おはようございます。 | Ohayou gozaimasu. | Good morning |

EXPLANATION

Typically used in the morning hours before noon. However, the kanji word is hayai (早い) which simply means "early." "Ohayou" can be said casually or "Ohayo gozaimasu" to be polite. Kanji: お早うございます。 Ohayou gozaimasu.

| 2. | こんにちは。 | Konnichiwa. | Hello |

EXPLANATION

Translated as "hello," and can be used at any hour. However, you most commonly use it during the daytime. Kanji: 今日は。 Konnichiwa.

| 3. | こんばんは | Konbanwa. | Good evening |

EXPLANATION

Translates as "good evening" and is used in the evening or at sunset. Kanji: 今晩は。 Konbanwa.

| 4. | おやすみなさい。 | Oyasuminasai | Good night |

EXPLANATION

Supposed to be used before going to bed or taking a rest.
"Oyasuminasai" is the formal way of saying this phrase, informal version is Oyasumi.
Kanji: お休みなさい。 Oyasuminasai.

| 5. | ようこそ | Youkoso | Welcome |

EXPLANATION

Greeting given upon someone's arrival.

Review ☐Awesome ! ☐Excellent ! ☐Good ! ☐Average ! ☐Poor !

Note:

ESSENTIAL JAPANESE GREETINGS

6.	さようなら	Sayounara	Good bye

EXPLANATION
Goodbye (for a long period of time).

7.	いってきます。	Ittekimasu	I'm leaving

EXPLANATION
Specifically, for when someone leaves the house or office. Kanji: 行ってきます。

8.	いってらっしゃい。	Itterasshai.	Please go and come back

EXPLANATION
Used daily, but only at the home, office or somewhere where people are based, since it only makes sense when they will go and come back later. Kanji: 行ってらっしゃい

9.	ただいま。	Tadaima.	I'm back home

EXPLANATION
The phrase you can say when person returns home. Kanji: 只今。

10.	おかえり。	Okaeri	Welcome home

EXPLANATION
Okaeri – おかえり : the shortened version of the interjection, "Okaerinasai"
which means "welcome home" or 'welcome back. Kanji : お帰り。

11.	ひさしぶり	Hisashiburi	Long time, no see

EXPLANATION
Said to a person whom you have not seen in a long time. Kanji: 久しぶり

Review ☐Awesome ! ☐Excellent ! ☐Good ! ☐Average ! ☐Poor !

Note:

ESSENTIAL JAPANESE GREETINGS

| 12. | おつかれさまです。 | Otsukaresama desu. | Thanks for your hard work |

EXPLANATION
Does not have a particular meaning, but expresses the appreciation of your co-workers' hard work. Kanji: お疲れ様です。

| 13. | はじめまして。 | Hajimemashite. | Nice to Meet You. |

EXPLANATION
Said to someone you are meeting for the first time. Kanji: 初めまして。

| 14. | どうぞ, おさきに | Douzo, osakini. | Go ahead / After you. |

EXPLANATION
An indication of Japanese people's respect for each other. You can translate "douzo, osakini" as "after you," but also "please go first," "go ahead," etc.
Kanji: どうぞ、お先に

| 15. | じゃあ また。 | Jyaa mata. | See you. |

EXPLANATION
This is gender-neutral, so both women and men use it.

| 16. | また あした。 | Mata ashita. | See you tomorrow. |

EXPLANATION
Friends say it at the end of a school day or the end of the evening to mean "I'll see you again tomorrow." Kanji: また明日。

Review ☐Awesome ! ☐Excellent ! ☐Good ! ☐Average ! ☐Poor !

Note:

ESSENTIAL JAPANESE GREETINGS

| 17. | がんばって。 | Ganbatte. | Do your best. |

EXPLANATION

"Good luck!" "Do your best," "Try hard!" etc. Kanji: 頑張って。

| 18. | きをつけて。 | Kiwotsukete. | Be careful / Take care. |

EXPLANATION

A warning or encouragement to "Be careful," "Take care," "Watch out," etc.

| 19. | ごめんなさい。 | Gomennasai. | I'm Sorry. |

EXPLANATION

I'm sorry; Casual expression of apology. Kanji：御免なさい。

| 20. | すみません。 | Sumimasen. | Excuse me. |

EXPLANATION

"Excuse me" or "Sorry." In daily conversation, "Suimasen" is used overwhelmingly often. Is also used as a light apology. The polite form is "Sumimasen." Kanji: 済みません。

| 21. | おめでとうございます。 | Omedetou gozaimasu. | Congratulations. |

EXPLANATION

A polite form of congratulations on a favourable occasion such as a birthday, wedding, graduation etc.

| 22. | おたんじょうび おめでとう | Otanjoubi omedetou. | Happy birthday. |

EXPLANATION

"Otanjoubi" is the polite form of "tanjoubi" (たんじょうび) meaning "birthday" and "omedetou" means "congratulations" The polite version is "otanjoubi omedetou gozaimasu"

Review ☐Awesome ! ☐Excellent ! ☐Good ! ☐Average ! ☐Poor !

Note:

ESSENTIAL JAPANESE GREETINGS

23.	ありがとうございます。	Arigatau gozaimasu.	Thank You.

EXPLANATION

"Thank you" in formal situations, but when your relationship with the person is close and casual, ありがとう can be used for both present and past tense. ありがとうございました Which means "Thank you for what you've done".

24.	ごちそうさまでした。	Gochisousama deshita.	Thank you for the meal

EXPLANATION

After finishing a meal, this phrase is spoken to offer gratitude to the person who prepared the food. It basically means "I really enjoyed this meal Thank you"

25.	しつれいします。	Shitsurei shimasu	Excuse my interrupting

EXPLANATION

Shitsurei shimasu is most commonly used in the workplace. It is used in the sense of "excuse me" in this case. For example, if your cell phone rings and you need to answer it, you can say "Shitsurei shimasu", You can use"(しつれいしました) in the past tense after you have had the phone call to express "sorry for being rude".

26.	おまたせいたしました。	O matase ita shimashita	Thank you for waiting

EXPLANATION

The phrase can be translated to "Thank you for waiting", "I am sorry to have kept you waiting" or "We apologize for the delay" Waiters, shop assistants and office workers say the expression all the time.

27.	もしもし	Moshi-Moshi	I'm going to talk

EXPLANATION

"Moshi-Moshi" means "I'm going to talk" and is mostly used in a phone call.

Review ☐Awesome ! ☐Excellent ! ☐Good ! ☐Average ! ☐Poor !

Note: